Food through the Ages

About the Author

Mike Gibney is Professor Emeritus of Food and Health at University College Dublin. He previously held posts at the University of Sydney Veterinary School and the Medical Schools of Southampton University and Trinity College Dublin. He is a fellow of both the Nutrition Society and the American Society for Nutrition, and a Fellow of the International Union of Food Science and Technology. His research interests are in both public health nutrition and molecular nutrition with over 350 peer reviewed papers published in leading scientific journals. He has served on expert committees at national, EU and UN levels. He is the author of *Something to Chew on: Challenging Controversies in Food and Health* and *Ever Seen a Fat Fox?: Human Obesity Explored*.

Food through the Ages

A Popular History

Mike Gibney

The Liffey Press

Published by The Liffey Press Ltd
'Clareville', 307 Clontarf Road
Dublin D03 PO46, Ireland
www.theliffeypress.com

A catalogue record of this book is
available from the British Library.

ISBN 978-1-8383593-7-9

Photos are courtesy of www.foodiesfeed.com or www.istockphotos.com.

Printed in Spain by GraphyCems.

Contents

Preface

I sometimes hear parents or the media food police bemoaning the fact that most children don't know where milk comes from. Dreadful! They know it first comes from the supermarket and then they find it in the fridge. They also know it comes from farms but are no more interested in any further detail than they are of seeking the computer code of their favourite video game. Tut-tut, the parents think. But let's imagine I asked an average parent where did salami come from? I suspect that a sausage might be mentioned or maybe a cured meat. But why is it so dry and what are those white spots in it, and is pepperoni the same as salami? The reality is that very few of us really know how food gets to the point of sale, be it on the high street or in the farmers' market.

When we drink our favourite coffee, we might think of coffee plantations in far-off equatorial parts of the world and have some idea that fair trade for coffee farmers is worthy of support. Most people don't picture a coffee tree, three metres in height. Nor would they think of the delicate buds that sprout out of each branch in early spring, that eventually become green and when they become cherry-coloured are gently picked, leaving the bud intact to grow more berries, and that these cherry berries are gently ruptured and allowed to ferment to yield two coffee beans. Nor would they know that when the beans are roasted, two audible cracks can be heard marking key stages in achieving the perfect roast coffee. Neither are they likely to know that it was the Arabs and then the Turks who perfected coffee and that Europe would wait another 1,000 years to enjoy this brew. And then again, like the child and the provenance of milk, does it matter knowing the background to everyday foods?

The basic tenet of this book is that the more we know about the origins and history of the foods we eat, the more we can appreciate them beyond their role as functional ingredients in some dish or other. Also, there's an aesthetic pleasure in understanding the role that spring and autumn monsoon winds played in sailing ships to and from Arabia to the coast of Malabar in southwest India in search of precious spices, in appreciating that the multitude of pasta shapes is not the legacy of whimsical engineers but rather the invention borne out of the necessity to best match pasta shapes to different sauces, or in recognising the ingenuity of early humans in mastering fire and its use in cookery. All of these help us to better understand and appreciate the foods we eat.

And the reason I have a poem at the outset of each chapter is in a similar vein: to remind the reader that this is a book about the love of food. Each poem is intended to produce a heightened emotive state to help the reader better engage with that chapter's contents.

Having spent my entire academic career in the laboratory-based discipline of human nutrition and metabolism, I lack any formal training in history and apologise to scholars of that subject for my many historiographic shortcomings. To food historians in particular, may I apologise in advance for the few gaffs you may find (all mine) in this extensive exploration of the story of food.

Bon appétit.

Acknowledgements

This book started off with the intention of combining a book on the history of food with recipes for each of the foods. My original idea was to work with the many outstanding chefs in the town of Kenmare in County Kerry. In seeking advice on the project, reservations were expressed about the idea of combining history with recipes. In food terms, it was deemed to be neither fish nor fowl.

Nonetheless, my many friends in Kenmare worked with me in the early stages and I wish to thank them sincerely for their encouragement: Lynn Brennan who was to be the local organiser, John Moriarty of the Park Hotel who was a key advisor, and chefs Maura Foley (Shelburn Lodge), James Coffee (The Park), Aileen Crean O'Brien (Tom Crean's) and Martin Hallissey (Packies).

Dr Kantha Shelke, from Johns Hopkins University and author of the Edible Series book *Pasta,* was very helpful in critically reading early drafts of several chapters.

My sister, Dr Rosemary Gibney, deserves my sincere thanks. She was very helpful in the search for a willing publisher, took on the task of securing copyright permission to reproduce several poems and helped in the tedious task of proof reading.

My wife Jo, to whom this book is dedicated, was a great source of encouragement and was particularly keen on the idea of a poem for each chapter.

My thanks are due to Peter O'Connell of POC Media for his guidance in the promotion of this book and to Ros Murphy at Phoenix Graphic Designs for his patient work in designing the book's cover. And of course my sincere thanks are due to the team at The Liffey Press and in particular David Givens. He made such a difference to the structure of the book and was quite simply a pleasure to work with.

Thank you all.

For Jo

Chapter 1

The Great Descent

The Hermit's Song

(Anonymous, Irish, eighth century)

To what meals the woods invite me
All about!
There are water, herbs and cresses,
Salmon, trout.
A clutch of eggs, sweet mast and honey
Are my meat,
Heath berries and whortleberries for a sweet.
All that one could ask for comfort
Round me grows,
There are hips and haws and strawberries,
Nuts and sloes,
And when summer spreads its mantle
What a sight!
Marjoram and leeks and pignuts,
Juicy, bright.

In order to understand and appreciate the modern food chain and the origins and etiquette of dining, it is necessary to go back to the beginning, to the period when humans left the tree tops, setting in train the evolutionary trajectory to humankind as we know it today. There were several fundamentally important events that occurred in the tens of millennia since the first hominids abandoned the forests: the discovery of fire, the introduction of cooking, the ability to preserve food, the emergence of social norms, the division of labour and the merging of smaller into larger social units. Our food chain, our food markets, our cooking, our tableware, our table manners and our dining etiquette all began back when the ape-person emerged to become more person than ape.

From the Forest Canopy to Terra Firma

Our most immediate primate ancestors were the chimpanzees and their close cousin, the bonobos, who found their food along the fertile tree tops of the forests. Leaves, nuts and fruit would have been a very important part of their diet, which would also include birds' eggs and insects. Whilst the idyllic life of the jungle, as described in Rudyard Kipling's *Jungle Book*, or its Walt Disney animation, might make us all happy and warm, life swooshing through the tree tops was not without its perils. Great storms and fires would frequently decimate the natural habitat of these primates and hunger, even perilous hunger, was almost certainly a common consequence. Some chimpanzees and bonobos began to abandon the tree tops setting in train the rapid descent of pre-humans from the tree-tops and the slow ascent of hominids into the homo sapiens that we know today.

These hominids would now live on land, hunting small animals with simple tools and, in time, they learned to hunt and trap larger animals and to shape spears to catch fish. They would gather wild crops, nuts, fruits, berries and eggs. Between the periods of more-ape-than-human to that of more-human-than-ape, many changes occurred in the physique of this new hominid. They abandoned the four-legged life of the early apes for the two-legged biped of

Photo credit: gorodenkoff

homo erectus, freeing their hand for all manner of complex tasks. They grew taller so they could see further into the distance. Their dentition changed because they no longer used their mouths in fighting and their gut adapted to the transformation of food through cooking. Their brains grew in size and above all in complexity, making it possible for them to use their newly found hands to make tools and traps for hunting.

Hunting

Today's stereotype of these early hunters is of warriors stealthily pursuing their prey across great plains. But animals do not live alone. The more vulnerable types, with the least effective defensive systems such as springboks, buffalo or deer, exist in great herds. Those animals who have the greatest offensive skills, such as lions, tigers or leopards, exist in smaller packs but hunting such powerful animals was a very risky business. Hunting rabbits and other small animals would provide no threat but equally would provide little nourishment for a community. The most desired meat was that of large animals. These early hunters had time on their side, they had curiosity and they had patience. They observed the pattern of migration of herds of wild animals and set about trapping them.

At first it might be no more complex than a carefully camouflaged hole in the ground for a single animal to tumble into. But why go for one? Why not bigger trenches? These would work only if the herd's exact path in their migration was known. So these early hunters found ways with fire or fallen trees to direct these herds on their migratory route to the traps they had constructed. The two best documented of these techniques come from the Native American peoples. The Northern Peigan, in Alberta, Canada and the Piegan Blackfeet in Montana, USA used a technique known as a buffalo jump to trap and kill buffalo. The kill involved herding the buffalo toward a precipice, and the most celebrated of these, a UNESCO heritage sight, has the strange name of 'Head-Smashed-In Buffalo Jump'.

Bull buffalos are stubborn and cows with calves don't roam too far. So when the calves were weaned, the mainly cow-calf herd could be enticed toward the precipice to fall all of 10 metres to their death. In contrast to bulls, their protective instinct is to run rather than to turn and charge the predator. Lanes were constructed with poles and vegetation to funnel the herd to the site. The most fleet of foot warrior would don a buffalo skin and wear a hollowed buffalo head over his own. The tribe would move in from the sides and from behind and the warrior would begin to run toward the edge. To frighten the herd, the tribespeople would have mock-up wolves heads. The herd would follow the buffalo lookalike warrior and, when in full flight, he would dive into a protected crevice and allow the herd to run over the edge. No doubt, this was a technique mastered over time and some braves would have been killed in the stampede. Indeed, this is where the name 'Head-Smashed-In' is believed to have originated.

Another Native American tribe that used such drives were the Beothuk in Newfoundland. In spring they hunted seal as they migrated and in early summer they would gather at river traps to catch migrating salmon. They would also fish, hunt sea birds and collect bird eggs. In autumn they came together for the great caribou drive. The caribou were funnelled towards rivers with the use of cut trees and other vegetation while warriors waited in canoes with sharpened arrows and spears to wound and kill the now vulnerable animals as they struggled to cross the river.

Gathering

There is a common belief that while men went out to hunt, women pottered off every so often and came back with whatever foods they managed to forage. The acquisition of foraged foods would thus be somewhat random, dependent on the generous compliance of nature and the weather. The truth is far from that. Foragers fought nature to acquire their plant-based foods. That was the only sensible route to ensuring a satisfactory supply of the non-meat component part of their diet.

A second misconception is that hunter-gatherers were nomadic. Some were but others not and, even among the nomadic, their journeys were driven by a detailed understanding of their wider surrounding ecosystems and the seasonal arrival and departure of wild plant crops. In time, these crops would be used to expand their nutritional resource. Thus, if it was known that at a certain month, a particular plant food was abundant, it is highly likely that some enterprising gatherers would attempt to take cuttings and plant them in the hope that when they next returned to this region, a more bountiful crop would be available.

It is also believed that at any given encampment, gardens would be set up, specifically to attract and then trap nosey animals or birds. Thus while we think of classic hunter-gathering and the eventual dominant role of settled agriculture as sequential periods, we miss· the many millennia when these systems operated side by side in both settled and nomadic communities.

Among the non-agricultural food security measures that were adopted in the era of the hunter-gatherer were hunting, harvesting, planting, husbandry of crops and animals, pest control, habitat management such as thinning, clearing, creating ponds and the use of fire to clear areas and to rejuvenate ecosystems. Settled agriculture and hunting-gathering co-existed and were inter-dependent. Quite simply, foraging was not left to chance and any romantic notion of subsisting on a natural supply of fruits, berries and nuts is naïve. Archaeological investigations reveal that in a representative central European site, the following were the ten most recorded plant foods encountered: Crab apple, hazelnut, strawberry blackberry, raspberry, beechnut, common nettle, oak, acorn and cherry.

Fire

Without doubt, one of the greatest achievements of humans that no other animal species has ever rivalled is the harvesting of fire. It transformed our entire evolutionary path. It is estimated that humans began to work with fire about 400,000 years ago and that the use of fire for cooking dates back to then. It is impossible to

Photo credit: gorodenkoff

know how humans came to capture fire but in the very dry climatic conditions of the time, random forest fires would have been common and fires started by lightening might also have been a route. From the dying embers of such fires, playful youths might have swung smouldering tree branches about and observed them re-igniting.

Indeed, the English poet and essayist, Charles Lamb, in his *Dissertation Upon Roast Pig*, tells the story of a swineherd Ho-Ti and his son Bo-Bo. While Ho-Ti was in the nearby forest collecting food for his pig, Bo-Bo, fond of playing with fire, allowed his fire to get out of control, quickly engulfing their home and killing their pig. While Bo-Bo pondered the fury of his father, a most tantalising aroma filled the air. His curiosity was aroused and he set out to move the dead pig. In doing so, he burned his fingers and popped them into his mouth to ease the pain. But some of the scorched skin was attached to the finger and, according to Lamb, 'for the first time in his life (in the world's life, indeed, for before him no man had known it) he tasted – crackling!'

7

A tall tale possibly, but most likely the effect of fire on food was an accidental discovery. The advantages of fire soon became apparent. Heat killed bacteria and destroyed natural plant toxins so food was safer. It helped gelatinise starchy foods and vegetables to make them less chewy and easier to eat, and it helped release flavours and aroma from the main ingredients of a dish and also from the native herbs and spices that became seasonally available. Research indicates that the counter rubbing of wooden sticks was the most common method of starting a fire, and still is today among nomadic indigenous peoples. Early US military opinion was that the Apache tribe of native Americans could light a fire in just 8 seconds using two wooden sticks. Charles Darwin observed the Tahitian natives lighting a fire:

> *They then proceeded to make a fire, and cook our evening meal. A light was procured, by rubbing a blunt pointed stick in a groove made in another, as if with intention of deepening it, until by the friction the dust became ignited. . . . The fire was produced in a few seconds: but to a person who does not understand the art, it requires, as I found, the greatest exertion; but at last, to my great pride, I succeeded in igniting the dust.*

The Advent of Cooked Food

Primitive cooking involved many techniques from simply roasting on a spit above a fire to burying heated stones in the holes in the ground to create an oven or the boiling of water using stones heated by fire. Darwin describes the process of cooking in Tahiti:

> *The Tahitians having made a small fire of sticks, placed a score of stones, of about the size of cricket-balls, on the burning wood. In about ten minutes the sticks were consumed,*

and the stones hot. They had previously folded up in small parcels of leaves, pieces of beef, fish, ripe and unripe bananas, and the tops of the wild arum. These green parcels were laid in a layer between two layers of the hot stones, and the whole then covered up with earth, so that no smoke or steam could escape. In about a quarter of an hour, the whole was most deliciously cooked.

Archaeological digs in the southwest of Ireland revealed another approach to cooking in that period when cooking was not conducted in the dwelling itself. First, their dig revealed the elements of a hut which they re-constructed with thin poles, animal skins and string to yield a structure, not unlike a wigwam of Native Americans. This was thought to be a store for food to protect it from animal predators. Within the tent, they found evidence of what might have been a butcher's table. Outside the tent was evidence of the use of wooden branches to form the walls of a rectangular hole in the ground. The team reconstructed the pit with crude wooden walls based on the wooden branches they unearthed in their dig. Because the pit was in boggy soil, they sealed the junctions with moss, which meant that as water seeped in, the gritty bits of peat were excluded by the filter. Next they turned to a semicircle of stones which they could see must have been the hearth. They experimented with the process of heating stones in a large fires and found that layers of wood followed by a layers of stones with a second layers of wood and stones worked best.

Once the fire was advanced and at its height, the structure collapsed to yield super-hot stones. With fork-like wooden structures, the stones were cast into the water and within minutes the pit-water was boiling. As the boiling subsided, more stones were added. A 10-pound leg of lamb, wrapped in straw and tied with straw string was lowered into the pit of boiling water. It was allowed to cook for 'twenty minutes to the pound and twenty minutes over'. The lamb was cooked through to the bone, as good as in any of today's kitchens.

Fires attract attention from rivals so were often moved into mountainous caves, partly to hide them but also to maximise the use of heat at night since fires in the open warmed only those sleeping very close by. What followed then would also transform human evolution, for in the warmth of the cave and with ample food to cook, time could be devoted to social activities: story-telling, cave art, early music and dancing. This was the beginning of the great creative powers of humans, far in advance of the animal kingdom.

Central to the group was the fire and eventually the meal, and it is certain that rules existed as to how people should behave at such meals. These rules were designed to create an order so that the meal itself was never the source of discord. In time, another remarkable milestone was achieved in dining etiquette. A stranger would be welcomed to join the group for the meal. This practice of sharing a meal with a stranger and eating in a communal eye-contact environment is utterly unheard of in all other animal species.

Storing Surplus Food

Early humans began to preserve foods using many techniques that are still in use today in the modern processed food industry. Drying was fundamental to food preservation and early humans used the heat of the sun, fires and the freezing winds of the north to dry foods. Foods which were dried would lose water and shrink and thus be light and portable. At first, these dried foods would be eaten raw but as the techniques of using animal hides and bladders developed, the dried food could be soaked in water to rehydrate.

Native Americans prepared a food called pemmican. Very thin slices of meat from large animals would be dried in the sun, over a fire or in the wind. The dried meat was then pounded in a stone mortar and pestle and then mixed 50-50 with melted fat from cattle, pigs or bear. Some bone marrow would be added and some berries and ground nuts might be as well. It is then put into a sack made from animal skin, sewn up and sealed with fat. The package was about the size of a modern bedroom pillow and would sustain tribespeople for long periods. It was a very nutritious food, high in protein and fat with vitamins from the berries.

Drying houses became commonplace in northwestern Europe where neither sun nor arctic winds prevail. This involved the use of a fire in pits with heat funnelled away from the fire to pass over foods for drying. Biscuits became an essential provision for seafarers with the ship's biscuit known as 'hardtack'. Made with just flour and water, these highly dried biscuits could last for a very long time, assuming they could be kept dry, not always an easy task on ships.

Salting is another ancient method of food preservation. We are familiar with aubergines being sweated before cooking, a process in which coarse salt is rubbed on the outside to draw water out. This reduces the slightly astringent flavour of the aubergine. Nature doesn't like imbalances and when salt is rubbed on a slice of aubergine, water moves out of the aubergine to reduce the concentration of salt on the outside, a process known to chemists as osmosis. If the salt-sweated food is dried, further movement of water to the exterior can occur. Thus, frequently, salting and drying go together. Dry salting involves a piece of meat being covered with salt which is vigorously rubbed into the flesh, a process which was repeated several times. The meat is then stored in a container, buried in salt, or it could be hung to dry.

Wet salting, also known as brining, was used to prepare meat for longer preservation than dry salting. In a sense, brining is the other side of the coin to salt sweating an aubergine. The meat is placed in a solution where the salt concentration is orders of magnitude higher than the natural salt within the meat. Since the brine is watery, there is no reason for water to move from the meat to the exterior. Rather, the salts of the brine enters the meat and this inflow of brine brings with it whatever flavours might have been added to the brine. Cloves, cinnamon, ginger, peppercorns and the like were added to the brine and these flavours would infuse the meat. Saltpetre was in use by the ancients for medicinal purposes and as an addition to brine. The use of saltpetre in Europe was unknown in Europe up to the eighteenth century when gunpowder was adopted by the military. The addition of saltpetre to brine gives the meat a red colour and greatly enhances flavour during wet curing.

Other ancient methods of preserving food include pickling, where the food is added directly to vinegar or allowed to ferment in acid conditions favouring bacterial growth. Foods such as meat, fish or poultry exposed to smoke will absorb many chemicals in the smoke which contribute to preservation. Smoking also adds flavour and gently dries food. All of these methods were used by early humans and very often multiple methods were used in turn. Meat could be brine-cured, then smoked and finally hung up to dry. The preservation of food was essential to provide its even distribution over all seasons and to facilitate migration into far off lands.

The ancient science of food preservation is brilliantly covered by Sue Shepherd in her book, *Pickled, Potted and Canned*.

Division of Labour and the Growth of Social Units

When tribespeople left the encampment to hunt for food, they did so as a team. Some were very skilled at tracking animals, others at throwing spears, others in skinning and butchery so that large animals could be more easily transported back to base camp and, in case of an overnight stay, others would manage tents, fires and cooking. Other than social insects such as bees and ants, very few creatures are so efficient at maximising the mixed skills of communities. This division of labour meant that many had skills which did not require them in the hunting team, such as those who fashioned weapons, those who tailored clothes and travel bags from hides, those who could ensure adequate supplies of fuel and those who were skilled in managing the communal needs of the group. This division of labour would inevitably begin to create a social order where the worth of one person's labour became more precious and in time more valuable than another's.

As these communities grew, they would encounter other near-by communities. Being human, there would sometimes be conflict and the social unit would grow to encompass the conqueror and the vanquished. But, being human, they also formed bonds with other groups and were united within small clans which in turn were united with greater clans. In his book *Sapiens*, Yuval Noah Harari notes that when settlers arrived in Australia they encountered native hunter-gatherers. It was estimated that around half a million Aborigine people were divided into between 200 to 600 tribes, and that would put the number in a tribe at a rough average of just over 1,000. It is proposed that as many as 100 small social units existed within each tribe. All of these tribes had their own language and they all varied in their religious beliefs, customs and social norms.

There is no reason to believe that it was different in the past and in different locations.

The Dawn of Settled Agriculture

As hunting and gathering became more sophisticated, and as social structures grew in scale and complexity, early humans began to settle in one place and to create a greater emphasis on animal and crop husbandry and a lesser emphasis on hunting and gathering. At some stage, the domestication of large animals occurred, and it has been suggested that the transition started when humans began to develop their symbiotic relationship with herds of cattle.

Young bull and cow calves were taken from the herd and managed in settlements. Within a few generations these animals became docile and adapted to the animal husbandry techniques of the day, one of which was the milking of cows, goats and sheep. The nutritional value of milk soon became evident and helped tip the scales from herding to farming. In time, the techniques for processing milk were acquired bringing butter, cheese, yogurt and cream to early human larders.

Bull calves can be reared for slaughter ensuring an adequate supply of meat as well as hides for clothes, bones for tools and horns for musical instruments. They can also be yoked to pull heavy objects from ploughs to millstones. As noted, early humans had successfully learned to forage for plant food with a deep understanding of the times of the year when different fruits, nuts, seeds, berries, edible flowers and herbs became available and when root crops or the mushrooms and truffles of the forest floor were best harvested. The advent of animal farming would require early humans to also turn their domestication efforts to plant foods. They would have learned that seeds that were not eaten and which fell on the ground would lead to renewed plant growth the following year. Almost certainly, cereal crops were the first to be cultivated.

Whereas the hunter-gatherers cooked in the open and lived in crude tent-like structures, settled agriculture brought with it houses. Central to all homes was the hearth for cooking and socialising. Archaeological digs at Ballynagilly in Ireland revealed the largest late stone age house in Britain and Ireland. It measured 6 metres by 6 metres with the walls made of wood. The gable ends were made of wattle daubed with mud. The houses had a pitched roof which was thatched with a hole in the roof for the smoke to escape. There were two hearths, one within a hole in the ground and the other on the surface.

These Neolithic dwellers cleared forests inland from the rivers where they might have first settled and farmed wheat, barley and oats and would have kept pigs and cattle. In time, these settlements would grow and begin to resemble small villages and towns. The wealthier in this new hierarchical society would have had more sophisticated houses, built with stone and soon reaching to two and then three floors. Their cooking would have been separate from the living and sleeping quarters and they would be the first to acquire more advanced cooking vessels, pottery at first, then bronze and eventually iron. The constructions of these sophisticated houses was accomplished with the labour of poor peasants seeking to secure additional income. As these peasants learned the tricks of construction so too did their houses develop. In time, wood was partly replaced by stone.

But whereas the life of hunter-gatherers was quite egalitarian, the arrival of agriculture led to a new hierarchical structure in tribes, one in which those at the top dreamed of larger fields to yield even more food, not only to feed the community but also to allow a substantial surplus to be stored. This would have two benefits. Surplus crops could be traded for luxuries with passing traders and could also be used to feed small armies to take what wasn't theirs. Those at the bottom of the hierarchy were the forerunners of the serfs, those who toiled for meagre personal reward and whose toils fed the forerunners of the ruling class, the aristocracy. Research shows that the transition from hunter-gatherer to settled farmer led to a fall in height of six inches and a reduction of life expectancy from 26 to 19 years. The growth in population density, a major characteristic of settled agriculture, brought with it a dramatic increase in intestinal and respiratory diseases, in parasitic infections and quite likely in violent crime.

Photo credit: Nastasic

Migration

Settled agriculture began in the 'fertile crescent', a region of today's middle east from the Nile delta, northeast through Jordan, Lebanon, Israel and Syria and then south from Turkey through Iran and Iraq. The fertile crescent fostered settled agriculture, but it would soon reach a critical point where the food supply would struggle to meet the needs of all. Populations expand exponentially (2, 4, 8, 16 etc.) and land or food can be acquired arithmetically (1, 2, 3, 4 etc.). This is the old Malthusian dilemma. So, at a certain stage when population growth began to misalign with food availability, migration to newer areas began.

In time, the ice sheet retreated and, as it did, humans moved northwards. Archaeologists have studied this migration and have several conflicting theories as to how this evolved. One thing is certain: food was central to migration. To move northwards, there were two options – over land or by river. Pigs and cattle can be easily herded on expansive grasslands such as existed in the fertile crescent. But the journey northward by land would mean making a journey through the heavily afforested vegetation that followed the ice age. The herding of pigs and cattle through these forests would be possible but challenging.

Another option was to move by boat, either west along the Mediterranean coast toward Spain or northwards through the networks of rivers of the European continent: the Danube, Rhine and Elbe. One estimate is that migration via a river or sea would involve about 40 people, with 5 to 10 breeding pairs of cattle and pigs together with 250 kilograms of wheat. That would mean about 4 persons per boat with 10 boats each carrying 1 to 2 tons of provisions. A replica of a 10-metre long log boat uncovered near Rome in an archaeological dig was able to travel 30 kilometres in one day with a crew of 10 and ample space for cargo.

Migration was not just north but west along the Mediterranean and the north coast of Africa, south along the east coast of Africa, southeast to Asia and northwest to the plains of Russia. In each direction the agricultural landscape changed in temperature, in rainfall, in seasons, in elevation and in soil type. At each new stage, adaptations would take place in animal and crop husbandry. When considering late stone age migration, one must constantly re-member that the period covered very many millennia. Thus, many groups would have split off and lived for many centuries in isola-tion. As time went by, greater migration would take place and there would an exchange of genes and agricultural know-how. Thus, did our food chain begin.

Chapter 2

Bread and Breakfast

Extract from Ballad of an Irish Wheat Field
(Anonymous)

Walk softly, O man, past an acre of wheat,
With awe in your heart and your face.
Walk humbly, O man, and with reverent feet,
For strength slumbers here – Can't you feel its heart beat?
And beauty's own couch is an acre of wheat,
And holiness dwells in this place.
Breathe gently, O breeze, on the grain-heavy ears,
That drank long and deep of spring rain.
O breeze, ripple gently the yellow-tipped spears.
Our little ones, caught in the rush of the years,
Need growth that is stored in the wheat's golden ears
All mother-ripe now with smooth grain.

All of the main cereals, wheat, oats, barley, rye, maize and rice, share the same botanical heritage, in that they are all grasses. In the early period of the hunter-gatherers, the seeds of grasses would have been plucked for consumption. This practice was precarious since grass seed is designed to be loose fitting so that it can be blown in the wind to spread the crop. Left to its own, a field of grass will take over any free soil it can find.

Photo credit: Iakov Kalinin

As ever, in the evolution of food, some wise person would pay attention to the few grasses that might survive a storm or strong winds. In time, their curiosity was rewarded from repeated sowing and reaping by way of a stable grass that would not be spread by wind, giving rise to a crop that depended on man. The payback was a dependable supply of grains.

In the early stages of homo sapiens, tools were used to break up the hard grains and, in time, to separate flour from hulls. Cereals would become the most important component of the diet of humans from earliest times to the present. Mastering the use of cracked cereals and flour would give rise to breads, gruels and ale and, in time, mixed with honey, the earliest form of biscuits.

Milling

Milling quickly developed as one of the most important technological innovations in food processing. It started off with a large, flat stone with a slight hollow in the middle. The miller would put some grains in the hollow and then rub another stone back and forth to break up the grain. From there it graduated to the millers quern. This involved two flat stones maybe as thick as a fist. The bottom one was slightly convex and the upper one slightly concave. The bottom one was fixed while the upper one had a handle which allowed the miller to turn the upper wheel over the lower one. The two were held together by an axle and the wheat was fed down the axle to fall between the two stones. If the two stones were too close the wheat would get too hot, and if too far apart the wheat would fly everywhere as it was cracked. Getting that right was a special skill of the miller.

These stones were specially made and would have been expensive to purchase. The miller was thus a very important person in early society and milling was a process that all of the community relied on. The *Book of Deuteronomy* records that Moses declared:

> *No man shall take the nether or the upper millstone to pledge: for he taketh a man's life to pledge.*

The work of the miller gave rise to many phrases we commonly use today: the daily grind; nose to the grindstone; run of the mill; grist to the mill. The tedious task of turning a heavy grindstone by hand was eventually replaced with the use of an ox and then by water and wind power. After the industrial revolution, steam and ultimately electric power would bring us to where we are today. Crushing wheat or other cereals gave rise to a form of wholemeal flour and the more skilled the miller, the finer the flower. Wholemeal flour, whilst more nutritious that white flour, is in fact more perishable because of the fatty material in the germ. This was one of the reasons why millers sought to obtain ever whiter flour.

It has also been argued that white was seen as a sign of purity, of heavenly beings and of priests and imams and thus white flour was somehow nearer perfection than wholemeal flour. To obtain white flour, the crude milled wholemeal flour had to be sieved and this appears to have been achieved by weaving very thin elm or willow branches into flat lattices through which the white flour could pass while retaining the germ and hull. Whether it was white or wholemeal flour, whether it was from wheat, oats or barley, flour became the key ingredient of the many breads that would sustain humankind for millennia. So important was bread, that along with olive oil and wine it became quasi-sacred. At first, though, most breads were flatbreads

Flatbreads

In the beginning, crushed cereal seeds would be mixed with water into a thick paste and spread thinly on a hot, flat stone to cook. These flatbreads as they are known, were unleavened, that is they were baked without the use of yeast or other raising agents to cause the bread to rise. Pitta bread is one of the best known flatbreads, possibly of Bedouin origin. It involves a simple mix of water and wheat flour which is left to rise just a little and is heated at a high temperature such that the hot steam creates an envelope effect. When cool, pitta bread is somewhat crispy on the outside and soft inside and can be opened up to be filled with meats or other foods. Pitta bread was dominant in the middle east and eastern Mediterranean.

The Indian sub-continent also has celebrated flatbreads, most notably chapati (also known as roti) and naan. Chapati is made with flour, water, oil and salt and is worked into a dough from which small pieces are pinched off, rolled very thinly and cooked on a pan at high heat. Again, the hot steam release causes bubbles to occur on the outside giving a crisp, snappy bread. Naan bread is made with flour, yeast, sugar, salt, ghee, water and yoghurt and as such is a leavened bread. After it has risen, it is rolled out to a plate-like structure. It is typically cooked in a tandoori oven over a very hot bed of charcoal and traditionally the wet plate-shaped dough is stuck to the inside wall of the oven. The release of steam at the high baking heat, together with the leavening process, gives a soft bread with an airy inside.

Non-leavened flatbreads could be made with most cereal flour, and in many parts of the world the climate and soil conditions didn't favour wheat and rye and so oats and barley were frequently used. Bannock is a Scottish flatbread made from unleavened barley or oatmeal dough, traditionally cooked on a hot stone. Similarly, stotties are round flatbreads, about 3 centimetres in height which have their origins in Newcastle in the northeast of England. Today they are split when cooked to form a sandwich-like product containing bacon or eggs or indeed both.

Following the swift and widespread adoption of the potato in Ireland, several potato-based flatbreads emerged, of which boxty is the most celebrated. It is comprised of a mix of grated raw potato, cooked mashed potato, flour, buttermilk and egg, then cooked like a pancake on a griddle pan. Indeed, pancakes are a worldwide form of flatbread from French crepes to Russian blinis. Fadge is another Irish potato cake popular in the north of Ireland as are soda farls, made from the dough of soda bread, flattened and grilled or fried.

When the Spaniards arrived in the New World, they encountered Aztecs eating a flatbread made from maize corn which is today's tortilla. The Jewish tradition of eating matzo during Passover is traced back to the belief that, in their haste to escape the

Egyptians with Moses, the Children of Israel left their bread which was rising and were required to eat flat unleavened matzo bread. Flatbreads were simple to make but as food became more abundant and more varied, bakers would experiments with variations on the theme and one of the main outcomes of that curiosity is the pizza, a food with a long history

Pizza: Pitta with a Flair

If the leavened loaf is regarded as the ultimate in bread bakery, then the pizza and related foods are a half-way house. But its origins go quite a way back. The ancient Greeks and Turks made partially leavened flatbreads, but unlike the early bakers these were dishes in themselves and not just a means of eating other dishes as pitta and other flatbreads had been. The Greeks made a flatbread called plakuntos, which incorporated herbs and olives into the dough. The Turks made a similar product, pede, again a round, partially leavened flatbread that would be eaten with a variety of adornments of meats and vegetables.

The Romans showed little interest in baking but the prosperity of Rome enticed many Greek bakers to emigrate there and in time they had established over 300 bakeries in Rome. The Greeks were assisted by Gaul immigrants from France for in pre-Roman Gaul, the Greeks had a significant presence there, establishing the city of Marseilles in 600 BCE. The Greeks brought their plakuntos with them which became known in Latin as placenta, and was comprised of a flatbread incorporating cheese, bay leaves, olives and honey. In time the placenta morphed into the traditional dish of north Italy, focaccia, which is derived from the Latin word for hearth, *focis*. Focaccia spread throughout Italy with different regions each with its unique recipe.

In the twelfth century, when Saracen pirates raided the coastal region of Liguria, the citizens of the city of Recco took refuge on high inland mountain land and developed what we now call Focaccia Recco, a three-layered non-leavened flatbread. In the south of Italy, the province of Bari adopted focaccia as an essential part of its cuisine, again with each town having its own unique recipe. *Focaccia Blues* is a comedy/documentary on a real life battle between two brothers, Luca and Giuseppe Digesù, who owned a small focaccia bakery and the fast food giant McDonald's who opened a 500 seat franchise nearby. In the 2002 battle for the minds of the locals, the Digesù brothers won and McDonald's was closed.

West of Bari lies the Kingdom of Naples, a Spanish colony since the thirteenth century, which was the main port of trade with Spain. The city of Naples, with a population of 314,967 in 1814, was the third largest city in Europe after London and Paris. In the early seventeenth century, a completely new food, the tomato, arrived in Naples as part of the Spanish booty from their conquest of Central America. It was at this point that focaccia evolved into the pizza and it was among the poor of Naples who took to this new food.

As Spain's' wealth dwindled due to multiple military and naval campaigns, it was the Italian provinces like Naples that bore the biggest burden of taxation. Moreover, Italy suffered great famines in the 1580s and 1590s with plagues decimating the population in the early half of the seventeenth century. Milan, Naples and Genoa lost as much as half of their population. These twin events of the famine and economic downturn meant that Naples would suffer a very serious and prolonged recession. It also accumulated a significant population of homeless citizens, as many as 50,000, which were known as the Lazzaroni. It was they who popularised street food in Naples, particularly pasta and pizza. In the case of the latter, the Lazzaroni could buy pizza by the slice according to the money they had available. Pizza remained a peasant food for a long time and the homeless Lazzaroni were looked down on by the literati. Carlo Collodi, author of *The Adventures of Pinocchio*, described the peasants of Naples in 1877 as covered in mud and dust and in ragged clothes. He went on to describe the pizza of the poor:

> *Do you want to know what pizza is? It is a crumb of leavened bread dough, toasted in the oven, with a sauce of everything on it a little. That black of the toasted bread, that off-white of the garlic and the anchovy, that yellow-greenish oil and the fried herbs and those red bits of tomatoes here and there give the pizza an air of complicated filth that is perfectly fine in harmony with that of the seller.*

The modern guardians of the Neapolitan pizza, the Associazione Verace Pizza Napoletana (AVPN), have records of a 'pizza marinara' being sold in 1730. Naples was a busy port and money-strapped sailors were aplenty in the city, all looking for a cheap tasty meal. In 1889, King Umberto I, also known as Umberto the Good, was touring the recently unified Kingdom of Italy following the reign of his father the great Victor Emmanuel II, the first king of unified Italy. Whilst in Naples, his wife, Queen Margherita, asked about some local foods, reflecting the growing disdain for anything French, given that country's annihilation of its royalty. A local pizzaiolo, Raffaele Esposito, made up three pizzas for the Queen. The one she liked best was made with toppings of tomato, mozzarella and basil and looked distinctly like the Italian tricolour flag of red, white and green. The Margherita pizza was born. Even with this royal approval, the pizza would remain a simple dish for the Lazzaroni of Naples.

The AVPN, who control the standards of a Neapolitan pizza, have a number of requirements. The oven must be wood burning. The flour must be '00' grade (never wholemeal), the tomatoes must be plum tomatoes, only natural Italian mozzarella should be used and the cooking should involve a well-kneaded dough, cooked at temperatures of about 400-480°c. Any toppings must be natural so it's okay to include mushrooms or peppers, but apparently since it's not 'natural' pepperoni is out. Quite how the high priests of Neapolitan pizzas can see bread or cheese as 'unprocessed' or 'natural' is difficult to follow. Finally, the AVPN requires the pizza to be eaten on the premises where it is baked.

But Pizza is now a global food and few pizza makers have ever heard of the AVPN police! It is said that Italy gave America the pizza and that America gave it to the rest of the world. However, the poor

Photo credit: Jakub Kapusnak

of Naples arriving in the US would meet with strong anti-immigrant opinion. Samuel Morse, he of the Morse code, described Neapolitan immigrants as filthy, ragged, ignorant and lacking morals. He also identified with Carlo Collodi in lambasting the pizza:

> *. . . a species of most nauseating looking cake . . . covered over with slices of pomodoro or tomatoes, and sprinkled with little fish and black pepper and I know not what other ingredients, it altogether looks like a piece of bread that had been taken reeking out of the sewer.*

The first licensed pizzeria in the US was that of Gennaro Lombardi in 1905 on Spring Street in New York. This NYC pizza was thin-based and crispy-crunchy. Other pizzerias followed but they were very much a niche food and not something sought by your average American family of the time.

The famous Chicago-style pizza is said to have been developed by Ike Sewell at Pizzeria Uno on the corner of Ohio and Wabash streets during World War II. It had a much deeper base than the NY pizza and was intended to provide not a snack but a substantial meal. When the dough is ready, it is pressed well into an iron pan including the sides. The pizzaiolo seeks to end up with a deep soft centre, a little crusty at the bottom and quite well done at the sides.

American GIs in southern Italy fell in love with pizza and as they advanced northwards popularised the dish throughout Italy. But the big surge in the pizza market was in the post-war period when they returned home. Today, pizza is the fourth most craved-after food in the US, after cheese, chocolate and ice cream. Some 70,000 pizzerias in the US produce 3 billion pizzas a year, amounting to a daily output equivalent in size to 100 acres (about 80 football fields) generating the consumption of 350 pizza slices per second.

Bread

It is widely held that bread, as we know it today, first appeared in Egypt. As with many great leaps in culinary techniques of old, we can only imagine how this came about. Basically, a microbe was needed to convert some of the sugars of the dough into carbon dioxide gas which would be trapped by the network of gluten fibres causing the bread to rise into a soft loaf, quite different from the hard flatbreads. Two sources would emerge. One was a family of bacteria that converts sugar into lactic acid and carbon dioxide. The second option was to use yeast, which is a microscopic fungus and which converts the dough sugars to alcohol and carbon dioxide, the alcohol vaporising when baked. Both were somewhat haphazard and beyond the control of the baker but they quickly learned to keep over some dough to start the bread making process the following day. Brewers' yeast was also used to rise bread dough and both bakeries and ale houses were often co-located and the assizes governing their standards were frequently enacted and enforced in tandem.

The original bread was a sourdough bread which has become very fashionable at the moment. It is far more challenging than simple yeast bread because it is a mixture of lactic acid bacteria and yeast, and the former grow 100 time faster than yeast. Thus if not properly controlled, the bacteria can use up most of the sugars producing a very sour bread which fails to rise adequately because the yeast is hindered. In the course of time the biological rising of bread by yeast was replaced by the chemical production of carbon dioxide. Wood ash contains a chemical which was known as potash, literally the ash left in a container after wood had been burned to ashes. It is a rich source of the chemical potassium carbonate.

Photo credit: Galina Afanaseva

This ash would be mixed with water to extract the potash and that was used in sourdough bread where the acid produced by the bacteria reacted with the potash to give rise to carbon dioxide.

This technology was an ancient one of Native American tribes which was adopted by the new settlers. Baking soda is a compound which when exposed to acid will give rise to carbon dioxide. The acid can be obtained using bacterial fermentation such as in sourdough, or it can be achieved using sour buttermilk. The latter is the traditional method of Irish soda bread. The final innovation brought us baking powder which is effectively a dry mixture of acid and an alkali in crystal form, and when added to water quickly starts to produce carbon dioxide.

There are two basic structures to bread. The first is the outside crust which can be soft or crispy, dark or light, glossy or matt, smooth or cracked, and the final appearance lies in the skilled hands of the baker. Within the crust lies the heart and soul of the bread, its crumb. The carbon dioxide released in the baking process is trapped in a complex network of gluten proteins and starch. The nature of this network is determined by the processing of kneading. If it is loose, large air pockets, which are called eyes, will be created. Ciabatta is a very popular Italian bread and although it is most often considered part of the ancient Italian cuisine, it was in fact first produced by two Italian bakers, Arnaldo Cavallari and Francesco Favaron, as recently as 1982. The dough for ciabatta is almost a batter because it has a high water content and also contains olive oil. It is so wet it is not kneaded but occasionally stirred during the fermentation process.

In contrast, a French baguette has very fine holes giving a very soft crumb. The crust's texture is related to the level of moisture in the dough which determines the amount of steam that will be produced and in turn that breaks up the outer crust making it a little flaky, but the more important determinant of the crust, crispiness, is the length of cooking and getting that right is the baker's skill. In his book *Bread: A Global History*, William Rubel describes almost 50 types of bread from around the world: bagel, baguette, baps, blini, brioche, ciabatta, crumpets, matzo, muffin, naan, poppadum, pretzel, pumpernickel, rye, soda bread, tortilla and panettone, to mention a few. Any one of them can have variations. The dough for a long baguette can be woven to an 8-plaited loaf. Loaves can be baked in batches with each loaf sitting right beside the next loaf during baking. The bread rises higher and when taken out and separated, the 'batch loaf' is tall and the sides are not crusted but pale white like the interior crumb. A standard bread can be altered to a brioche bread by the addition of eggs, butter and milk. The variations on a theme are enormous.

William Rubel shares with George Orwell a disdain for the snobbiness of bread. Bread is of great significance in ancient Christian texts. Apparently, the term bread is used all of 492 times in the bible and is a component of 38 biblical verses. Rubel describes the obsession we have with white and purity, and how the further we move from white the less pure we get. This is reflected in bread. White bread was the purest form, more expensive, tastier and accessible only to the better off. Wholemeal bread would not rise as much and had a thicker and chewier crumb and was decidedly for the peasants.

The most widely used wholemeal flour was that of rye and it was used extensively in northern Germany, across eastern and up along northern Europe. Wholemeal wheat would have been used wherever wheat was abundant and breads based on barley and oats were always wholemeal. But for as long as there was wholemeal bread as a staple for the lower class, there was always a craving within these consumers for whiter bread. And as this breakthrough happened with lower bread prices and higher incomes, white bread consumption grew. The high priests of public health nutrition see this as a retrograde step and preach the absolute nutritional superiority of wholemeal bread. In a *Road to Wigan Pier*, George Orwell expresses strong views on poverty and wholemeal bread:

The ordinary human being would sooner starve than live on brown bread and raw carrots. And the peculiar thing is this, that the less money you have, the less inclined you feel to spend it on wholesome food. A millionaire may enjoy breakfast off orange juice and Ryvita biscuits; an unemployed man doesn't. . . . When you are unemployed, which is to say when you are underfed, harassed, bored and miserable, you don't want to eat dull wholesome food.

The bread snob also has strong views on breads made locally by artisan bakers as compared to industrially processed bread, even though there is not one jot of difference between the two from a nutritional point of view. They are both made from white flour, water and yeast. Rubel recalls a workshop on bread at an international food conference. The moderator theatrically threw a pre-sliced, pre-packaged supermarket bread into a nearby bin. As Rubel put it:

To hundreds of millions of families worldwide this was good bread. . . . To the group of people in that room it was not just bad bread. It was not food. It was trash.

All white breads, bar the brioches and other fancy breads, are nutritionally identical. To dismiss an affordable and convenient bread as trash is simply sinful. It is a bit like saying that an industrially produced pure lambs' wool sweater is inferior to that which was hand crafted from the very same wool.

Breakfast

Today, cereals play a pivotal role in breakfast and I don't just mean breakfast cereals. Toast is commonly consumed at breakfast as are pastries, such as viennoiseries, pancakes, bagels and baguettes. Pliny the Elder refers to the taking of breakfast in ancient Rome. In her history of breakfast, Heather Anderson notes that a typical

Roman breakfast would include bread, cheese, olives, nuts and last-nights leftovers, all washed down with a little wine. The lower classes and slaves ate a porridge with bread. The Greeks also enjoyed a breakfast which was mainly bread dunked in wine. As time moved on, the hour when breakfast might be consumed varied and social values were attributed to the eating of breakfast. This meal was seen as a necessity for the labouring classes, for children, the elderly and the infirm, and was by and large shunned by the well-heeled who were hale and hearty and quite lazy.

In the twelfth century, the Anglo-Normans confined their eating to two meals in the day: dinner was at nine in the morning and supper at five in the afternoon, which was incorporated into the popular rhyme.

> *To rise at five, to dine at nine,*
> *To sup at five, to bed at nine,*
> *Makes a man live to ninety-nine.*

By the fifteenth century, the number of meals had risen to four: Breakfast at seven in the morning, lunch at ten, dinner at four in the afternoon and supper between eight and nine in the evening.

From then up to the present day, breakfast would be part of the diets of all classes and would, in time, evolve to what we see of breakfast today. By the start of the eighteenth century the English wealthy classes dined on eggs, bread and meat for breakfast while poorer people confined themselves to oaten porridge. Sometimes the word 'stirabout' is used as something different from porridge, but they are one and the same thing.

In the Celtic countries of Ireland, Wales and Scotland, oats was a crop that thrived best under the dominant soil conditions and prevailing climate, and oatmeal flour was baked into porridge with

Photo credit: NANAV Café Bangalore

milk and butter and, when available, honey. Oats were always considered inferior to wheat with barley lying in between but closer to oats. Pliny the Elder reveals his utter ignorance of botany when he describes oats as a crop which emerges from the degeneration of wheat or barley due to poor soil, microclimate and husbandry.

In her book *The Land of Milk and Honey,* Brid Mahon points out that even under ancient Celtic law, where fostering of young boys was commonplace, the advice was:

1. The children of inferior grades are to be fed on porridge or stirabout made of oatmeal on buttermilk or water taken with stale butter and are to be given a bare sufficiency

2. The sons of the chieftains are to be fed to satiety on porridge made of barley meal upon new milk taken with fresh butter

3. The sons of Kings and princes are to be fed on porridge made of wheaten meal, upon new milk, taken with honey.

In his *Dictionary of the English Language,* published in 1755, Samuel Johnson defined the world of oats as follows: 'A grain, which in England is generally given to horses, but in Scotland supports the people.' He and his pal Boswell would make many tours of Scotland and seemed to enjoy taunting the Scots. At a dinner party, an elderly lady addressed Johnson thus:

> *'Dr. Johnson, you tell us, in your Dictionary, that in England oats are given to horses but that in Scotland they support the people. Now, Sir, I can assure you, that in Scotland we give oats to our horses, as well.'*
>
> *'I am very glad, Madam,' he replied, 'to find that you treat your horses as well as you treat yourselves.'*

The view of the English gentry of the inferiority of the Scottish reliance on oats was commented upon by another English notable, Adam Smith:

> *The common people in Scotland, who are fed with oatmeal, are in general neither so strong nor so handsome as the same rank of people in England, who are fed with wheaten bread. They neither work so well, nor look so well; and as there is not the same difference between the people of fashion in the two countries, experience would seem to show, that the food of the common people in Scotland is not so suitable to the human constitution as that of their neighbours of the same rank in England.*

The advent of tea and coffee meant that for the wealthy, breakfast didn't have to involve alcohol, but for the lower classes ale and sometimes wine were an essential component of breakfast. In the US southern states, maize became a popular breakfast cereal as grits. As incomes rose, particularly in the US, ordinary people were beginning to have bacon, eggs and sausages, or variations of that theme, and this would bring them into conflict with the Clean Living Movement. The 'clean living' movement is a term coined by Ruth Engs in 1990 to describe a widespread concern over the morals of the nineteenth century way of life. It is an all-embracing term covering single issue groups on alcohol intake, smoking, contraception, sedentary lifestyle, and diet, including meat, roughage, filtered water, tea and coffee. These movements would give rise to the Seventh Day Adventists and to the Mormons.

The most vocal critic of poor diet was Dr Graham Sylvester. He was a preacher, and while a young man was expelled from school for an alleged improper dalliance with a woman. His lecture to young men strongly emphasised the association of a poor diet with bad sexual habits (specifically 'self-pollution'!) among boys and became a national champion of vegetarianism. Meat, coffee and sweet biscuits, among other bad habits, caused the blood to heat leading to early development of 'a preternatural sensibility and prurience of the genital organs'.

The association between vegetarianism and both God and health spread rapidly across the US. In 1894, a Seventh Day Adventist vegetarian, John Harvey Kellogg, established a sanatorium in Battle Creek, Michigan. The clients were affluent and upper class. One day, a pot of cooked wheat was left unattended and became stale. Both John and his brother Will, in a 'waste not, want not' frame of mind, attempted to salvage something from this error and passed the wheat paste through two rollers to dry. It came out as flakes and both Kellogg's Cornflakes and the breakfast cereal industry were born and flourish to this day. The obsession of physicians for healthy diets for their fancy sanatoria continued in Europe. The Swiss breakfast dish, Bircher Muesli, was developed around 1900 by Swiss physician Maximilian Bircher-Brenner for his patients and is still a very popular breakfast throughout Switzerland and Germany.

Breakfast varies enormously around the world and is influenced by the trials, tribulations and triumphs of everyday life: lazy breakfasts on the weekend, on-the-go breakfasts in busy city life, special breakfasts in fancy hotels, breakfast with the kids in the mayhem of the early hours of the day and healthy, mindful breakfasts when the see-saw of dieting comes around. It's the same the world over. The traditions vary, but on a global basis breakfast is a meal which is low in fat, high in starch and micronutrients and is the foundation for a good day's nutrient intake.

Chapter 3

Soup

Extract from **The Ballad of Bouillabaisse**

By William Makepeace Thackeray

A street there is in Paris famous,
For which no rhyme our language yields,
Rue Neuve des Petits Champs its name is –
The New Street of the Little Fields.
And here's an inn, not rich and splendid,
But still in comfortable case;
The which in youth I oft attended,
To eat a bowl of Bouillabaisse.

This Bouillabaisse a noble dish is –
A sort of soup or broth, or brew,
Or hotchpotch of all sorts of fishes,
That Greenwich never could outdo;
Green herbs, red peppers, mussels, saffron,
Soles, onions, garlic, roach, and dace:
All these you eat at Terré's tavern,
In that one dish of Bouillabaisse.

In her excellent book on soup, Janet Clarkson points out that for almost every food you can think of, some group of people in some part of the world don't include it in their diet. But everywhere

39

in the world, soup is eaten and with endless variation in the ingredients. Many of human's early dishes were gruel-like, simple dishes of crudely ground grains soaked in water, maybe with fruit added as a sweetener when in season.

The transformation of gruels into soups was one of the earliest consequence of domestic fires. They say that the word 'soup' is derived from the verb 'to sop', which means to soak up a liquid, in this case a broth-like meal. Sopping involves bread and not only allows bread to be used as a device to take soup, but the two together meant that older, staler bread could readily be used to sop.

Today, we always associate soup with bread and many soup recipes build in bread-like elements into the dish. French onion soup has a slice of cheese on bread floating on top and the croutons used in many recipes again reflect this bread-soup link, including the German Schwarzbrotsuppe or Boston seafood chowder. As time went by and soup and bread became associated with poverty, the term 'to sop' gave rise to the use of the word sop as some appeasement of an individual to shut them up, so to speak. Soup, although mostly liquid, is eaten, not drank. Soups have a strong health connotation, seen as 'hearty' and 'filling'.

Texture and Flavour

No dish varies so much across the globe as much as soup, but we can start to categorize it in terms of flavour and texture. A consommé is as liquid as it gets in terms of mouthfeel. It is simply watery. It may ooze flavour but its dominant trait is its purity. In general, consommés are associated with meat soups and during the preparation of the soup, you can strain off the solid bits but when it cools it will be quite like a jelly of a wobbling fragile solid masses and occasional liquids. The jelly bit is due to gelatine which is a

Photo credit: Jakub Kapusnak

collagen-type protein found everywhere in bones, skin, flesh and offal. To clarify a soup rich in gelatine, the amazing technology of a protein raft is used. This is yet another example of how sixteenth century cooks mastered techniques without any knowledge of the underlying science.

The whites of eggs are mixed with some vinegar and crushed eggshells and added to the soup. As it boils the gelatine becomes entrapped in the coagulating egg whites and after a while the raft can be gently moved to allow a fine liquid to be decanted. Some soups are creamy, such as veloute-based soups where a roux is used to thicken the soup, while others can achieve this texture with complete pureeing. Some are served cold such as vichyssoise or gazpacho, and some are very spicy such as tom yum. Wikipedia lists 116 soups from around the world, many of which are found in multiple culinary traditions.

Great Soups of the World

Bouillabaisse is a traditional Marseilles soup. The word is derived from the word 'to boil (*bouilllir*) and to reduce (*abaisser*), and was made popular by the fishermen of Marseilles who would cook up the soup on the beach. The fish they added were those that would not be popular in the local fish market, mostly rockfish such as char, grouper, dogfish, stonefish or striped bass. As with many soups, bread is an essential ingredient and in Marseille the soup is poured on to a stale bread known as a marette and the soup is eaten that way. The fish are served on a separate plate. Alternatively, the soup can be served with croutons which have been dipped in a rouille sauce, a Provençal sauce made from chillies, garlic, bread and saffron.

Bisque is a class of fish soup which was originally based on finely ground seafood shells which were first roasted and then boiled. This double cooking may be the basis of its name, since *bis* is 'twice' in Latin. Nowadays, bisque inevitably refers to a lobster soup.

Chowders, have large chunks of fish and were a traditional dish of Breton sailors who adapted it to the salted cod of Newfoundland. The chowder was made by boiling the ship's biscuit, known as hardtack, with pieces of salted cod. In time, this chowder travelled to the east coast of the US and gave rise to the famous New England clam chowder, a favourite of President John Kennedy. The word is related to the French word for a cauldron, *chaudière*. In Boston, clam chowder is finished with milk, whereas in New York tomatoes are used to finish the dish.

Another famous US seafood soup is Gumbo, which is the official dish of the state of Louisiana and was brought there by west African slaves for whom the word for okra is gumbo. It is most

Photo credit: Jakub Kapusnak

often associated with shellfish and is thickened with okra and/or a powdered seasoning made from the dried ground sassafras leaves. Its base is a dark roux achieved by prolonged cooking of flour and water.

Shark fin soup is a soup made with different ingredients but is thickened by using the gelatine-like proteins derived from the fins of sharks. Many countries have banned the sale of foods containing shark fin.

Of the vegetable-based soups, minestrone is one of the most famous derived from the Italian word for soup, *minestra*, itself derived from the verb *ministrare*, to administer. These early soups were handed out most likely to the poor and were intended to be a substantial meal. What distinguishes minestrone from other minestra soups is the use of pasta and beans which help to thicken it. Borscht is another world travelled soup with its origins in the Ukraine. Cock-a-leekie soup of chicken and leeks is a Scottish signature dish while mulligatawny, derived from the Tamil words defining pepper broth, is an Indian soup brought back to England by its colonists. Leek and potato soup is very popular and it would eventually give rise to vichyssoise, a cold version of this soup. This is an American soup with a French name, Vichy being a town in central France and Oise a city to the north of France. It was designed by a French chef, Louis Diat, at New York's Ritz hotel. In 1950, he described its origins to the *New Yorker* magazine:

> *In the summer of 1917, when I had been at the Ritz seven years, I reflected upon the potato and leek soup of my childhood which my mother and grandmother used to make. I recalled how during the summer my older brother and I used to cool it off by pouring in cold milk and how delicious it was. I resolved to make something of the sort for the patrons of the Ritz.*

Some cynics would say that someone in the kitchen forgot to reheat a simple leek and vegetable soup and that Diat simply had the nerve to garnish it and serve it cold with a warm story of his childhood. Many bean-based soups can be found such as lentil soup or Tuscan bean soup. Notable animal-based soups are oxtail soup which is an ancient use of that part of an ox that isn't too easy to put on a plate. The tail is skinned and cut into small pieces and served as a soup with vegetables. The bone marrow in the tail added an extra medicinal touch to this soup which was popularised in London with the arrival of the Huguenots from France in the seventeenth century. One soup bearing the same name as a famous perfume is the Philippine dish, Soup Number 5. It has the look of oxtail but is made from bull's penis and testicles and was associated with the acquisition of strength.

And there are some other exotic soups such as bird's nest soup from China. Swiftlets, birds native to Asia, use their saliva to build nests high in caves in remote regions. Their saliva, when exposed to air for a short time, forms a gelatinous substance which is used to build nests. These are harvested at great risk and effort and require meticulous cleaning with tweezers to remove even the tiniest feathers. The value is enormous, about €10,000 per kilo. The nests are used in chicken-type soups to impart a remarkable consistency, and a bowl of genuine bird's nest soup will cost about €100. Today, special swiftlet nesting boxes are built to make the entire process safer and cheaper.

Soup and Health

Soups are rarely such delicacies and, mostly, they are the ultimate comfort food, especially on a cold winter's day. But it's when you're laid up in bed that soup really helps to comfort and the healing property of soup has been in vogue for millennia. Maimonides was a Jewish philosopher of the twelfth century located in Spain. He was of the view that chicken broth was ideal for the treatment of many ailments, but especially respiratory conditions. Indeed, in the Jewish tradition chicken soup is often referred to as 'Jewish penicillin'. 'How mad is that,' I hear you say. Well, maybe not so mad.

Dr Stephen Rennard, a chest physician in Nebraska, was so pestered as to the health-yielding properties of chicken soup by his Lithuanian wife that he conducted an experiment to explore this. He found that under test tube conditions, chicken soup did seem to suppress the activity of the blood cells (neutrophils) involved in the start of the inflammatory process. He published his study results in the prestigious medical journal *Chest*, a journal of the American College of Chest Physicians. Soup is warm, easy to eat and digest and is not over-filling. In his novel *East of Eden* John Steinbeck writes thus of chicken soup:

Photo credit: chas53

And Tom brought him chicken soup until he wanted to kill him. The lore has not died out of the world, and you will still find people who believe that soup will cure any hurt or illness and is no bad thing to have for the funeral either.

Soup and Charity

Wherever you read of the history of soup, you will encounter its use in the management of poverty. Quite a few people have earned fame in this regard. A young woman by the name Roxelana was recruited to be the concubine of Süleyman the Magnificent who ruled the Ottoman empire in the fifteenth century. She established the Haseki Sultan Imaret, the world's first soup kitchen, which fed 500 deserving souls a hearty soup every morning and evening. Patrick Colquhoun, a nineteenth century Scottish merchant and wannabe statistician, is remembered for two things: the creation of the first police force in England, the Thames River Police, and the establishment of London's first soup kitchen.

However, the doyen of soup for the poor was the celebrated Victorian chef, Alexis Soyer. Born in France he worked in London as the head Chef of the Reform Club, a gentleman's club with leftish tendencies. He wrote a major cookbook for those with limited ability to spend money on food. During the ravages of the Great Hunger that was the potato famine in Ireland, Soyer travelled to Ireland with a reformist approach to soup kitchens. At the time, soup kitchens, temporary shelters built of canvas and wood, were common for the ravaged and malnourished poor.

The starving throng would gather en masse near the makeshift sheds with a chicane-type entry system much as you see in any modern airport passport control line. They entered, 100 at a time, and sat 50 opposite 50 with a soup bowl riveted to the wooden table and with soup spoons attached to the bowl by chains. As soon as everyone was seated, grace was said, and soup consumption commenced. Precisely six minutes later, the bell rang and the first group filed out of the back door as another shift came in the front. Soyer's kitchen fed 8,000 people each day during the first few months. At the height of the famine, 26,000 people passed through daily.

Regrettably, some proponents of the Protestant faith required the recipients to renounce their Catholicism and to manifest their new faith by eating meat-based soup on Fridays, as well as accessing the protection of the local English militia. It was a practice denounced by the majority of Protestant churches. Taking the soup was a no-brainer for a parent, most often the mother, of starving children. Such poor souls earned the title of 'soupers' having 'taken the soup'.

Photo credit: danefromspain

Soyer set up many soup kitchens and used them to show off his patented designs for large-scale preparation of soups which he would eventually take to the military in the Crimean war. His standard recipe was as follows: 1 ounce of dripping, 4 ounces of diced beef without bone, 2 medium onions, thinly sliced, the peelings of 2 turnips, 15 green leaves, 8 ounces of flour, a teaspoon of brown sugar and 2 gallons of water. This would equate to about 60 calories per pint which might be a generous serving. The soup filled the belly of the destitute but it hardly slowed their wretched path to starvation and death. Soyer's book, *A Shilling Cookery for the People,* contained all sorts of recipes for those with little money. One such recipe was for sheep's head soup. It was a dish that remained popular among the poor in Dublin and the dramatist Brendan Behan recalls this soup with horror in his essay, 'The Confirmation Suit', published by *The Spectator*:

Aunt Jack made terrible raids on us now and again, to stop snuff and drink, and make my grandmother get up in the morning, and wash herself, and cook meals and take food with them. . . . When she was left alone it was a pleasure to eat with her. She always had cans of lovely things and spicy meat and brawn, and plenty of seasoning, fresh out of the German man's shop up the road. But after a visit from Aunt Jack, she would have to get up and wash for a week, and she would have to go and make stews and boil cabbage and pig's cheeks. Aunt Jack was very much up for sheep's heads, too. They were cheap and nourishing. But my grandmother only tried it once. . . . When she took it out of the pot, and laid it on the plate, she and I sat looking at it, in fear and trembling. It was bad enough going into the pot, but with the soup streaming from its eyes, and its big teeth clenched in a very bad temper, it would put the heart crossways in you. My grandmother asked me, in a whisper, if I ever thought sheep could look so vindictive, but that it was more like the head of an old man, and would I for God's sake take it up and throw it out of the window. The sheep kept glaring at us, but I came the far side of it, and rushed over to the window and threw it out in a flash. My grandmother had to drink a Baby Power whiskey, for she wasn't the better of herself.

Soup is offered on most western menus to be eaten at the start of a meal. Not so in Asia. It may be served at the beginning but it is more likely to be served as the final dish. With big banquets in China, many soups might be served in one meal, some of which may be savoury, others sweet. Soup may be part of every cuisine but its global variation is enormous.

Chapter 4

The Delights of Dairy

The Cow

By Robert Louis Stevenson

The friendly cow all red and white,
I love with all my heart:
She gives me cream with all her might,
To eat with apple-tart.

She wanders lowing here and there,
And yet she cannot stray,
All in the pleasant open air,
The pleasant light of day;

And blown by all the winds that pass
And wet with all the showers,
She walks among the meadow grass
And eats the meadow flowers.

Dairy foods have been part of the human diet since the dawn of agriculture and milk was very sought after given its highly nutritious profile. However, milk is very perishable and so its role in the human food chain required it to be processed to forms that would keep for some time. The auroch was the original bovine that eventually gave rise to a multitude of cattle breeds. It was a monstrous animal described by Julius Caesar in his *History of the Gallic War* as 'a little below an elephant and of appearance, colour and shape of a bull' and describes how young German warriors would hunt these beasts using hidden pits to trap and kill them. Both large and small aurochs are depicted in cave paintings at Lascaux near Montignac in France and, although the aurochs were extinct by the seventeenth century, they formed the stock from which almost all modern cattle breeds emerged.

Cattle would become the main species providing milk for human consumption but others had advantages. Sheep and goats can manage steep mountains in foraging for food whereas the heavy cow just isn't suited to hilly, rugged terrain. Camels were the main source of milk for the pastoral Bedouins and the yak became the bovine of choice in the Himalayas and eastwards to Mongolia. Many different breeds of cattle emerged and for good reasons it must be said. The Kerry cow, native to Ireland, is much lighter than most dairy breeds and is thus best suited to the west coast where annual rainfall is high. Because of their weight, they do less damage to the wet soil. The Jersey breed is also small, allowing a higher stocking rate than heavier cattle and they are prolific lactators yielding a milk rich in dairy fat.

Milk in History

Milk and the cows are heavily featured in myths and in religions. The Upinshads are a set of sacred texts designed to help Hindus to achieve spiritual balance, and one of these, the Chandogya Upanishad, espoused the ethic of non-violence, including non-violence to animals. The sacredness of the cow in India is not simply due to this ethic of non-violence, but also to the fact that the cow was associated with several Gods such as Lord Krishna, who created the cow and Kamadhenu, the goddess of cows, depicted in an ancient sculpture as a beautiful female torso on a cow's body with the cow displaying both wings and a peacock tail. In her book *Milk: A Local and Global History*, Deborah Valenze described the Graeco-Roman tale:

> *Milk belonged to the gods; it was the elixir of immortality. One sip from the breast of the chief female goddess, Juno, could confer divinity and an endless life. . . . According to legend, the stars of the Milky Way – plentiful but unobtainable – represented droplets of Juno's milk, scattered when Jupiter stealthily installed his illegitimate and mortal offspring, Hercules, at the breast of his sleeping wife. The infant's energetic sucking woke the goddess and she pulled away, startled. But it was too late to avoid a divine mess: her let-down reflex sent milk spraying into the heavens, where the fluid congealed into stars, and down to earth, where it sprouted lilies.*

Interestingly, this mythology of Juno, the peacock of the goddess Kamadhenu and the stars of the milky way is drawn upon in Sean O'Casey's play *Juno and the Paycock*. Captain Boyle explains the preference of sailors for the word 'Blowed' rather than 'Blew':

> *Joxer: Aw, it's a darlin' word, a daarlin' word.*
>
> *Boyle: An', as it blowed an' blowed, I ofen looked up at the sky an' assed meself the question – what is the stars, what is the stars?*
>
> *Joxer: Ah, that's the question, that's the question – what is the stars?*

Both the Bible and the Koran refer to milk, the former when it describes the land of milk and honey, and the latter when a glass of milk is consumed at Iftar, the end of the daily Ramadan fast. One of the great legends involving milk is that of the wolf who nursed Romulus and Remus, the founders of the city of Rome. Across the species of lactating mammals, there is a common general pattern of nutrients: fat, sugar as lactose, proteins (casein and whey), and minerals and vitamins. However, the balance of the main nutrients varies according to the need of the species.

Hooded seal milk is 50 per cent fat compared to just 3 per cent in cow's milk. In the dangerous ice packs of the arctic, seal pups are nursed for just four days or so and they must pack in as much body fat as possible in that short period. They double their weight in that short period consuming about 17 pounds of milk per day. In contrast, Rhino milk contains only 0.3 per cent fat but the nursing period is very long, about two years. The Kangaroo is unique in having the ability to nurse both older and nascent joeys at the same time with milks of different composition being secreted from either of the two teats, one in the pouch and one outside.

Photo credit: Melanie Dompierre

Milk can give rise to many dairy products but fresh milk would have been the mainstay of the diets of those herding dairy cattle, sheep or goats. However, because milk is so perishable, it was processed into a variety of dairy products, the most simple of which would have been sour milk and such fermented milks are found all over the world. When butter is produced from milk, the byproduct would today be called skimmed milk but was traditionally known as buttermilk, which was allowed to ferment before drinking.

Yogurt

Yogurt was almost certainly the first modification to milk to increase its shelf life. It is often said that yogurt developed when herdsmen stored milk in sacs made from animal intestine and found that the milk thickened into some form of yogurt. This seems unlikely. It may help explain the development of cheese, but yogurt is quite a different thing. It requires inoculation with very specific lactic acid bacteria. They convert the sugar of milk into lactic acid which gives yogurt its sour, tart taste.

Photo credit: Jakub Kapusnak

Decomposing plants and fruits create the right conditions for the growth of these bacteria and almost certainly this is where yogurt began – the accidental contaminations of milk with perhaps a fruit which was beginning to decompose. In time, these lactic acid bacteria would be found wherever milk featured, such as on the teats of animals or in milking pales.

Early humans had all the time in the world to try out new ways of modifying foods; indeed, they had millennia to do it. Pliny the Elder noted that the 'barbarous nations', for whom milk was a central part of their diet, simply didn't make cheese and 'yet they understand how to thicken milk and form there from an acrid kind of liquid with a pleasant flavour, as well as a rich butter'.

There are many yarns about yogurt. For example, it is said that Genghis Khan had his warriors drink fermented mares milk as they roamed the steppes of central Asia. Another is that the French King, Francis I, was given yogurt on a visit to Turkey by Sultan of the Ottoman Empire, Suleiman the Magnificent to cure his diarrhoea. But perhaps the biggest yarn of all would come from no less than Professor Élie Metchnikoff, a Russian zoologist who worked in the Pasteur Institute and was awarded the Nobel Prize in 1908 for his work on natural immunity. On June 8, 1904, Metchnikoff gave a public lecture on 'Old Age' and is reported to have claimed that:

> *Interestingly, this microbe is found in the sour milk consumed in large amounts by the Bulgarians in a region well-known for the longevity of its inhabitants. There is therefore reason to suppose that introducing Bulgarian sour milk into the diet can reduce the harmful effect of the intestinal flora.*

Well, the key phrase here is 'to suppose' because neither then, nor now, was there a shred of evidence to support the theory that yogurt prolonged life. Moreover, experts on his life refer to his personal interests in the commercialisation of yogurt manufacture.

Butter

Butter is likely to have its origins in the transport of milk on horseback where the milk was stored in an animal hide, not animal intestines. In milk, the fat exists as tiny droplets wrapped in thin protein-rich membranes, designed to repel one another which allows the fat to be suspended in water. When milk is jostled about, as would happen in such horseback journeys, the fat globules collide, the outer membranes get broken down and the droplets begin to merge with each other into increasingly larger droplets, eventually yielding butter. The next step was to control this random process and early methods involved a stick with a paddle at the bottom where a small rope was twisted around the stick. One person pulled one end of the rope, then another pulled the other end. As this churning process was repeated, butter was formed.

The simple technology of churning milk became a little more sophisticated. The buttermilk, just milk minus the now solid butter, is drained off and the butter is washed several times to remove all the buttermilk. The butter is now worked on by hand to thoroughly mix it and to allow salt to be added. The butter is shaped using small paddles into the traditional rectangular shape of butter. In his poem 'Churning Day', Seamus Heaney beautifully describes the emergence of butter during churning as 'gilded gravel' and 'coagulated sunlight'.

In India and neighbouring countries, the warm climate would readily lead to a deterioration in the quality of butter with a distinct rancid smell. To overcome this, butter was melted and slowly cooked at a low temperature to evaporate off the water, thereby increasing its shelf life. This form of butter is known as ghee. Given the sacred nature of the cow in the Hindu religion, ghee is perceived as an important feature of many religious functions from sacred candles to burial pyres.

Cheese

Cheese offers the best way to preserve milk for long periods. It is a remarkable example of how food production, today a precise science, began as an art form. Little Miss Muffet certainly knew her curds and whey but not nearly as well as the cheesemaker did. This form of milk processing very likely began with exposure of milk to the guts of animals, specifically to the fore stomach of calves. When a calf suckles its dam, the milk enters the forestomach and is immediately acted upon by the digestive enzyme rennet. This causes the milk to coagulate to form a solid curd, about the size of an American football. The liquid part of the milk is expelled from the solid curd, and flows onwards for digestion. The curd is digested more slowly because it has a complex structure and to extract all of the vital nutrients requires a rather sophisticated process.

There are three ways to make cheese. One is the use of the calf enzyme rennet, another is the use of lactic acid bacteria and the third involves a combination of heat and bacteria. The first day or so of cheese making is critical and the three different processes focus on acidity, water content and salt. By varying these factors, we arrive at different cheeses. Lactic acid bacteria are central to most cheese-making and early cheese makers would have discovered that if the used some whey from the previous day, the process of curd formation was speeded up. They would not have known that it was the lactic acid bacteria in the whey which got things going. Today, specially cultured strains of these bacteria are used as a starter culture.

The sole use of lactic acid bacteria to rapidly produce acid conditions makes for a weak curd with a lot of water and favours cheeses which are eaten freshly, such as cottage cheese, fromage frais and cream cheeses. The lactic acid bacteria and heat combination leads to less water retention and less acidity and this gives rise to ricotta cheese. Finally, rennet, which usually involves some lactic acid bacteria being added, yields a harder curd with the least water of the three approaches. Within this first day or so, the initial curd undergoes a series of processes to get it ready for maturation. Almost all of these processes are designed to squeeze out as much liquid whey as possible.

The process of ripening is known as affinage and the person who oversees this is an affineur. They manipulate the cheese to control moisture and air through washing, piercing and turning. Columella, the Roman agriculturalist, describes an ancient approach to cheese making.

> For which reason, the country-people do not indeed suffer the moisture to drop slowly from its own accord; but when the cheese becomes a little more solid, they put weights upon it, that whereby the whey may be squeezed out. When taken out of the moulds or baskets it is put in a dark cold place so as not to spoil; it is arranged on perfectly clean boards, sprinkled with ground salt to draw out the acid liquor; when hardened, it is pressed even more forcefully to compact it; then it is treated

again with roast salt and again pressed. After nine days of this treatment the cheeses are washed and arranged without touching one another, out of the light, on wicker trays made for this purpose, to dry out somewhere; then they are stacked close together on the shallow shelves in a room that is closed and out of the wind.

This is not a million miles from what happens to this day in preparing the great cheeses of which there are thousands. Wikipedia lists 46 varieties of blue vein cheeses alone! Each cheese has its own story, and each is distinguished by a slight or significant variation in cheese making.

Let's begin with smelly blue vein cheeses such as English stilton, French roquefort and Italian gorgonzola. About five or six days into the formation of the coagulated curd, the cheese is inoculated with a special fungus known as *penicillium roqueforti*. The cheese is then sealed to keep air out and stored under strict conditions of

Photo credit: gresei

air and temperature for about five weeks with regular turning and salting. The final stage is called piercing in which the cheese curd is punctured to let air in, and this now changes the internal environment to favour the growth of the mould. About two months later, the cheese is ripe with the mould penetrating throughout the curd, giving it a distinctive flavour.

The Swiss cheese emmental has unique holes throughout its structure and for the last century or so the theory was that when all the lactose in the milk had been converted to lactic acid, new bacteria came to the fore and fermented the acid which gave rise to the gas, carbon dioxide, thus creating holes. However, recent data from the Swiss research agency Agroscope, using CT scanning, have shown that tiny dust particles, mainly hay, are responsible for the holes. That, however, seems quite unlikely. Modern Swiss dairying is not very different from anywhere else in the world with sterile modern milking parlours and with milk collection in the summer months when cows are grazing grass. And if hay is the culprit, why aren't other cheeses riddled with holes? So, the mystery of gruyere and other holed Swiss cheeses continues.

Camembert, it is said, was created by Marie Harel, a French cheesemaker in the eighteenth century. Like brie and cambazola, camembert are surface-ripened cheeses, unlike almost all others which ripen from the inside out. When the curd is formed it is sprayed with a fungus, *Penicillium camemberti*. The fungus forms an outer rind and moves into the cheese, breaking down proteins and releasing fat, which is what makes these cheeses creamy. The mould will still be at work in your kitchen and that's why these cheeses ooze their innards out. Most cheeses are sold in blocks, but these cheeses are individually formed into round shapes and generally sold as such.

Greece and Cyprus are famous for two unique cheeses. Feta cheese is characterised by its high salt level. When the curd is finally formed, it is cut up and dry-salted to achieve a salt level of about 3 per cent compared, for example, to cheddar cheese with just 0.5 per cent salt. For haloumi cheese, the curd is heated in hot whey which kills off the lactic acid bacteria. The curd is broken up to release the whey and what's left looks like white scrambled egg. Because this cheese has very little acid due to the heating stage, the main minerals of milk, calcium and phosphorous leach out of the maturing curd. Thus the proteins that are in the curd form a very tight network which means that this cheese is unique in that it doesn't melt when heated.

Photo credit: bhofack2

The most noted English cheese is cheddar and its manufacture involves a very traditional process known as cheddaring. When the curd is formed it is broken up into very small particles which causes maximum expulsion of the whey. The curd is left for a short period and congeals into a large coagulum. Pieces are cut about 1 foot square and laid one on top of the other until maximum expulsion of whey is achieved. The curd is then broken up, salted and put in a cheese press which gradually applies pressure, releasing even more whey. The cheese is left to ripen giving a very hard cheese with a long shelf life. After coagulation, the resulting curd is cut into small pieces and the whey is separated from it.

For mozzarella, after the curd is formed, boiling water is added which is stirred with a paddle until it congeals into a large soft and elastic mass. The skill in making mozzarella lies in the hands of the cheesemaker who can tell when the mass is ready to be lifted. It

Photo credit: Monika Grabkowska

comes out in a long stretched mass which is then drained and put into holders to make it congeal. Eventually, the curd is soft and elastic and the cheesemaker makes ball-like shapes which are kept in whey.

And finally, there is one of the great cheeses, parmigiano reggiano, popularly known as parmesan. This cheese is very hard and very strongly flavoured. About 900 years ago, Benedictine and Cistercian monks in the province of Parma and the surrounding regions of Reggio Emilia fostered dairy farming. They used salt from the nearby town of Salsomaggiore and developed their unique cheese. The curd is put into circular metal moulds, each of which holds 50 kilograms of curd. It is then wet-salted and stored for three years and turned over every week. On completion the curd shrinks to a hard cheese half its original weight.

Photo credit: fcafotodigital

The cheeseboard is an essential part of a good dinner, but here we have an old Anglo-French divide. The English finish their dinner with cheese served after dessert and the French do the opposite. The popular theory is that red wine was frequently served in France with the entrée and that any remaining red wine would be best consumed with cheese. Then dessert would be served with a sweet wine. The English had their pudding first, followed by cheese and generally men remained at the table to drink port, smoke cigars and gossip or engage in polite conversation. The English had a limited number of cheeses, mostly hard, whereas the French had many dozens of cheeses, from soft to hard, from smoked to mouldy. Emile Zola, in his novel *The Belly of Paris*, published in 1873, described a cheesemongers shop in Les Halles, Paris.

> *But it was upon the table that the cheeses appeared in greatest profusion. Here, by the side of the pound-rolls of butter lying on white-beet leaves, spread a gigantic Cantal cheese, cloven here and there as by an axe; then came a golden-hued Cheshire, and next a Gruyere, resembling a wheel fallen from some barbarian chariot; whilst farther on were some Dutch cheeses, suggesting decapitated heads suffused with dry blood, and having all that hardness of skulls which in France has gained them the name of 'death's heads.' Amidst the heavy exhalations of these, a Parmesan set a spicy aroma. Then there came three Brie cheeses displayed on round platters, and looking like very like melancholy extinct moons. Two of them, very dry, were at the full; the third, in its second quarter, was melting away in a white cream, which had spread into a pool and flowed over the little wooden barriers with which an attempt had been made to arrest its course. Next came some Port Saluts, similar to antique discs, with exergues bearing their makers' names in print. A Romantour,*

in its tinfoil wrapper, suggested a bar of nougat or some sweet cheese astray amidst all these pungent, fermenting curds. The Roqueforts under their glass covers also had a princely air, suffering from some unpleasant malady such as attacks the wealthy gluttons who eat too many truffles.

Contrast this with that great English foodie, Mrs Isabella Beeton, who in her book *Beeton's Cookery*, published in 1863, launched this attack on fancy cheeses:

It is well known that some persons like cheese in a state of decay and even 'alive'. There is no accounting for taste, and it may be hard to show why mould, which is vegetation should not be eaten as well as salad, or maggots as well as eels. But generally speaking, decomposing bodies are not wholesome eating and the line must be drawn somewhere'

So much for French cheese!

Cream

The final use of milk in our food supply is cream, and there is no processing needed to get cream from milk: if left alone, it will float to the top. Clotted creams are popular in England. Legend has it that when the 'giants' of ancient Briton were defeated by the invading Romans, they retreated to Cornwall and Devon. One of them, Blunderbuss, exiled one of his four wives who was banished to a cave. She saved a ship from hitting the rocks by lighting a fire and was duly rewarded by the ship's captain with the recipe for clotted cream. One of the most celebrated creams is Chantilly in which the cream is whipped with sugar and vanilla. Whipped cream was a reasonably common component of sweet dishes among the wealthier classes, but the addition of the new and expensive sugar and vanilla gave it an added dimension. Chantilly cream

Photo credit: Vero Manrique

was invented by Francois Vatel who was the head chef at Prince de Condé's Chateau de Chantilly. In 1671, the Prince threw a banquet for the French royal family, but on the fateful day the delivery of the fish Vatel had ordered was wholly inadequate for the size of the banquet so Vatel, an obsessive compulsive, fell on his sword and died. Apparently, the rest of the fish arrived a few hours later.

Ice cream began with the Arabic technology of preserving ice harvested from mountains and frozen rivers. Some would argue that the Arabs learned this technology from the Chinese for, apparently, as far back as the Tang dynasty they were consuming frozen flavoured milk. The Arab tradition would have arrived in Europe via their colonies in Spain and Italy, and it was the Italians who took these flavoured to heart. Filippo Baldini wrote a treatise on sorbets, *De'sorbetti*, in 1775 where he outlined the use of different salts in enhancing the freezing of iced drinks.

The transition from iced drinks and sorbets to ice cream didn't involve rocket science from cooks. Custard goes right back to Roman times and involves cream, milk, eggs, sugar, flour and flavourings. The flour thickens the custard and if omitted it would be runny. But it could be frozen and taste just as delicious. And so, ice cream was ready to formally arrive. However, the big difference between custard and ice cream, apart from temperature, is the process of churning. As the mix is cooled, it tends to form large ice crystals, but if the cooling process also involves churning the ice crystals become tiny, yielding the wonderful mouthfeel of ice cream.

The early manufacture of ice cream was arduous. One began with a wooden box containing ice and salt which would house and cool a metal dish containing the ingredients for ice cream. The lid was put on which covered both the box and metal pot and it was repeatedly shaken. After a while, the lid was removed and the developing ice cream was scraped from the sides of the pot and re-arranged neatly to repeat the process of hand churning. In 1843, Nancy Johnson from Philadelphia was awarded a patent for a mechanical churner which greatly speeded up the manufacture of ice cream, and from there ice cream took off. Prior to Johnson's invention, Italian immigrants to the UK and USA sold ice cream on the street and made the product widely available and popular, particularly as a treat for children. These ice cream vendors were known as hokey-pokey men, and their name has been traced to their street cries of 'O che pocco' or 'Oh so little'.

It is not unreasonable to say that without milk, whether it be cow, goat, sheep or camel, human development would have been very different, if not imperilled. Milk abounds in essential nutrients not widely available in other foods, at least not at the same level. A typical glass of milk contains just over 200 milligrams of calcium and you'd need six servings of mixed cooked beans to achieve that, or ten servings of broccoli. But, not all cattle yield milk. The male of the species was put to work in field in mills and wherever strength was needed. They did, however, serve as another important food – meat – alongside that of many other animals favoured for their flesh.

Chapter 5

Meat and Poultry

The Health-Food Diner
By Maya Angelou

*No sprouted wheat and soya shoots
And Brussels in a cake,
Carrot straw and spinach raw,
(Today, I need a steak).*

*Not thick brown rice and rice pilaw
Or mushrooms creamed on toast,
Turnips mashed and parsnips hashed,
(I'm dreaming of a roast).*

*Health-food folks around the world
Are thinned by anxious zeal,
They look for help in seafood kelp
(I count on breaded veal).*

*No smoking signs, raw mustard greens,
Zucchini by the ton,
Uncooked kale and bodies frail
Are sure to make me run*

to

Loins of pork and chicken thighs
And standing rib, so prime,
Pork chops brown and fresh ground round
(I crave them all the time).

Irish stews and boiled corned beef
and hot dogs by the scores,
or any place that saves a space
For smoking carnivores.

When the great apes descended to terra firma, they had a largely vegetarian diet but were very much flexivores. They would eat eggs, unfledged birds and insects and they sought out high protein, nutrient-dense animal-based foods. On the ground this would have extended to slow moving vulnerable prey such as insects, snails, turtles and the like. In time they learned to trap small prey such as rabbits and eventually to hunt with increasingly sophisticated methods. Very early humans benefited greatly from the nutritional aspects of meat, fish and poultry: high quality protein, highly available iron, zinc and calcium, vitamins and essential fats. All of these contributed to the growth of the brain of early hominids and to their increasingly sophisticated societies.

But it was more than that. As the early hominids lost their hair, a major advantage in shedding troublesome lice that bedevil furry primates, they were of course happy to live naked in the warm regions where early hominids emerged. But as the population growth outstripped the food supply, migrations began to reach climates where clothing was needed, be it the cold desert nights or the winters of northern Europe. It is thought that in the beginning, winter hair shed by animals combined with soft dried leaves would have been used as bedding in caves and tents. In time, early humans exploited this to make felt, which is wind-proof, rain-proof and sun-proof. But in the earliest of times before animals were domesticated, the availability of shed animal hair was haphazard so when humans started to undertake significant hunts, animal hides took the place of crude felt. Animals yield more than clothing and food. Their horns were used for drinking, their stomachs to store liquid and their bones for weapons, sewing needles and tools.

The enhanced intellectual ability that was made possible from animal-based diets would, in time, cause a re-think of the rights and wrongs of killing animal for food. Pythagoras was an early advocate of a meat-free diet and this approach to food became known as a Pythagorean way of life. It was only in the nineteenth century did the word vegetarian appear. Eastern religions such as Buddhism and Hinduism introduced a strict set of dietary rules which prohibited the flesh of living creatures. They had the advantage of a long tradition of growing pulses and of the use of multiple spices to embellish vegetable dishes. Vegetarianism took off in Europe and the US in the nineteenth century, frequently associated with stricter religious beliefs. One of America's founding fathers, Benjamin Franklin, was a vegetarian for a long time until he was becalmed at sea near Block Island just off the coast of Rhode Island. The crew caught a large haul of cod and set about cooking them. Franklin, who had loved cod, gave in to temptation and ate some, noting in his autobiography:

> *I had formerly been a great lover of fish, and, when this came hot out of the frying-pan, it smelt admirably well. I balanced sometime between principle and inclination, till I recollected that, when the fish were opened, I saw smaller fish taken out of their stomachs; then thought I, 'If you eat one another, I don't see why we mayn't eat you.' So, I dined upon cod very*

heartily, and continued to eat with other people, returning only now and then occasionally to a vegetable diet. So convenient a thing is it to be a reasonable creature, since it enables one to find or make a reason for everything one has a mind to do.

Beef

Domesticated cattle and sheep have contributed to our cuisine since time immemorial and, from the point of view of history, nothing has changed from the earliest of times to today. An animal is killed, butchered and the flesh cooked in multiple ways. Fashions of course have come and gone, and for many the recent fashion of ultra-lean beef is a backward step, for it is in the fat of animals that

Photo credit: Pivofy

the flavours of pastures and wild mountains are to be found. Fat, or marbling as it's called since it looks like marble with speckles of white in a red matrix, also improves tenderness, juiciness and other such desirable flavour characteristics.

Whilst the lean beef campaign dominated the diet conscious, a small counter movement favoured a highly marbled beef from Japan known as wagyu. In fact, *wagyu*, is the Japanese for cow but among Japanese cattle there are four breeds that actively store fat in muscles giving it a highly marbled structure: Japanese Brown, Black, Shorthorn and Poll. This type of wagyu beef is graded on the yield of meat per animal and the Beef Marbling Standard. To qualify as one who can rate this kind of beef requires three years of training. Of the breeds that have this marbling feature, the best known is that from the prefecture of Kobe. Wagyu can of course be sourced elsewhere in Japan, but the industry of Kobe has cleverly branded their beef. And they get a premium return. A 12 ounce steak will cost somewhere around $100 to $150. By all accounts, if properly cooked, it melts in the mouth.

One variation on the typical steak is steak tartar, known in Europe as Steak Americane. One myth is that the tartar horsemen would put beef under their saddles to reduce saddle sore but that is not so. In Jules Verne's 1880 play, *Michel Strogoff*, based around the Russian Tartar battles, a correspondent of the *Daily Telegraph* by the name of Blount tells the innkeeper what he would like to have for supper. Blount sets out his list and the Tartar inn keeper regrets that he can only offer koulbat. Blount asks, 'What is this thing called . . . koulbat?' to which the inn keeper replies, 'A pate made with minced meat and eggs.' Verne's work coincides with the medicinal use of raw meat, such as its juice being used to treat haemophilia, as described in a report to the *British Medical Journal* of 1908. Recipes began to appear for finely minced raw beef with raw eggs to moisten the dish. It is thus likely that the koulbat of Jules Verne play in the Tartar Inn provided an excellent name for this new dish. Steak tartar was born.

The nineteenth century German chemist, Justus von Liebig, often cited as the father of modern chemistry, began to study meat and its composition. Apparently he was visited by a colleague whose young daughter fell gravely ill and von Liebig nursed her with regular servings of aqueous chicken extract. The child survived and von Liebig began to explore the extraction of material from meat. He mastered the large-scale production of beef extract but because beef was expensive in Europe and it took 30 kilograms of beef to make 1 kilogram of extract, the production could never be commercially viable. He sought a partner to find ways to make it a commercial proposition and in 1862 was contacted by George Giebert, based in Argentina. Large-scale refrigeration was not operational at the time so the large herds of Argentinian ranches were killed solely for their hides. Now the extract could be made commercial. Giebert established a production plant at the port of Fray Bentos. At first the meat extract was thick, dark and syrupy. Argentinian beef now had a real commercial value but only the choicest cuts were used for the extract so the trimmings of meat were there for the taking and Giebert saw the opportunity to use them for corn beef production. The global brand of Fray Bentos Tinned Corned Beef now became a major component of the diets of many armies.

In 1908, Liebig and Giebert developed the technology that moved the extract from a thick liquid syrup to a dried cube that could be sold for a penny. He coined the new product Oxo, a palindrome of the word 'ox'. Bovril was developed in 1870 by John Lawson Johnston, a Scotsman living in Canada who won a contract from Napoleon III to feed his troops with tinned beef during the Franco-Prussian war. Transport and storage proved to be a problem so Johnston, possibly drawing on von Liebig's product, created a beef extract. The name Bovril was based on the word 'bovine' and the word 'vril', which was a fictional electromagnetic force which energised a race known as Vril-ya in a popular novel of the time,

The Coming Race. At about the same time in Switzerland, Julius Maggi had a similar vision to Liebeig and solved the problem of the high price of beef by using the proteins of pulses, creating the famous Maggi cube.

Lamb

In days gone by, lamb was a meat that was far more likely to be served to the rich than the poor. Whilst there is no wagyu among lamb breeds, there is the Kobi approach of branding. Lambs reared on the rugged mountains and hills of Connemara have earned a special distinction by the European Union with the award of the Protected Geographical Indication status. Hill lamb embraces the flavours that come from wild plants and heathers, unique to these hills. Lamb has very significant roots in the Judeo-Christian religions. The book of Exodus tells the story of a series of terrible plagues involving the death of all firstborn sons. God told the Jews to paint their doorposts with lamb's blood so that the angel of death would 'pass over' their homes. With the conversion of some Jews to Christianity, the eating of lamb at the Jewish feast of Passover was adopted as a traditional dish for the Christian feast of Easter. Lambs were generally white and whiteness was associated with purity, and they were a first choice for sacrificial offerings.

Pork

The pig is a different kettle of fish, as they say. The pig is not meadow-dependent and is a scavenger. It will eat left overs, peelings, rotten fruit and vegetables, mouldy bread and scraps of any sort. Moreover, if the pig has access to a woodland, it will scavenge for acorns, nuts, mushrooms, insects and anything that will yield nutrients. We can gain an image of the role of pigs and poultry in the lives of the peasant class from the writings of Arthur Young in the eighteenth century regarding his tour of Ireland:

The country is cheerful and rich; and if the Irish cabins continue like what I have hitherto seen, I shall not hesitate to pronounce their inhabitants as well off as most English cottagers. They are built of mud walls eighteen inches or two feet thick, and well thatched, which are far warmer than the thin clay walls in England. Here are few cottars without a cow, and some of them two. A bellyful invariably of potatoes, and generally turf for fuel from a bog. It is true they have not always chimneys to their cabins, the door serving for that and window too. If their eyes are not affected with the smoke, it may be an advantage in warmth. Every cottage swarms with poultry, and most of them have pigs.

It wasn't just country folk who kept pigs; they were also to be found in cities. Samuel Pepys records a dinner he had with the head of the admiralty, Sir John Minnes, on October 30, 1616, where a topic of conversation was the conundrum of 'how it comes to pass that there are no boars seen in London, but many sows and pigs'. The *Norwich Book of Custom* records in detail the damage that urban swine could do:

Whereas great injuries and dangers so often have happened before this time in the City of Norwich and still happen from day to day in as much as boars, sows and pigs before this time have gone and still go vagrant by day and night without a keeper in the said town, whereby divers persons and children have been hurt by boars, children killed and eaten, and others when buried exhumed, and others maimed, and many persons of the said town have received great injuries as wrecking of houses, destruction of gardens of divers persons by such kind of pigs upon which great complaint is often brought before the said Bailiffs and Community imploring them for remedy on the misfortunes, dangers and injuries which have been done to them.

The habit of the pig to devour living animals, and as noted above to kill children, is the basis for the eschewing of pork by the Jewish and Muslim faiths. In the Christian bible, Leviticus 11:1–2, Moses and Aaron instruct the children of Israel exactly what foods may or may not be eaten. Because blood was considered life, it was forbidden to eat blood or to eat animals such as the pig who would happily eat blood. Deuteronomy 12:23 makes this clear:

Only be sure that thou eat not the blood: for the blood is the life; and thou mayest not eat the life with the flesh.

And the Qur'an (2:173) says:

He has only forbidden to you dead animals, blood, the flesh of swine, and that which has been dedicated to other than Allah.

Pigs were slaughtered in months with an 'r' in them and every part of the pig was used for some form of food. Indeed, it is said that the notable eighteenth century food writer, Grimod de la Reynière, declared that the only part of a pig that cannot be eaten is the 'oink'. The slaughtering of a pig involved the help of many neighbours. Two year old pigs are hardy creatures and squeal ferociously when threatened, so slaughtering a pig was no easy job. Immediately after slaughter, the pig was suspended by its hind legs and its blood collected, mixed with pork fat, cereal or chopped onions and herbs and squeezed into the pig's intestine. The meat of the pig, pork, can be cooked as such, but to provide food for those long winter months with an 'r' in them, most of the pig was preserved. Ham is the meat of the hind leg and bacon is meat from any other part of the pig. Both these cuts were usually dry cured with salt and sugar.

Of the famous hams in the world, three stick out: Ibérico and Serrano ham from Spain, and Parma ham from Italy. A special breed of pig is used for Ibérico ham, black in colour including its hooves. This black hoof, the *pata negra*, is the trade mark of Ibérico ham.

Pigs are about 10 months old when they are released into the unique ecosystem of Spanish Dehesa forests, where pastures are littered with great oaks. Dehesa ecosystems were established as far back as the fourteenth century and were intended to foster live-stock farming. The oaks shed their acorns in autumn and winter and these acorns or, in Spanish, *bellota* are the real secret of Ibérico ham.

Photo credit: Maurizio Odiardo

Jamón Ibérico de Bellota involves pigs gorging themselves on acorns, up to 10 kilograms per day. The latter will command twice the price of standard Ibérico ham. The hams are cured with sea salt which reduces bacterial growth and draws water out of the hanging ham. The cool winter air and the drying effect of the salt slowly lead to a major transformation of the ham, a process that will take up to four years.

The other famous Spanish ham is Serrano, from the Spanish word *sierra* for mountain, and it is in the mountains that this ham is produced. It differs from Ibérico ham in that multiple breeds of pigs could be used and because there are few acorn-rich oak trees in the mountains. As with Ibérico, Serrano hams are dry cured for many years in mountain air.

Parma ham comes from the province of Parma in Italy's Emilia-Romagna region. The pigs, the Duroc breed, are fed a diet of barley, maize and the whey obtained during the making of that regions famous cheese, parmigiana reggiano. It is dry cured with salt much like its Spanish counterparts, a process that can last for 100 to 1,000 days. The longer the cure, the more flavoursome the ham. It is the ham of Parma that is sold as prosciutto, much loved in antipasto.

Sausages

Europe has a bewildering variety of sausages. Traditionally, pork for sausage making was chopped by hand into fine pieces and, in some cases, like mortadella, the pork meat was pounded into a smooth pulp. Salt is then added and this salt acts as a preservative and flavouring agent. A third key role of this salt is that it leads to the breakdown of some of the meat proteins which then act as a binding agent. Herbs and spices are then added according to local

Photo credit: Jakub Kapusnak

traditions. Finally, the mixture is forced into its casing, traditionally pig intestine.

For some sausages, the quantity of salt is strictly limited to that which allows water to be drawn from the meat, but not enough to stop natural bacteria fermenting the meat mixture. This leads to slightly acidic conditions. When air dried, which is the tradition in the warm climates of the Mediterranean, the acid and salt are concentrated giving the sausage a distinct flavour. Smoking may be added to the process of drying.

Salami is a generic term for Italian sausages that are dried and fermented giving them a long shelf life and are consumed without cooking. Every city in Italy has its own traditional recipe for salami making. Naples has its salsiccia napoletana picante, a salami which is rendered spicy with paprika. Calabrian soppressata is another spicy sausage with the addition of fennel seeds and is first partially dried, then placed underneath weighted wooden boards to expel water and then allowed to continue drying. Chorizo is also a dried sausage strongly flavoured with paprika. Pepperoni is a US invention and was first recorded in New York in 1919 when the spicy Neapolitan salami was adopted to include peppers and also differed from the traditional Italian salami in being very finely ground. Traditional Bologna mortadella is an emulsified sausage, of a pounded cured pork paste with pistachio nuts, black pepper and myrtle berries and with a good quantity of pork fat cubes. Mortadella is a an example of a sausage moving toward a luncheon meat.

As with Italy, Germany is famous for its sausages but generally these are fresh and need to be cooked before eating. Frankfurt has its frankfurter würstchen which is boiled after it is encased giving it a good shelf life and of course was made very popular in the US by German immigrants. It is ideal for street food as it is already cooked and simply needs light boiling to re-heat the sausage. Wiener würstchen was a Viennese adaptation of the frankfurter with beef mixed with the pork. Munich's weisswurst is a white sausage involving a mixture of pork, veal and pork fat, seasoned with parsley, pepper, lemon and salt. As with the frankfurter, it is pre-boiled. Perhaps the best known of German sausages is bratwurst which was first recorded in Nuremberg in the fourteenth century. It is not pre-boiled which makes it vulnerable to spoilage and, traditionally, was prepared in the morning and eaten by noon. Its distinct flavour comes from the inclusion of marjoram.

In the 1850s, some 800,000 Germans emigrated to New York bringing with them their traditional foods. One such was a sausage from Frankfurt. The Frankfurter became known as the dachshund sausage given its long body similar to the dog by that name. Then it became known as the hot dog or even just a dog. In about 1860 the first frankfurter sausage was sold by a German immigrant out of a food cart in New York. A decade later, a German immigrant opened the first hot dog stand on Coney Island. Soon consumers were given a glove to help them with the heat and the dripping sauces, and that quickly led to the hot dog being held in a bun.

England also has its notable sausages. The Cumberland sausage, from the county of that name, goes back half a millennium and is distinguished by the fact that the pork is roughly chopped giving it a unique texture. Lincolnshire is another English sausage, also characterised by its chunky texture and the addition of sage to the process.

Poultry and Fowl

The domestication of the precursor of today's hen goes back to the eighth century BCE in Asia and eventually became part of all global cuisines. It is a particularly attractive animal, especially for peasant households, as it is capable of picking and pecking its way around pastures and woodlands, will eat scraps and is a rapid converter of food into lean meat. Chicken meat is used for sausages in the Muslim world, but generally chicken is cooked in dishes flavoured with all forms of herbs, spices and sauces. It is quick to cook and is seen as good for health.

When chicken isn't in a dish, be it in one adorned with korma, tomato sauce, shawarma, pollo rojo or white wine, it is quite likely to be breaded and deep fried. Deep fried chicken was a traditional Scottish dish which was a very special treat as it needed a good spring chicken and lots of expensive oil. American slaves brought their chicken farming practices to the US and they were allowed to keep and eat chickens. They too had deep fried chicken breaded with spice which soon took on among the white community and hence we have Kentucky and southern fried chicken.

Winter time was the season for the hunting of wild fowl and, again, because preservation was not possible, a disproportionate consumption ensued. For landowners, hunting brought pheasant, woodcock, pigeon, guinea fowl and the like, but not of course turkey. The meaning of turkey then and now is very different. Colonial explorers of the day discovered a bird in Madagascar that was like a guinea fowl, only much larger. It was delicious with ample white breast and tasty brown leg meat. It was seen as a real luxury back in the day. It was imported into Europe either through Turkey or India. Thus, what the English called turkey was just a big exotic

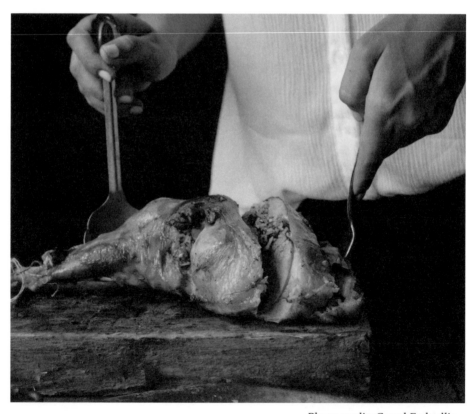

Photo credit: Gunel Farhadlio

bird imported from Madagascar via Turkey, originally called Turkey bird and then just turkey. The French regarded the same bird as having its origins in India which became *oison d'Inde*, goose from India, abbreviated to *dinde*, the modern French word for turkey. But whereas there may be some truth in this account, as ever with food history there is another side to it. The turkey we know today had its origins in Central America for the turkey was central to the cuisine of the Aztecs and other native peoples of Central and South America. The Spanish explorers brought this bird home and in time it was adopted as the turkey in England and the *d'Inde* in France.

In England, goose was regarded as a significant social step up above lowly beef. The goose also provided superb feathers for pillows, the finest quills for writing and, most importantly, the tail and wing-tip feathers for arrows to guide flight. The inn keepers of England ran goose clubs for its patrons, beginning with the purchasing of young geese to be communally raised on local commonage via a weekly subscription to the club. But for the landed gentry, it was this exotic imported bird from Turkey together with a range of hunted domestic fowl that they focused on for Christmas and, for them, the social ladder required as much culinary ostentation as possible. One way to impress was to go as far as possible in the process of engrastation, nowadays called 'stuffing'. It would not be uncommon to have the flesh of a partridge stuffed into the cavity of a pigeon and for the whole pigeon to be stuffed into the cavity of a goose and then to top it all to stuff the multi-stuffed goose into the turkey.

In the Cajun region of the United States, Paul Prudhomme, the famous Louisiana chef, whilst working at a carvery, decided that the turkey was boring. He set out in the mid-1980s to improve it and invented and patented the now famous Cajun treat, the Turducken. This is a duck stuffed with a hen and in turn the stuffed duck is stuffed into the turkey – turkey-duck-hen, 'Turducken'. The Turducken wasn't the first phenomenon of stuffing smaller de-boned birds into bigger de-boned birds. In 1807, the French food critic, Grimod de La Reynière (one of the first of this species!), described 'roast without equal' – a bustard stuffed with a turkey, a goose, a pheasant, a chicken, a duck, a guinea fowl, a teal, a woodcock, a partridge, a plover, a lapwing, a quail, a thrush, a lark, an ortolan bunting and a garden warbler: 17 birds in all!

Eggs

When we talk about eggs, we inevitably are referring to hen's eggs, but the eggs of other avian species are also used from quails to geese to ducks to bantams, among others. There are few foods as versatile as the egg. It can be boiled, fried, poached or scrambled. It can be combined with bread to make French toast and it can be used to make an omelette or a quiche. Whole eggs are used in the preparation of cakes, cookies, brownies, bread doughs, waffles, pancakes, muffins and pastries. When mixed with sugar in biscuit and cake baking, eggs help emulsify the fat and water and they trap and hold air.

Egg yolks are used to make custards, pastry cream, cakes, ice cream, creme brûlée and curds. They are natural emulsifiers, acting to help fat and water mix to a smooth consistency. Egg whites are used to make meringues, pavlova, chiffon cakes, macarons, marshmallows, marshmallow fluff and frostings. When egg whites are whisked, they trap much more air than whole eggs, air which when cooked give a solid structure with a high level of air trapped inside – the wonderful mouthfeel of a meringues: first crunch and then melt. In his book *Eggs*, the renowned chef Michel Roux writes,

Photo credit: Jakub Kapusnak

'When I hold an egg in my hand, I feel that it represents the image of the universe, and it awakens and increases my respect for life'.

There are both simple and classic dishes where the egg is the centrepiece. Eggs Benedict are said to have been created at New York's Delmonico restaurant by the chef Charles Ranhofer, when a regular client complained about the lack of imagination in his egg dishes. Thus were Eggs Benedict created: an English muffin with a piece of bacon (Canadian by tradition), a poached egg and Hollandaise sauce. Eggs Florentine are apparently so-called because the Florentine Catherine de Medici brought a love of spinach to Paris when she married the future King of France. Eggs Florentine are often described as much like Eggs Benedict where the bacon is replaced with spinach, but Michel Roux insists that it is sauce mornay that should be used in Eggs Florentine and he would also include tongue. If this form of egg was possible in the days of the Medicis, then certainly, the Delmonico invention of Eggs Benedict was simply an adaptation of an earlier recipe. Eggs are wonderful but rotten eggs stink. So how do you gauge the freshness of an egg? Michel Roux has a simple test:

> *If you are in any doubt about the freshness of an egg, do the following simple test: Drop the egg into cold salted water (100g/3½oz salt to 1 litre/4 cups water). If the egg sinks, it is 'extra fresh'; if it remains suspended in the water, it is about 2 weeks old; if it floats, the egg is not fresh enough to be eaten and should be thrown away.*

Eggs have a small pocket of air, but if left for long periods there will be an increasing movement of air into the egg and a corresponding movement of water out of the egg.

Salmonella poisoning is life threatening and poultry can be infected with salmonella. However, modern poultry farming uses a combination of eradication and vaccination programs to eliminate salmonella from poultry flocks. Nonetheless, when making a sauce which involves raw uncooked eggs, it is wise to buy them from accredited suppliers. Tiny blood spots can appear in eggs arising from small bleeds in the hen's reproductive system. They are far more common in brown than in white eggs and the occurrence of a blood spot in an egg means it is not kosher and will not be eaten by those of the Jewish faith. It goes back to the issue raised with the non-kosher nature of pigs, in that blood is life and thus cannot be eaten.

Chapter 6

Fish and Shellfish

Extract from Wynken, Blynken, and Nod
By Eugene Field

Wynken, Blynken, and Nod one night
  Sailed off in a wooden shoe,–
Sailed on a river of crystal light
  Into a sea of dew.
'Where are you going, and what do you wish?'
  The old moon asked the three.
'We have come to fish for the herring-fish
  That live in this beautiful sea;
  Nets of silver and gold have we,'
    Said Wynken,
    Blynken,
    And Nod.

Our meat from the avian world is largely limited to chickens, turkeys, ducks and geese while that from quadrupeds is largely either, cattle, sheep, pigs or goats. When it comes to fish and shellfish, the sky is the limit. In Jules Verne's *Twenty Thousand Leagues under the Sea* the narrator, Professor Aronnax, remarks to Captain Nemo: 'You're in love with the sea,' to which he replies:

Deeply in love! The sea is the be all and end all! It covers sev-
en-tenths of the planet earth. Its breath is clean and whole-
some. It's an immense wilderness where a man is never alone
because he feels life stirring all around him. The sea is simply
the vehicle for a prodigious, uncanny mode of existence; it's
simply movement and love; it's living infinity, as one of your
poets put it . . . and those countless legions of fish, an infinite
order of creatures totalling more than 13,000 species, only a
tenth of which belong to fresh water.

From the tiny anchovy to the large whale sharks, fish come in all shapes and sizes, some clever, some not so smart, some pretty and others downright ugly. Humankind has always sought food from the seas, oceans, lakes and rivers and, in the beginning, it involved no more than gathering immobile shellfish along the seashores in coastal deltas at low tide. The early hunter gatherers had great patience, great powers of observation and were incredibly curious. All are the key skills of fisherfolk. They understood tides and the seasonality of marine life. They recognised the toxicity of algal blooms and learned to avoid high risk areas. They learned many tricks from diving birds or bears snatching leaping salmon. But they were, above all, cautious and, in the beginning, they could access fish and seafood without the need to set sail on the high seas.

Before Boats

As the tide ebbs, fish will become stranded in rock pools and make for an easy catch. Catfish, who enjoy the brackish waters where sea water meets fresh water, were particularly likely to be so trapped and archaeologists have uncovered two million-year-old catfish bones at a hominin site near Lake Turkana in northern Kenya. The carp spawns in shallow waters for a very limited period each year and there is now clear evidence that this pattern was understood by primitive hunters who would return to these spawning grounds annually. Archaeological evidence indicates that huge hauls of carp were caught and dried for later consumption. Early humans were so observant and clever that they mastered the art of trout tickling. Brian Fagan in his book, *Fishing: How the Sea Fed Civilization*, describes the process:

> *The fisher, seeing the tip of a fin or a moving tail near a rock in the water, kneels and passes his fingers under the rock until he feels the fish's tail. Then he tickles his prey's underside with his forefinger, moving his hand along the body with infinite care. When his fingers are under the gills and the fish is in a trancelike state, he grabs it and jerks it out of the water . . . fish tickling is a subtle art, no doubt first learned by chance. It would have been entirely within the abilities of a Neanderthal.*

Earliest fishing tackle evolved in time with a strong but flexible length of wood from some tree with a pointed end. Fisherfolk learned the power of refraction whereby light coming from the fish changes direction when it emerges out of water. A person above the water is led to think that the position of the fish is nearer the surface than its true position. But time, reflection and practice would have taught them that lesson. If a fish is speared, it can wriggle free and escape alive but injured. So the next innovation was to tie a thin but sharp barb to the end of the spear. The fishhook was born. In time came double barbed spears, then fibre nets, snares, traps and fishing lines.

Fish farming was practiced in China, as early as 3500 BCE and three millennia later a civil servant, Fan-Li, published a textbook on aquaculture, *The Classic of Fish Culture*, with detailed instructions on the construction and maintenance of fishponds, brood selection and nutrition. Indeed, records exist of criminal charges for the 'rustling' of fish. The reign of the Tang Dynasty (618 to 906 CE) is particularly significant in the history of world aquaculture. The first emperor in the Tang dynasty was named Li (Li Yuan, 618-626 CE), which is also the Chinese name for the common carp, the most widely used fish in aquaculture at the time. Li issued a decree prohibiting the culture of the common carp. Far from creating an obstacle to the industry of fish farming, it turned out to be a blessing. Other carps such as the silver carp, the big-head carp, the grass carp and the mud carp were introduced and it was discovered that these fish lived in different strata in fish ponds and ate different foods. Polyculture was discovered. To this day, China accounts for two-thirds of all global aquaculture.

The Romans built large fish farms fed mainly by sea water but their interest in aquaculture was more a display of opulence and grandeur among the wealthier classes than as a significant source of food. They would construct lengthy walls out to sea which would be fed by fresh water at high tide. Throughout Europe, similar structures were built in rivers and deltas to yield weirs in which migrating fish could be trapped. Ponds were inland water masses created by humans whereas lakes were natural aquatic structures. The man-made Fleet Pond in Hampshire in the UK covers 21 hectares and is surrounded by another 30 hectares of wetland and dry heath. The pond was formed in the twelfth century by building embankments which re-directed streams flowing from nearby hills to the low-lying land at Crookham Common. These ponds were stocked with fish by the monks who managed them. Wild fowl began to nest along the wetlands and heaths, adding another source of food to the locals.

The shoreline, river weirs and fish farms were enough to meet the needs of populations relatively close to the sea. But early humans were inventive and almost certainly crafts of one form or another emerged, enabling fishers to move into deeper water for fish. The next phase of fish and shellfish in the human food chain would begin.

Seafaring

Almost certainly, fishing came before boats or other water craft but once constructed, smarter crafts moved fishing to new levels and that in turn drove the fishing-vessel cycle. The sea was mastered

Photo credit: Istock

beginning with simple raft-like vessels capable of manoeuvring in shallow coastal waters and in rivers, lakes and ponds. Simple papyrus reed boats would have been used to undertake longer sea journeys. The ancient Egyptians built skiffs from papyrus reeds tied together first in small and then larger bundles. The reeds were hollow, and the trapped air contributed to better buoyancy and this technology spread across North Africa and the Middle East.

In Ireland similar one-man skiffs were built from inter-woven wooden lattices, covered in one or more layers of animal hides. These vessels, known as curraghs, were light enough to be carried by one person but in time they evolved into much larger vessels. The Twelfth Century Book of Rights records that the King of Cashel would annually supply the High King of Ireland with 'ten ships with beds'. Papyrus boats were sturdy and in 1970 the Norwegian adventurer Thor Heyerdahl demonstrated such by building a traditional style papyrus boat and sailing it from Morocco to Barbados.

In time, the animal hide sail emerged as did the rudder and the stabilising keel. Boats grew in size and journeys across the seas became longer. From that point onward, the technology changed little other than smarter ways to construct the hull, the sail, the keel and the rudder. Multi-deck, multi-sail ships were eventually replaced by steamships and they in turn were replaced by today's diesel-driven trawlers and fish factories with the most advanced technology on board. For the ancients, fish were either eaten fresh or quickly preserved in any one or more of several traditional technologies, all of which still operate today.

Preserving Fish

Fish adapt to different temperatures as they move between the upper and lower parts of their habitat. The range is somewhere around 5°c to 15°c. When a fish is landed, its natural microbial population will respond to the warmer dry land temperature and begin to spoil the fish. Fish preservation can be achieved by salting, drying, smoking, pickling or canning, and often more than one method is used. For this section, I draw heavily of Sue Shephard's book, *Pickled, Potted and Canned*, and will deal with one fish species to illustrate these various approaches to preservation.

Cod was fished off the Atlantic coasts along the eastern European seaboard and to the north around Scandinavia, right up to Iceland. In the early middle ages, the most successful cod fishing was the reserve of Basque whalers who, in the pursuit of their prey, fell upon the cod-infested seas off Newfoundland. It was a secret the Basques kept to themselves for several centuries. But so convinced were European entrepreneurs of the existence of a westward passage to the East, awash with precious treasures, that great investment was made to go one step further than Columbus. At the turn of the sixteenth century, John Cabot (born Giovanni Caboto), undertook three separate westward voyages where he sailed the eastern shores of what he would call Newfoundland and continued south to Chesapeake Bay in today's Virginia. A few years later, in 1534 CE, the French mariner Jacques Cartier set sail to discover the elusive western passage, and after twenty days he navigated around the gulf of St Lawrence, circumnavigating what we now know as the islands of Newfoundland and Prince Edward. The French and English disputed ownership of Newfoundland but France ceded it to England in the Treaty of Utrecht of 1713.

Cabot and later Cartier would report back on the incredible density of cod in the seas of Newfoundland and south to Boston. The long held Basque secret was discovered. Soon great fleets set sail for Newfoundland in search of cod. The French had the upper hand over the English in that they had a much greater supply of salt. Their ships could stay much longer at sea, salting the cod as it was taken aboard. Because of their very low levels of body fat, cod is ideal for preservation by salting. The heads were removed and kept for a stew. The fish was then gutted and the backbone removed. The fillets could now be salted. Their livers were kept for cod liver oil and the tongue was preserved to be eventually deep fried, still a delicacy in Newfoundland. The cod's bladder was used to prepare isinglass used for clarifying beer and wine. When the cod ships returned to France, the salted cod was immediately dried to yield a hard product stable for quite long periods. Because the English were limited by their access to large quantities of salt, their catch was lightly salted and then taken back to the shores of New-foundland and dried. This required labour and thus the English colonised the new lands and in time this would allow them discover other areas rich in cod. One such place was Boston and its famed Cape Cod. The traditional dish of Boston is scrod, purportedly an abbreviation of sacred cod.

Herrings exist in massive shoals across the Atlantic and North Sea and have been fished from the earliest times. Herring rise to the surface after dark to eat and digest plankton and return annually to the same region to spawn, the best time to catch herring. The Hanseatic League organised a large herring fishing industry in the Baltic Sea that thrived for some time and then collapsed. Minor changes in tidal patterns can be caused by the construction of new ports and harbours and such minor perturbations can cause herrings to simply abandon traditional feeding areas.

The collapse of the Baltic herring shoals facilitated the Dutch in developing a very large herring fishing industry to the west of the Baltics in the North Sea. They say that Amsterdam was built on herring bones. One of the reasons why the Dutch were so successful in herring fishing was the discovery by William Beukels at the end of the fourteenth century that partial evisceration of the fish prior to salting greatly increased the flavour of the fish and also facilitated preservation over much longer periods. The stomach, heart, liver, and part of the intestine were removed leaving both the pancreas and little stomach pouches called the pyloric caeca. If the pancreas, rich in digestive enzymes, was damaged, the fish would be discarded as this would lead to rapid spoilage. As the fish was salted, the enzymes in these leaky stomach pouches leached out and produced a softening of the flesh yielding a cheesy or gamy flavour.

Rollmops are a favourite Dutch way to eat herrings. The salted herring is soaked in water with several washes and smothered in mustard. They are then rolled up with a pickled gherkin in the center of the roll which is held in place held in place with a toothpick. They are then put into a glass jar and immersed in a marinade of made vinegar, water, chopped onion, peppercorns, bay leaves and mustard seeds. Stored in a cool place for five days or so, rollmops are a delicious treat. The herring is also subject to another method of preservation, smoking, to produce kippers. The salted fish was washed, re-salted for a short period, washed again and then skewered with a wooden rod, twenty-five fish to the skewer, and smoked over oak chips. Smoking causes drying so the fish were left to drain for a few days and re-smoked. These two-day cycles were repeated three to four times. Red herrings were similarly smoked but were not eviscerated before smoking which led to a red colour, a process developed by a Northumberland fish merchant, John Woodger, in 1843.

The salmon is generally regarded as king among fishes, for it has to master both rivers and oceans at different stages of its life. The earliest records of salmon fishing relate to the Jomon civilisation of Japan. Archaeologists have uncovered traps, spears and boats, both hollowed out and planked, dating back to 3,500 BCE, some 400 years before Egypt's first Pharaoh. The salmon was admired for its knowledge, its energy and its determination. Native Americans carved pictures of salmon into rocks, and it was believed that if you rubbed such a stone you would be gifted with these much-admired salmon attributes. The ancient Celts believed that every time a salmon leaped from the water, it gained in knowledge and one of the greatest of ancient Celtic sagas surrounds the warrior and ad-venturer Finn McCool (Fionn mac Cumhaill) who helped the druid Finnegas to hunt for the mythical salmon of knowledge, a salmon

Photo credit: Jakub Kapusnak

that had eluded him for seven years. Finn caught the salmon and, when cooking it, burned his thumb which he quickly put in his mouth to sooth, instantly gaining this elusive knowledge. From then on, sucking his thumb drew upon the great knowledge of the salmon.

The late nineteenth century saw the emergence of the canning industry, and whilst the canning of salmon started in Aberdeen it moved to the US where the supply of salmon was orders of magnitude greater. Such was the global demand for nicely preserved salmon in natural brine or oil in a sealed tin, that stocks of salmon were depleted rapidly. The Columbia River is the largest river in the Pacific Northwest region of North America and it was here that the first river-based canneries began under the stewardship of Andrew Hapgood and two brothers, George and William Hume, who rapidly became multi-millionaires. But over-fishing of all the northwest pacific coastline and rivers led to a rapid depletion of salmon. Fresh salmon was a fish which was associated with wealth. William Hume, who foresaw and then witnessed the depletion of salmon stock in these rivers, wrote that salmon was 'a luxury of which none but the wealthy could partake' and also that it was 'doubtful if but few in that State of his age had ever seen one.' Tinned salmon was always a second best to the real thing which remained expensive to the average citizen.

Posh Fish

Caviar is posh. It is the most highly regarded delicacy of marine life. But it wasn't always so. The sturgeon is a large fish which bottom feeds and is hard to capture. It existed at the time of the dinosaurs but when the earth cooled, the land-based dinosaurs became extinct, while the sturgeon lived on. Inga Saffron, in her book *Caviar*, describes the sturgeon thus:

> *It remains a big, slow-moving beast, sweetly curious about the goings-on above its head and lumpenly passive when it runs into danger. Scientists call the fish a living fossil because the sturgeon have changed little over the millennia.*

The great association of Russia with caviar is linked to the rules of the Orthodox Christian church, whereby over 200 days a year were to be meat-free. A second factor was the large quantity of sturgeon in the Caspian Sea who migrate up the Volga to spawn. Sturgeon roe is not especially tasty when raw although, as I have often said, hunger is a wonderful sauce. When sturgeon roe is lightly salted, it becomes what we know today as caviar; the salting greatly improves its flavour.

Although caviar was shipped from Russia to western Europe, the old problem of spoilage remained and the quality of the sturgeon was highly variable. Indeed, many proverbs at the time warned of its dangers, such as the Venetian proverb: 'Whoever Eateth Caviar Eateth Salt, Dung, and Flies.' Louis XV was offered caviar by an emissary of Peter the Great and was so repulsed by the taste that he spat it out on the fine carpets of Versailles.

However, it was a Greek sea merchant who unlocked the simple technology to reduce the spoilage of caviar on its long westward journey. Ioannis Varvarkis, a Greek revolutionary and merchant seaman, re-fitted his boat with cannons and joined the Russian navy when hostilities with the hated Turks were looming in 1774. Peace broke out and Varvarkis lost his boat to the Turks when he tried to sell it in Istanbul. Penniless, he made his way back across 2,500 miles to arrive in St Petersburg. A chance meeting with Catherine the Great's lover, Prince Grigory Aleksandrovich Potemkin, earned him a royal audience and was given gold in recompense for the loss of his ship and unlimited tax-free rights to fish the Caspian sea. He built huge boats to fish the Caspian Sea and started to explore the export of caviar. He learned from Cossacks that the linden tree had smooth staves that were impermeable and which would greatly enhance long-term storage of these delicate, lightly salted fish roe storage. That discovery would revolutionise caviar production and its rarity, high cost and unusual taste made it a food of the elite.

Salmon and prawns were often associated with well-to-do. Those who held somewhat socialist views but were at a level of wealth above the ordinary citizen were referred to as 'smoked salmon so-cialists' and the sponsors of big sporting teams who attend games in comfortable surroundings with prime views are often referred to as the 'prawn sandwich brigade'. In *Ulysses*, James Joyce refers to Dr George Salmon, the noted mathematician and theologian whose statue greets the visitor to front square of Trinity College Dublin:

> *Provost's house. The reverend Dr Salmon: tinned salmon.*
> *Well tinned in there. Like a mortuary chapel. Wouldn't live in*
> *it if they paid me.*

In this instance, with typical Joycean cheek, he does not refer to real tinned salmon. The term 'tinned' in Dublin slang was used to describe the well to do.

Sitting in the Dublin pub, Davy Byrnes, James Joyce's hero of *Ulysses*, Leopold Bloom, comments thus on oysters and in doing so raises the issues of snobbery (The Red Bank restaurant was very exclusive), of oysters as an aphrodisiac and the old adage of an 'R' in the month, or as he call it an 'ar':

Photo credit: lensmen

Yes but what about oysters. Unsightly like a clot of phlegm. Filthy shells. Devil to open them too. Who found them out? Garbage, sewage they feed on. Fizz and Red bank oysters. Effect on the sexual. Aphrodis. He was in the Red Bank this morning. Was he oysters old fish at table perhaps he young flesh in bed no June has no ar no oysters.

The oyster was a shellfish widely available to coastal communities. However, as has been pointed out by Jonathan Swift: 'He was a very valiant man who first adventured on eating of oysters'. And the English poet John Gay was of the view that a steel palate was needed for the first oyster eater:

The man had a sure palate cover'd o'er
With brass or steel, that on the rocky shore
First broke the oozy oyster's pearly coat
And risqu'd the living morsel down his throat

Jonathan Swift would appear to have gone on to enjoy oysters and to perpetuate a view that oysters stirred sexual desire:

Charming oysters I cry:
My masters, come buy,
So plump and so fresh,
So sweet is their flesh,
No Colchester oyster
Is sweeter and moister:
Your stomach they settle,
And rouse up your mettle:
They'll make you a dad
Of a lass or a lad;
And madam your wife
They'll please to the life;
Be she barren, be she old,
Be she slut, or be she scold,
Eat my oysters, and lie near her,
She'll be fruitful, never fear her.

Poisonous Fish

It makes sense to avoid any food that is known to be poisonous to all, but in Japan there has been an ancient right of passage in the consumption of fugu, otherwise known as puffer fish or blowfish. To protect themselves from predators, these fish suck in water and can rapidly increase their size into a ball two feet in diameter, a tall order for any predator. This fish contains a poison, 30 times more lethal than cyanide, and is served only in specialised restaurants prepared by chefs who train for three years to get a Fugu license. Most deaths from this toxin occur when the fish is prepared inexpertly in homes.

Fugu was eaten by the Jomon civilisation 5,000 years ago and blowfish bones have been found on various middens or mounds of fish bones and shells. During the Tokugawa Shoganate (1603-1868), the consumption of fugu was banned in the district of Edo, now Tokyo, but it flourished in the western province of Yamaguchi where Shogun had no authority. As the nineteenth century drew to a close and the Shogun's power faded, fugu returned to Edo but when that era was replaced in 1868 by the Meiji Restoration, the ban on fugu consumption was again enforced. Twenty years later, that ban would be lifted by the first Prime Minister of Japan, Prince Itō Hirobumi, who was born in the Yamaguchi region, famed for its love of fugu. Apparently, he was served fugu unbeknownst to himself and, when it became known, he realised that in the proper hands this fish is a safe delicacy.

Shellfish are enjoyed by many people, but for some can lead to an acute onset of life threatening symptoms, which we know to-day as food allergies. Indeed, the word was coined by a Viennese paediatrician, Clemens von Pirquet, in 1906. It is comprised of two

Photo credit: nedjelly

Greek words, *allos* and *ergon*, meaning 'changed' and 'reaction'. The Greeks recognised that some foods were poisonous to all but others were dangerous for just a small proportion of people.

The first case history of an allergic reaction to shellfish was that of the Belgian physician Jean Baptiste van Helmont, who described an asthma attack after eating fish. In 1698, Sir John Floyer wrote a treatise entitled *Food of Asthmatics* and noted how a fish allergy could lead to the production of 'a viscid chyle, which stops in the lungs in the spitting asthma, and that oppresses them'. It is often said that we should not eat oysters and other shellfish when there is an 'R' in the month, meaning that such foods should be avoided from May 1 to August 31. This 'R' in the month rule is attributed to William Butler, physician to King James I, who in 1599 wrote a cookbook, *Dyets Dry Dinnen*, which was more comical than serious. He did so in the hope of winning the love of his third cousin, Lady Anne Bacon.

'The oyster,' he wrote, 'is unseasonable and unwholesome in all monethes, that have not the letter R in their name, because it is then venerious', meaning it was spawning at this time. At this stage the oyster is laden with eggs and the flesh fades in consistency, making it much less attractive to eat. He adds that the 'exciteth appetite, and Venus: nourisheth little'. There is another reason for the 'R' in a month rule besides that of spawning, and that is that in the summer months toxic algae can bloom and such toxins can be concentrated in shellfish.

Fish, back in the day, looked after themselves. The fisherfolk applied their guile to catching them. For the cultivating farmer, harvesting was low risk unlike that of the fishing scene, but their guile was in replacing the harvested plant foods. It is to these foods we now turn.

Chapter 7

The Garden, Orchard, Hedgerow and Forest

The Mushroom is the Elf of Plants

By Emily Dickinson

The Mushroom is the Elf of Plants –
At Evening, it is not –
At Morning, in a Truffled Hut
It stop upon a Spot

As if it tarried always
And yet its whole Career
Is shorter than a Snake's Delay
And fleeter than a Tare –

'Tis Vegetation's Juggler –
The Germ of Alibi –
Doth like a Bubble antedate
And like a Bubble, hie –

I feel as if the Grass was pleased
To have it intermit –
This surreptitious scion
Of Summer's circumspect.

Had Nature any supple Face
Or could she one contemn –
Had Nature an Apostate –
That Mushroom – it is Him!

Twenty minute drive from Manhattan lies a farm that grows herbs and vegetables. Nothing surprising about that, you might say, except that the farm is in the heart of downtown Newark, in a disused multi-story building where plants are grown in this vertical farm under blue light, with precision delivery of water, nutrients and heat. Across the globe vertical farming is taking off, and literally so in Dubai airport where the world's largest vertical farm now serves the vegetable and herb needs of airline catering. If that is the future, then what was the past like?

Unlike livestock, the variety of which can be counted on one hand, our plant food is enormously varied. In today's world the variety is bolstered by sophisticated post-harvest storage and rapid transit to supermarkets, continents away from the farms in which produce is grown. But in ancient times, our plant food offered a very limited choice. Different climates and soil conditions meant diverse plants in various parts of the world, and it would take trade and imperial conquest to widen the plant food chain. But that was very dependent on who you were. Almost 80 per cent of the English medieval population were peasants, eking a livelihood from small patches of land and toiling on the lord's manor who would retain the choicest of land and, of course, the bulk of it.

Farming: Open and Closed

In the beginning, Europe was mainly a mass of forests. Over many millennia, some were cleared and the land cultivated. We know that over 5,000 years ago, the ancient Celts had each field contained within stone walls. Some 6,000 years later, the Domesday book of William the Conqueror recorded 35 per cent of land as arable, 25 per cent as pasture and meadow, 15 per cent as woodland and 25 per cent as bog or marsh.

This was the era of manorial feudalism and each peasant had some land allocated by the lord of the manor. This land existed as patches, hither and tither, the idea being that all peasants would have a mix of good and poor land. To pay for the rent of this land, peasants would give a fraction of the output to the lord of the manor as well as time serving as a farmhand on the lord's own land, the demesne. Most of the land would have been tilled for wheat and barley, for bread and beer respectively. A peasant might own a cow which would be grazed on the commonly owned pasture and meadow. All true ownership of land lay with the king and he allocated it as a reward for military or religious service.

A royal survey of the village of Elton (Cambridgeshire) in 1257 recorded that the lord of the manor owned 1,900 acres of arable land, of which 450 acres were for his personal demesne. The remaining land was allocated to 113 peasants averaging 13 acres for each tenant. Life was hard for peasants. Over the period 1334-1381, Edward III imposed no less than 30 tax hikes to fund his wars with France, ultimately leading to the Peasants' Revolt in 1381. A Kentish priest by the name of John Ball played a leading role in the revolt and expressed his fervour strongly:

> *The lords are clad in velvet and camlet lined with squirrel and ermine, while we go dressed in coarse cloth. They have the wines, the spices, and the good bread: we have the rye, the husks, and the straw, and we drink water. They have shelter and ease in their fine manors, and we have hardship and toil,*

the wind and the rain in the fields. And from us must come,
from our labour, the things which keep them in luxury.

He was hanged, drawn and quartered under the watchful eye of the King.

In 1349, the Black Death killed 30 per cent of the population of Europe and the population of England fell from 4 to 2.5 million. The resulting shortage of labour would have a lasting effect on agriculture. Tillage is labour-intensive but livestock are much less demanding of time and effort. At the end of the fifteenth century, England had nearly three times more sheep than people. The powerful lords and abbots increased their land by simply ousting peasants and purloining commons and meadows, described by Thomas More in his description of the ravages of extensive sheep farming:

> *They consume, destroy and devour whole fields, houses and*
> *cities. For noblemen and gentlemen, yea and certain abbots,*
> *holy men no doubt, not contenting themselves with the year-*
> *ly revenues and profits . . . leave no ground for tillage: they*
> *enclose all into pastures, they throw down houses, they pluck*
> *down towns and leave nothing standing . . .*

As with John Ball, he was summarily executed. The poor of rural England migrated to cities and enlisted in the army leaving behind a diminishing labouring class who, perversely, could now command a higher wage. Fields became enclosed and commonage reduced. For the remaining peasants, gardens assumed great importance to their nourishment.

The Garden

The allocation of land specifically for the growth of vegetables, herbs and flowers was fostered by religious orders. Monks and nuns lived a cloistered life free from the demands of the outside world, and to that end they developed gardens both to feed themselves and to adorn their church with flowers. They became very skilled in all forms of gardening and passed these skills on to the villages around them.

Recorded history tells us much about the gardens of the wealthy but little of those of the peasants. English peasant villagers would have a front area, adjacent to the road, with a small number of farm animals in pens. Peasant gardens or crofts were raised above the flood plain and bounded by dykes and ditches, measuring about half an acre. This would not be sufficient to feed a family but would be a major addition to the meagre amounts of food that they could buy with their earnings.

Cabbage, lettuce, leeks, spinach, kale and celery would be common vegetables for cultivation. Herbs would also be grown, quite often in pots to embellish a somewhat boring diet dominated by barley-based gruel. Peas and beans, rich in protein and micronutrients, would be grown in summer, dried and saved for the lean time of winter. And lean times were commonplace and seasonal in the medieval era. Eventually, cities emerged and new markets were created, boosting trade in food. Roman conquests transformed the gardens of Rome, and Pliny describes the plant food from a region of Tunisia:

> *Here, beneath a palm of enormous size, grows the olive, beneath the olive the fig, beneath the fig, again, the pomegranate, beneath the pomegranate the vine, and beneath the vine we find sown, first wheat, then the leguminous plants, and after them garden herbs – all in the same year, and all growing beneath another's shade.*

Photo credit: Jakub Kapusnak

Vegetables native to many far-off places found a new home across Europe, including aubergines, cucumber and chicory from India; saffron, cauliflower, kohlrabi, broccoli, asparagus, beet, radish and celery among many that originated in the lands bordering all parts of the Mediterranean sea; and the artichoke, yam and okra from Africa. In time, when the spoils of the Inca and Aztec conquests were made available, yet another flood of vegetables arrived in Europe such as chillies, squash, French beans, cassava, potatoes, tomatoes and maize. Many of these earlier imports across Europe were adapted in the local cultivation, and for the well to do there was quite a range of vegetables available, such as onions, parsnips, fennel, garlic, parsley, shallot, watercress, endive, lettuce, beetroot, cabbage, leeks, carrots, artichokes, long-beans, broad-beans, peas, lentils and asparagus, a list quite befitting any modern greengrocer's stock. The arrival of the Huguenots into England brought new expertise in vegetable growing.

The medical theories of Galen, which dominated food choice for centuries, held that vegetables should be first cooked, but he had one exception – lettuce. Up to the sixteenth century, salads were eaten with most, if not all, ingredients cooked. Bartholomew Scappi, the sixteenth century chef, records the preparation of three salads, all involving cooking. Nonetheless, salads or 'sallets' were well recognised as delicate dishes in the seventeenth century. In 1699, John Evelyn presented at length a paper to the Royal Society of London, of which he was founding secretary, on the subject of salads, not something the Fellows of that august body might hear these days:

> *And now, My Lord, I expect some will wonder what my mean-*
> *ing is, to usher in a trifle, with so much magnificence, and*
> *end at last in a fine receipt for the dressing of a sallet with an*
> *handful of pot-herbs!*

In time the theories of Galen faded and the culinary skills of chefs increased; salads as we know them today began to emerge: Salad Niçoise from the city of Nice; Waldorf salad created at New York's Waldorf-Astoria Hotel in 1896; Caesar salad created by Caesar Cardini in 1924 in Tijuana, hoping to entice alcohol-parched Californians to enjoy salad and Tequila; and Cobb salad which was designed in 1937 at the Hollywood Brown Derby restaurant. It became a signature dish named after the restaurant's owner, Robert Howard Cobb. Salads are very culinary specific across different parts of the world from a feta cheese-based Greek salad to a mozzarella and tomato salad from Italy or Fattoush from Lebanon.

Unlike the meagre gardens of medieval peasants, those of the manors and monasteries were highly sophisticated, usually combining a lesser garden for vegetables and herbs and a larger ornamental garden bedecked with beautiful, flowers, shrubs and trees. There were three gardens areas in a typical monastic settlement. The first was the walled cloister garden with pristine lawns interspersed with paths, all designed to facilitate quiet ambulatory meditation. Next came the cellarer's garden where vegetables and herbs were cultivated, and finally, the physic garden where all forms of medicinal herbs such as opium poppies, mandrake, foxglove, henbane, liquorice, comfrey and myrrh were grown, the monasteries often serving as early hospitals.

Many of the gardens of the wealthy would also have had glass houses and the origins of their construction can be traced back to the Roman emperor, Tiberius. His doctors prescribed a cucumber a day for his ailing health. However, whilst that was fine in the summer sunshine, it was a problem in the dark cold days of winter. The plant was protected by growing it in a wheel barrow covered in an opaque material with the wheel barrow moved indoors and outdoors to maximise sunshine and warmth, scarce commodities in a Roman winter.

The Italian glasshouse developed in complexity, learning from the experiences of Korea where glasshouses were built above a pit which was filled with hot air pumped from a nearby fire, giving underground heating. Today, vertical farming, extensive glass-house farming and the use of poly-tunnels lead to a high output of vegetables which can be shipped around the world, abolishing the seasonal shortages that affected consumers in times gone by. If vegetables were a necessity, however, fruit was a luxury.

Orchards and Hedgerows

Our ancestors had one advantage over us. They had time, oodles of it. They would experiment, observe and adapt every aspect of the food chain, and they would discover that although fruit was tasty, it would not sustain the calorific price of hard work. Nonetheless, as ever from the Garden of Eden, fruit is very tempting and humans have an innate sweet tooth. Archaeological digs reveal widespread consumption of crab apples across Europe. Fruit trees were cultivated by peasants, the produce of which more often ended up in the preservation of the fruit as an alcoholic beverage: apple cider in the UK; apple and pears in calvados in Brittany; slivovitz from plums in Eastern Europe; gin from juniper berries; and wine, port and brandy from grapes and berries. Fruits and berries were also preserved in jams and marmalades, generically known as preserves. The first recipe for jam appears in the first known cookbook, *De Re Coquinaria* (*The Art of Cooking*), which dates from the first century CE:

> *Pick out perfect quinces with stems and leaves, place them in a vessel, pour over honey and defrutum and you will preserve them for a long time.*

The arrival of affordable sugar in the sixteenth century increased interest in various forms of preserves. Jams and marmalades from many fruits, sometimes infused with herbs, are described by the Duchess of Northumberland in her little book on jams, jellies and marmalade. The recipes are derived from the archives of Alnwick Castle and originate with Edith Beale's recipe book of 1576, Miss Beale being the great-great-great-great grandmother of the first Duchess of Northumberland.

The list of fruits is extensive and includes fruit grown in Northumberland, such as apples, pears, damsons, quinces and various berries, and also fruit imported from warmer climes, particularly citrus fruits. The latter, and indeed many vegetables, were introduced to Europe through the Muslim empires of the Umayyad and

Photo credit: Jules Kitano

Abbasid dynasties, whose rule covered vast tracts of land bordering the north and south coasts of the Mediterranean Sea. We know from Pliny the Elder that techniques such as grafting were well understood in ancient times and would have been further developed in the orchards of the monasteries and lords.

Apples were the most popular of fruits in Europe, largely because they were quite suitable to the climate of this continent. In England, apples were divided into two broad categories, cooking apples and eating apples. Raymond Blanc, head chef at Le Manoir aux Quat' Saisons in Oxford, writes:

> As a chef and a Frenchman, I don't make this simplistic and confusing distinction between cooking and eating apples. It is crucial to me to push the boundaries to understand how to achieve the best flavours and textures from every individual apple, in order to give my guests the best, most sublime apple experience. So I set my own five specific tests. I wanted

to know which apple would give the best juice and how each variety would behave when pureed, baked whole, in a tarte Maman Blanc or a tarte tatin.

Picking berries was a regular treat for city children who would fill cans and buckets of blackberries from hedgerows on quiet country roads. The Royal Horticultural Society also lists cherries, cherry plums, damsons, elderberries, rosehip and hawthorn as berries that are found in hedgerows at different times of the year. Garden berries include raspberries, gooseberries, redcurrants, blackcurrants and strawberries. For some reason, berries attract a lot of folklore. Jacob and Wilhelm Grimm collected German fairy tales and in 'The Three Sisters', the youngest and most beautiful of the three wins the heart of a handsome prince. In Cinderella style, her less beautiful older sisters send her out to the woods to pick

Photo credit: Yana Kozlova

berries, accompanied by a sinister witch, dressed as a maid who sneaks away leaving the young vulnerable princess to flounder in the dark woods. The Celtic tale of the fairies of Dooros woods and the land of the giants all centres on the little red berries that were the secret diet of the fairies.

Nuts

Nuts are high in protein and low in water and can be readily preserved by drying. They represented an important food for peasant households to take through the hungry winter. Hazelnuts were widely consumed across Europe and could tolerate very poor soils. In one study, a typical hazelnut tree or bush was found to have about 1,000 green-coloured nuts in the last week in August, and two months later a total of 850 were collected from the ground. The flesh of hazelnuts, when ground, gives a smooth buttery paste which in the Piedmont region of Italy was incorporated with chocolate to yield a tasty spread which many children worldwide know today as Nutella.

Almonds were highly prized and expensive ingredients in many cooked dishes, but also provided an almond butter and an almond milk which were consumed in place of dairy produce during religious fasts. Like many of these choice expensive foods that came from the east, their price fell after the Black Death decimated the population of Europe and some former serfs and peasants could demand higher wages. Now affordable to those less well-off, early cookbooks abound in recipes involving almonds, toasted, ground flaked and whole for main courses, desserts and biscuits. Sugar-coated almonds were eaten as comfits at the end of the meal.

Chestnuts were widely available across Europe and were consumed in a variety of ways. The flesh of the chestnut is softer than

Photo credit: Jakub Kapusnak

most nuts because it is higher in starch. Chestnuts roasted on an open fire, lovingly captured in the Christmas song, are widely sold as street food around Europe. Marrons glacés, sugar-coated chestnuts, are a very old form of confectionery. Chestnut flour was often mixed with potatoes in seventeenth century Italy for making gnocchi.

Walnut trees were widely distributed across Europe by the Romans and whilst their nuts were of great nutritional value, it was walnut wood which became a favoured wood of furniture makers. Many other nuts would enter the European market from Asia and central America including those of hickory and pine, popularised by native Americans, pecan nuts from the US, peanuts from South America, macadamia nuts from Australian aboriginal tribes, mongongo from Africa, pistachios from Persia and gingko nuts from China. Of course, nut shells can be bashed with any tool to get at the kernel, but to do it properly nutcrackers were invented, first wooden and then metal.

Food of the Forests

Besides, berries, nuts and fruits, early humans foraged in forests and woodlands for mushrooms and truffles, both of which we think of as vegetables but are in fact fungi. The world apparently was divided into those countries who were innately suspicious of mushrooms and those that readily adopted them into cooking. But beyond their culinary role, mushrooms have been used for centuries for their hallucinatory properties. The Spanish Franciscan friar, Bernardino, described the use of hallucinatory mushrooms by the Aztecs in his sixteenth century book, *Historia General de la Cosas de Nueva Espana*:

> *Coming at the very first, at the time of feasting, they ate mushrooms when, as they said, it was the hour of blowing of the flutes . . . they ate mushrooms with honey. When already the mushrooms were taking effect, there was dancing, there was weeping . . . some saw a vision that they would die in war. . . . be devoured by wild beasts . . . become rich . . . wealthy and become slave owners . . . slave owners. . . . And when the effects of the mushrooms ceased, they conversed with one another, spoke of what they had seen in the vision.*

To the Christian missionaries, this was the work of the devil. For many in ancient times, mushrooms were the work of the grim reaper. Poisoning was rife in ancient Rome but mushrooms were probably only used as a cover for a more lethal plant-based poison. Agrippa used this ruse to do away with her emperor husband, Claudius. Among the mushroom-loving countries was France, and mushroom poisoning, accidental as opposed to deliberate, was so common that regulations were introduced into the famous food market Les Halles in Paris in 1808, allowing the Gendarme to establish a mushroom inspection service. Mushrooms have a strong meaty or umami taste and the darker the mushroom, the meatier the effect. Indeed, mushrooms harvested from the forest would frequently have been favoured during periods of religious fasts. Among the most commonly used mushrooms in western cuisine are the button, portobello, oyster, chanterelle and porcini varieties. Because mushrooms are fungi, not vegetables, they can grow wherever there is rotting and decaying vegetation. They secrete enzymes which break down the surrounding detritus and then absorb the nutrients for growth.

The empires of Rome and Persia, the Crusades and trade with the east all embellished the diets of early settlers with new and exotic foods. Some of these are very prominent in our modern diet and it is to these and their eastern provenance that we now turn.

Photo credit: AscentXmedia

Chapter 8

Rice and Noodles: The Eastern Carbs

Toiling Farmers

(Child's poem, Tang dynasty)

Farmers weeding at noon,
Sweat down the field soon.
Who knows food on a tray?
Thanks to their toiling day.

The patience of poverty. In rice fields, backs bent forever.
Amazing, man outoxens the oxen and still smiles. The
mystery of India, say Indologists. – Günter Grass

Wild rice was foraged in Asia along the banks of rivers and streams. Early hunter-gatherers would always have associated rice as a crop that thrives in shallow water. Indeed, intermittent floods and droughts would have taught these early peoples much about the agriculture of rice and its strong affinity for watery soils. The earliest record of rice agriculture can be dated back to 10,000 to 14,000 years ago along the Pearl and Yellow rivers of China. Wild rice was domesticated and evolved into a strain of rice which accounts for the vast majority of rice eaten today, oryza sativa.

The process of domestication was not simply the adaptation of a new variety. It also involved the slow development of rice cultivation in what we know today as paddy fields (the Malay word for rice is *padi*). Early farmers, who would have harvested rice along the shallow banks of streams, decided to extend this by digging canals inland from rivers and streams.

When the canal was full, simple dams would retain the shallow water, the level of which could be regulated by opening or closing the dam linking it to the stream. One can also envisage a reservoir into which water from the main canal would be drained, in effect providing the canal with a tap and plughole: a tap from the stream and a plughole to the reservoir. That is the basic principle of paddy irrigation.

It involves water capture through rainfall or rivers, wide canals to grow the rice and reservoirs to drain the water from the canal. Finally, from the last reservoir will run a canal to a point downstream from the point of input from the stream or river. Because streams and rivers flow on a downward gradient rather than flow with lunar tidal forces, the point of water entry and exit to and from the paddy field irrigation system must be far enough apart to allow drops in elevation to be of sufficient scale to support a good flow when needed, but not so great that the task of constructing canals becomes unmanageable.

The paddy fields are drained before the seedlings are planted and the muddy earth ploughed with the aid of the water buffalo. Water is returned for growth and drained again for harvest. No doubt, this description will be faulted by some wizard in paddy field irrigation, but this is the gist of this odd agricultural or aquacultural system. Irrigated rice from paddy fields accounts for 75 per cent of global production, rain-fed rice production accounts for

20 per cent, and upland dry rice production, mainly from South America and Africa, account for 5 per cent.

Working the Paddy Field

Traditional rice farming accounts for the vast majority of rice produced in Asia and is an extremely labour-intensive form of agriculture. In his book *Outliers: The Story of Success* Malcolm Gladwell explores the work ethic that is central to rice growing. A typical paddy field is small, about 100 yards square and to feed a family of several generations with just two to three paddy fields per family requires great attention to detail at all stages of rice production, and to attain that detail, great cooperation and coordination is needed from all the extended family. Just to plough one hectare of a paddy field will require the farmer and water buffalo to walk about 80 kilometres. That same hectare of rice will require up to 2,000 hours of labour. If it takes, on average, 120 days to grow rice from planting to harvesting, that translates into 17 hours a day, seven days a week. That can only be achieved with the full commitment of the wider family to share the load. As the Filipino folk song goes:

> *Planting is never fun*
> *Bend from morn to set of sun*
> *Cannot stand and cannot sit*
> *Cannot rest for a little bit*

Unlike wheat, rice strains can be very different and the farmer must hedge his bets about which strains to select, usually selecting a mix which can cope with varying climatic conditions. Each strain needs to be spaced exactly to its needs when the young seedlings are taken from the nursery for planting. And right throughout the cultivation, the farmer must manage the irrigation system to

Photo credit: istock

optimise growth and minimise weeds. Wheat, in contrast, can be sown and then be left to soak up the seasonal sun and rainfall until harvest time. Not so with rice.

In rice-eating cultures, there is a strong link between rice and a deity. Dr S.D. Sharma, a leading rice scientist from India, recalls an event from his childhood. His father, a religious man, having consulted his sacred texts, decided that on this particular year the success of the rice harvest would be best if his son would lead the ceremonial planting. This occurs on a specified day in the lunar calendar. All of the family completed their bath and dressed in their finest clothes. They brought gifts for the Goddess of Wealth to the rice field which they reached as dawn broke. Having placed a statue of the Goddess in a tiny patch of the field, his father prayed thus:

> *O Goddess of Wealth bless us with a rich crop of rice this year so that we have enough to eat and enough to sell to meet all our needs. Bless us with happiness and prosperity.*

His father then asked Sharma to symbolically plough a small area, plant the rice, and irrigate it. They then bowed before the Goddess and returned home.

This reverential approach to the cultivation of rice is typical of the strong association with the gods. Right throughout Asia, the rice crop is celebrated with many festivals to various Gods. Dewi Sri is the Goddess of rice in Bali and is honoured at the harvest festival. This Goddess exists in three forms: one who gave birth to rice, another who protects the rice and yet another form that harvests the rice. In the Philippines, the rice god is male, the god Humidhid, while in Japan Inari is the Shinto god or goddess of rice. In Osaka, at a Shinto shrine, is a paddy field where on June 14 every year, the rice planting ceremony takes place as it has done so for over 1,700 years.

The Long and the Short

There are two major types of rice, distinguished by the structure of the dominant starch within their grain. Long-grained rice has most of its starch organised into straight chains or filaments, and when cooked it absorbs water, elongates and can more than double its length. A small amount of the global output of long-grained rice is associated with the aromatic or fragrant rice strains, Jasmine from Thailand, Laos, Cambodia and Vietnam and Basmati from India, Pakistan and Bangladesh. They share the same fragrant compound giving the rice a buttery or popcorn flavour and they enjoy a premium price, up to two to three times that of normal rice. Moreover, like Champagne or Parma ham, Jasmine and Basmati are protected names. In the US, they have imitations like Jazzmen and Texmati rice. Jean Baptiste Tavernier in his travels in India in the seventeenth century, wrote of Basmati rice:

All the rice which grows in this country possesses a particular quality causing it to be much esteemed. The grain is half as small again as that of common rice, and when it is cooked, snow is not whiter than it is, besides which, it smells like musk and all the nobles of India eat no other.

Short-grained rice has its main form of starch organised into complex three dimensional webs, and when cooked this rice absorbs water, swelling rather than elongating. Long grained rice which elongates on cooking is favoured in those cultures where rice is eaten by hand, usually using something like chapati bread to scoop up some rice with bits of meat, fish or vegetables. Thus, this long grain, fluffy type of rice is popular, for example, in the Indian sub-continent. In South East Asia, where rice is eaten with chopsticks, the preference is for the shorter grain rice with the highly branched starch making the rice stickier and easier to eat with chopsticks.

Risotto

Although risotto is often regarded as another form of rice, it is simply a culinary term describing a specific approach to cooking rice. To achieve this, short to medium grained rice is preferred where the main starch type is the highly branched form, which swells when cooked. The most commonly used rice is arborio, named after the town Arborio in the Po valley north of Turin. Halfway between the Alps and the Mediterranean lies a large plain known as Pianura Padana, and in spring it is flooded by melting alpine glaciers. The water level is managed much as in Asian paddy fields, and at the end of the season the water is returned to the sea. Rice was grown in Italy from about the fifteenth century and the sole strain of rice was called nostrale. A wide variety of rice strains is believed to have

Photo credit: Thirawatana Phaisalratana

been brought to Italy by a Jesuit priest returning from the Philippines in the mid-nineteenth century, and almost certainly arborio rice began to dominate. Cooking arborio rice is quite different to boiling or steaming it.

The first phase in making a risotto is the toasting of the rice. This involves preparing a 'sofrito', slowly fried onions and garlic in a butter and olive oil blend. The rice is then added, and the heat is turned up. The rice grains get toasted by the oils and at the same time absorb much of the flavour of whatever is used in the sofrito. The grains become translucent which ensures that they are sealed by the fats, facilitating a slow release of starch as the dish evolves.

Since the secret of the risotto cooking process is the slow release of starch to create the creamy liquid, an essential element of risotto, this toasting, as the heating with fat is called, is critically important. From then on, the rice is cooked with small additions of the cooking liquid, usually wine, while being constantly stirred.

The stirring causes the rice grains to rub against each other, giving a gradual release of starch into the dish. The gradual addition of the cooking liquid ensures that the rice grains remain in close contact with one another, again facilitating slow starch release.

At the end, butter and cheese are added and the fats therein bind with the starch, much as in making a dough, to thicken the consistency of the final product. There are many chefs who argue that neither toasting nor stirring are necessary for a perfect risotto. Indeed, many argue that the liquid which will gel the rice grains does not have to be added slowly. Maybe. But there is something nice about the cooking of risotto, a sense of intimacy requiring your undivided attention from start to finish.

Paella

If the cooking of risotto is radically different from Asian rice cooking, then Spanish culinary rice traditions are yet more different. The most popular rice used in Spain is the bomba strain and the most popular dish by far is paella. The origins of Spanish rice can be traced back to Alexander the Great who is credited with introducing rice into Mesopotamia, a region of Western Asia situated within the Tigris–Euphrates river system in the northern part of the Fertile Crescent. From Persia it spread to Syria, Asia Minor and Egypt. From these Arab regions, rice cultivation spread to Spain and Sicily around the ninth century, both strongholds of the Muslim empire.

By the tenth century, rice had become a major crop in Spain in the region of Valencia. The Romans had earlier introduced significant irrigation systems in this region which may have played a role in the regional origins of Spanish rice cultivation. The Spanish name for rice, *arroz,* has its origins in the Persian name for rice, *al orz.*

The advent of the Christian conquest of the Muslim caliphate wrought significant changes to rice cultivation. Rice was seen as a Muslim food and proximity to irrigated rice fields were believed to be a threat to public health, particularly associated with malaria and the breeding ground of the mosquito.

From the fifteenth to the eighteenth century, rice production in Spain waned but did not disappear. The aristocracy were particularly fond of a custard-like sweet dish made of ground rice, cinnamon, sugar and almonds. The eighteenth century saw a huge growth in the population of Valencia and with it a resurgence of rice cultivation, but in new irrigated pastures, well away from heavily populated towns and cities.

The origin of the term paella is open to debate. One line of thought is that it is derived from *par ella* or 'for her'. Another is that the Arab for left over, *baqiyah*, is the origin, and finally there is the belief that the term is derived from the pan it is cooked in. This may be linked to the choices that peasants had in cooking rice for

Photo credit: Studioimagen73

paella. The rice growing areas were some distance from towns and the cultivation of rice would have involved many labourers, either hired or part of a family. The only fuel available for fires were light branches and large twigs which could be collected in the vicinity of the rice fields. Such fuel burns very fast and so rice was cooked is a special pan which was wide and shallow, the depth not to exceed the first joint of the thumb. The shallow pan is designed to allow the socorrat (from the Spanish for 'singe') to develop. This is a cara-melised crust of rice which should form on the bottom of the paella and its formation is detected by the crackling sound that can be heard as the socorrat is formed.

As the paella is cooking with its rice, seafood, meat or vegetables, the top part can be kept moist by adding wine, stock or water to spots of dryness here and there. Unlike risotto, there is zero stirring in the making of paella. Bomba rice, the most popular of the Spanish paella rices, is unique in that as it is cooked, it absorbs water to swell to three times its original volume, without either bursting or leaking starch. Thus, whereas risotto can be almost poured, paella is definitely grainy.

Rice in the US

There is a legend as to the arrival of rice to the United States. Ap-parently, on the island of Madagascar lived a warrior who fell in love with the King's daughter. The King was not a happy camper and the young couple fled to the other side of the island and set up home which included a paddy field. The King's army eventually caught up with the couple and the young warrior was sold off to a slave trader and taken to the US. His daughter, confined to house prison, escaped with a sack of rice and set off in a canoe in the hope of finding peace somewhere else. Exhausted by the sea and the sun, the young princess was rescued and taken aboard a ship and assigned to the cook's galley. On arrival in the port of Charleston, the ship's captain engaged with the great explorer of the Carolinas, Henry Woodward, who was delighted to be offered the young princess's rice. To that end he sent on board his slave to retrieve the sack of rice from the young woman. Thus, were the warrior and his love, the princess, re-united and presumably they lived happily ever after or as happy as any slave can be. Or so the story goes.

The initial cultivation of rice in the US was achieved through the use of water derived from tidal rivers about ten miles upstream from their deltas. For some time, the rice industry in the Carolinas flourished and even established export markets in Europe. However, it was a high cost crop and after the US civil war, the economic viability of this industry waned. Rice production began to move to Louisiana where the soil was highly amenable to irrigation for rice agriculture. From there it spread to parts of Texas and Arkansas and, following the Californian Gold Rush and the influx of some 40,000 Chinese immigrants, the San Jose region began rice production. The US is a small player in terms of global rice production at about 2 per cent of the total, but in terms of exports the US is much higher than that accounting for 12 to 13 per cent of globally traded rice. Of course, in most Asian countries the great majority of the rice produced remains within the domestic market.

Noodles

Rice is a main staple in Asia but so too are noodles which are made from many starchy foods but particularly wheat and rice. Wheat-based noodles were dominant in Northern China and the Chinese became masters of the chemistry of gluten, the wheat protein that gives wheat dough its great malleability. Indeed, in the sixth century they had managed to isolate gluten and used it to shape many dishes, and in particular to make vegetarian dishes more appealing. Wheat-based noodles were known as mian and thus the origin of chow mein or 'stir-fried noodles'. This was a dish of the working classes and remained so until quite recent times. Boiled noodles were eaten as far back as the Han dynasty and the Emperor had a designated official, the *t'ang guan* or boiled food officer.

Today, 80 per cent of all noodles consumed in China and other East Asian countries are prepared and consumed at home. Rice noodles are equally popular in Asia and the story is told of the invasion of Southern China by King Qin Shi Huang whose north Chinese troops could not cope with the rice dishes of the South. An enterprising chef tackled the issue and managed to develop a mill which forced ground rice mixed with water through a tiny hole in a lower mill stone feeding the rice paste directly into boiling water. The troops were happy and rice noodles were invented.

Photo credit: Alex Souto Maior

There are two main types of rice noodle. Qiefen is a translucent noodle made from very thin sheets of rice noodle dough cut into long strips, not unlike tagliatelle. Zhafen noodles are extruded through a narrow orifice, not unlike vermicelli or angel pasta. In Middle Eastern cuisine, vermicelli rice noodles are lightly fried and are included as a small component of boiled rice to enhance its fluffiness.

Almost all the rice we consume is white rice which has been milled to remove the outer husk or bran. Although it is popularly believed that brown rice is nutritionally superior, this is not so clear when you get down to the nitty gritty. Brown rice comes out slightly better in nutritional comparisons, although the differences are marginal. In countries with a very high reliance on rice for energy, eating brown rice might begin to be advantageous. However in Asia, white rice is believed to be easier to cook, to have a more desirable texture and to have a superior aroma compared to brown rice. In the west, anything that makes food easier to prepare is quickly taken up so boil-in-the-bag rice is very popular as are rice cookers. Rice remains a major source of starch in Asia, the Middle East and parts of Africa. As Auguste Escoffier, the most famous French chef of the last century put it, 'Rice is the best, the most nutritive and unquestionably, the most widespread staple in the world'.

Chapter 9

Tea, Theft and Opium

Of Tea, Commended by Her Majesty

By Edmund Waller

Venus her myrtle, Phoebus has her bays,
Tea both excels, which she vouchsafes to praise,
The best of Queens, and the best of herbs we owe
To that bold nation which the way did show,
To the fair region where the sun doth rise,
Whose rich productions we so justly prize,
The muses friend, tea does our fancy aid
Repress those vapors, which the head invade,
And keep the palace the soul serene
Fit on her birthday to salute the Queen.

The story of tea involves two great powers, China and England, one inward-looking, the other highly imperial, both extremely arrogant. The opening poem of this chapter was written for the birthday of Queen Catherine of Braganza, wife of the English King, Charles II, who was responsible for the popularity of tea in that country. According to Chinese legend, when heaven and earth split, the universe was ruled by 12 Emperors of the Earth, followed by 12 Emperors of Mankind, followed by a succession of sovereigns leading eventually to the three sovereigns or the three august ones.

These would provide humankind with the skills needed to survive. One of these three, Shen-nung, was the divine cultivator who imparted all the skills needed to till the land.

There are many legends and myths on tea which have been passed down the generations in China, and they all have one thing in common. Tea was always associated with the Divine and always had a very special place in Chinese tradition. So great in fact, that the Chinese kept the skills of cultivation and processing secret for millennia, unlike the Arabs who let the cultivation of coffee slip from their hands. At first, tea was used like other herbal infusions in China as a medicine, but by the sixth century it became a popular beverage of the common people. Its cultivation and processing was passed on by word of mouth. Whilst the commercial centres of China were using bank notes and coins by then, those in far-flung rural settings used tea as a currency.

Tea Farming

The first written text on the cultivation of tea, its processing, its associated equipment and on the ceremony of drinking tea was written by Lù Yǔ in about 761 BCE. This comprehensive book, *Ch'a Ching*, comprised many volumes and made Lù Yǔ famous and a friend to the Emperor. Great statues were built to him and many poems written in his honour.

Tea continued to grow in popularity and China grew in sophistication. This was disrupted by the invasion by the Mongols, first by Genghis Khan who conquered large parts of China, and then by Kublai Khan who took complete control of China establishing the Yuan dynasty from 1279 to 1368 CE. A four-tier caste system was established with the native Chinese at the bottom. He attempted an invasion of Japan with disastrous consequences.

When the Ming empire restored China to the Chinese, their psyche was forever shaped firstly, to be suspicious of foreigners, and secondly, to have no taste for imperialism. China became strongly inward-looking, regarding their civilisation as the most superior in the world. Westerners began to come to China but only by invitation and always with supplication to the Emperor and the Emperor's civil and military representatives. Visitors would prostrate themselves before these dignitaries, a process known as the kowtow, from the Chinese *ketou*. Tea drinking had expanded outside China into the Arab world and was soon traded by the Europeans, especially the Venetians. It was not until the early seventeenth century, however, that tea began to arrive in Europe in significant quantities.

Tea may have arrived in Europe but it did so as the finished product without the attendant agricultural and processing know how and wherewithal. All tea comes from one plant, *Camelia sinensis*, and the various types of tea are created by varying the method of processing. Southeast China is where the tea bush first originated. If left to their own devices, tea bushes would grow into trees too high for hand picking so farmers crop the plant to just over waist high. The leaves are about the length of your hand and about as wide as the length of your little finger. The edges are serrated and have short white hairs underneath. The leaves are picked by hand as they are today and the choicest tea is from leaves picked from the first growth. Two other pickings with declining tea quality would follow into late summer.

From Leaf to Tea

Tea is processed immediately after harvesting. The most processed of the teas is black tea, the least processed is white tea with green tea in between the two. The tea leaf, when freshly plucked, is quite brittle and can easily be broken which would essentially spoil it for tea production. So the first stage in processing is to allow the leaves to dry out a little so that the leaf can be folded and twisted and will not break anywhere. The next stage is to bash it about a bit, mainly to cause internal disruption in the leaf. The dominant smell is that of freshly cut grass. The leaves feel a little moist and oily, but this is not a milling or laceration process, more a gentle disruption to let the natural enzymes in the leaf initiate oxidation. Just as the flesh of an apple turns dark brown on exposure to the atmosphere, so too does the tea at this stage.

When the oxidation process is finished the leaves are dried in direct sunlight or under simple hot house conditions. The leaves are now black and dry and ready for shipping to the point of sale or export. White tea, the least processed of all teas, is so called because this tea involves the freshest of new leaves which have a white down on the opened buds – the newest growth on the tea bush. The freshly plucked tea leaves are allowed to dry for about two days and because there is no disruption of the leaves, there is no oxidation process. White teas have a pale green or yellow colour when infused and a very delicate flavour and aroma. In the case of green tea, after the leaves are plucked they are heated, usually by steam, to deactivate the oxidising enzymes that are the key to processing black tea. The leaves are rolled for a period then quickly dried and this cycle continues until the leaves are crisp The infusion of green tea gives a green or yellow colour, and flavours range from toasty, grassy, pan-fired teas to fresh-steamed green teas with mild, vegetable-like astringency. Oolong tea has the most complicated process and is between the unoxidized green tea and the fully oxidised black tea. The leaves are withered and rolled to release some moisture and to have some cell disruption. The fermentation period is short and the leaves are then dried under heat.

The vast majority of the tea we consume is produced using a system known as CTC, or cut, tear and curl. The leaves are withered until they are pliant and are then passed through a machine with sequential cylindrical drums designed to literally cut, tear and curl the leaves so that they achieve a uniform size. They are then passed along on a conveyor belt on which cool air is pumped to allow complete oxidation without over-heating. When dried they are perfect for use in tea bags.

Photo credit: Gunel Farhadli

Enter the Europeans

In China, at about the time that the Europeans were beginning to show an interest in tea, these processing methods would have been very traditional. The finished teas were packed into a brick sized shape. Getting this black tea down from high altitudes to the plains where the cities, markets and ports are found is a rough job. In his book on China, Henry Wilson describes the arduous task of taking heavy loads of tea down the mountains by coolies. They would carry loads of tea weighing up to 370 pounds (168 kilos) on specially constructed rafts, which the coolies carried on their backs. The raft had an in-built central rod to allow them rest without having to undo their harness. Once again, we see that without cheap or forced labour, the luxuries of coffee, tea, sugar and chocolate would be impossible.

One of the most useful accounts of the start of European tea consumption, with England the foremost consumer, is from the report by John McGregor to the English House of Lords:

> *The first accounts we have of the use of tea are from a journey attributed to two Arabian travellers who are said to have visited China about 850. They mention a drink called 'Chah' and that an excise tax was levied on its consumption. They drink a kind of black water, prepared from a decoction of a certain shrub, called Cha or Chia, which the Usbeck Tartars import from China.*

McGregor points out that the first tea imports to Europe were by the Dutch, and notes that even though the Portuguese had rounded the Cape of Good Hope in 1497 and had an ambassador appointed to Beijing in 1517, they did not bring significant quantities of tea to Europe. The Portuguese diplomats, after much kowtowing to the

Photo credit: Gunel Farhadli

Emperor, finally got permission to establish what was then called a factory which we would now call a trading centre in Macau in 1586. The Dutch East India Company was established in 1602 and was responsible for trade in Asia, initially in spices but expanding into coffee, sugar and textiles. It traded on its own terms since it had a large army and navy, and was both the victim of battles, such as their defeat in the naval battle with the King of Cambodia in 1642-1644, and the perpetrator of atrocities, such as the massacre of the entire population of Liuqi Island off the coast of Taiwan in 1636. But it is to another East Indian Company that we turn to explore the history of tea in Europe, but especially in England.

English Tea

Catherine of Braganza, a Portuguese royal, married King Charles II in 1661 and brought with her a dowry of £500,000, access to

Portugal's colonies including Brazil, Portuguese East Indies (East Timor) and, for good measure, she threw in Tangiers and Bombay as a gift. She was a lifelong tea drinker and Charles II had been raised in Holland and certainly was consuming tea then.

Catherine made tea fashionable in London and the good and the great of that city took up tea drinking as a very trendy thing. It wasn't just the tea itself but the whole ritual: silver tea pots, bone china cups and with handles, silver spoons, sugar thongs and sugar bowls and beautifully carved wooden tea caddies. She made it fashionable to drink tea with three fingers and with the pinky, or little finger, clearly extended. This goes back to the three-fingered dining by the wealthy and the five-finger dining of the *hoi polloi*. Originally, hot bowls, only affordable by the wealthy, require holding with as few fingers as possible, leading to the little finger or 'pinkie' protruding outwards. The handle for the tea cup was invented in 1707 by the German chemist Johann Friedrich Bottger. Catherine also moved England toward tea drinking with her gift of Bombay, which would headquarter the East Indian Company and ensure them a major role in the acquisition of tea for the tea-loving English.

And how was she regarded by her subjects? She sadly reigned during the Popish Plot, a hysterical belief that papists, led by Jesuits, were threatening to install a Catholic King of England. Actually, Charles II was Catholic but hid it. Two of the most ardent anti-Catholics, Titus Oates and William Bedloe, believed that the Catholic Queen was an easy target and on the November 28 formally charged Catherine with treason in the House of Commons: **'I, Titus Oates, accuse Queen Catherine of conspiring the King's death and contriving how to compass it.'**

The evidence was pathetic and King Charles stood by her. However she would face a wave of such accusations for many years until after King Charles' death, eventually returning to Lisbon. To gain some idea of the disdain by the public to the royal circles, consider the popular rhyme written about Louise de Kerouaille, Duchess of Portsmouth and a key political figure in the royal court. Louise had a long standing affair with the King and made no attempt to hide it. Because she was a Catholic with a lowly royal French background, she was hated even more than Catherine. This rhyme tells it all:

> *Portsmouth, that pocky bitch,*
> *A damned papistical drab,*
> *An ugly deformed witch,*
> *Eaten up with mange and scab.*
>
> *This French hag's pocky bum,*
> *So powerful is of late,*
> *Although it's blind and dumb*
> *It rules both church and state.*

The King was also cavorting with another of his staff, Nell Gwyn, a former actress and not a Catholic. She was once confronted by some angry Londoners thinking she was the Duchess of Portsmouth. Employing her best theatrical skill she quipped: 'Pray good people be civil, I am the Protestant whore.'

The East India Company and the Opium Wars

The Tea Queen gave England tea and effectively she gave India to the East India Company who settled into her bequeathed city of Bombay, and in time colonised India and transformed Indian agriculture. When first imported, tea was treated as a medicine and wasn't taxed. Once tea drinking became popular, taxes were imposed as tea was now seen as a luxury. The first tax appeared in 1660.

Photo credit: Jakub Kapusnak

By the eighteenth century, the tax on tea exceeded 100 per cent and William Pitt, the English Prime Minister, believed that almost half of the tea consumed in England was smuggled in. At first, the imports of tea were modest and not of sufficient size as to merit inclusion in the annals of the Revenue Commission. By 1697, official records show an annual import of 22,416 pounds of tea. In the next four years, the imports trebled and ten years later that figure was doubled with imports reaching 282,000 pounds. By the mid- nineteenth century, almost 32 million pounds of tea were imported into Britain.

All of this tea was brought to England by the East India Company, who from 1669 had exclusive rights to import tea to England. The Company, as it was known, was established in 1601 and initially began trading in pepper. In time, the pepper market became flooded and the price plummeted. The Company then turned to Indian textiles, calico, gingham, silks and fine muslin. Trade in the East Indies was complex. The Company would take Indian textiles to Indonesia and the Molucca Island and exchange them for exotic spices which were shipped back to London for auction.

The Chinese, however, had no interest in Indian textiles and a means had to be found to trade with China to meet the great English thirst for tea. Moreover, the Chinese would only accept silver as a form of payment. The Company had to find a way to unlock the Chinese protectionist stance. The key to that would be opium.

China's middle class bureaucrats enjoyed smoking tobacco and would add a little opium to spice up the kick. In time, the tobacco was dispensed with and wealthy Chinese developed a taste for the elaborate paraphernalia for smoking opium: boxes, knives, spoons and pipes made from the finest of materials and very much a status symbol.

The Company decided to develop an Indian opium agriculture and issue licences for the growth of poppies. The company would pay the peasant growers up front for an agreed tonnage of opium. But getting it into China would be a challenge and the only route would be to smuggle it in. The opium was sold to smugglers in return for silver on a weight for weight basis, silver for opium. Now the merchants had silver to pay the Chinese for tea. The smugglers sold the opium to dealers who sold it on to the common people through their narcotics network. This could only work if key custom officials at the port of Canton, and their inspectors on the rivers where opium was transported, turned a blind eye to this activity, which they readily did with the help of a kick-back. By 1839, the entire tea imports into England were paid for through opium grown in India. In 1836, there were 12.5 million opium addicts officially recorded in China, approximately 5 per cent of the adult population.

In 1729, the Qing dynasty under Emperor Daoguang made the use of opium illegal which had the same hopeless success rate as seen today. Fifty years later, another law was enacted, this time with the death penalty as punishment for opium use, but this was equally unsuccessful. In 1830, in a continuing effort to thwart the import of opium, the stockpiles of the drug in the East Indian Company's warehouse were destroyed. This would spark a series of opium wars in which the vastly superior English naval forces were triumphant.

The English detested the arrogance and protectionism of China. In 1816, Lord Amherst was appointed as ambassador to China but refused to kowtow to the Emperor, that is, in his words, 'to knock heads nine times against the ground'. The Emperor was insulted and expelled the entire embassy requiring a diplomatic note to be delivered to the King of England:

> *I have sent these ambassadors back to their own country without punishing them for the high crime they have committed.*

England was now without a diplomatic post in Imperial China. Quite simply, the English didn't like the Chinese. This is recorded in a report to the English Privy Council for Trade and Plantation, prepared by John McGregor, a retired Secretary to the Board of Trade, and presented to both houses of the UK parliament in 1849. McGregor's comments clearly reveal the UK's disdain for this empire:

> *In the scale of social beings, they cannot, whatever may be their arrogance, be admired for their dignity or morality of character. Cowardice must form a predominant feeling among them; and unfortunately, cunning among mankind is too frequently as closely allied to cowardice and immorality, as it is absent in the brave, wise, dignified, and virtuous.*

That same report also gives us an impression of how the English imperial mind worked. McGregor writes:

> *According to natural reason, it appears, morally and justly, not irrational to conclude that the Almighty Creator never bequeathed any portion of this world exclusively to any one branch of the human family; that he created the earth for the universal use and habitation of his creatures; and that when one nation denies the peaceable liberty of inter course to another, the natural law of right justifies the enforcement of that inter course among the families of mankind.*

The tea merchants lobbied London to conduct such an enforcement and so the opium wars began. Over a two-year period the English Navy took the archipelago of Chusan, the Bogue Forts that protected entrance to the Pearl river and, moving northward, took the ports of Xiamen, Ningpo and Zhapu, the city at the Mouth of the Yangtze river. In 1842, total capitulation by China ceded the island of Hong Kong to the English victor in the Treaty of Nanjing. This treaty also gave the English access to the ports of Canton, Xiamen, Foochow and Ningpo. Not satisfied with this success, a second opium war led again to an English victory and to the treaty of Tientsin in 1858 which legalised opium. Britain would continue to sell opium to China until 1911 when an international convention outlawed trade in opium.

The Great Tea Theft

Several events occurred which forced the East India Company to rethink their strategy regarding the trade in tea. They lost their monopoly rights to trade in India in 1813 and in China in 1833. Aware of the fortune to be made in selling tea to England, they began exploring the growth of tea in India. Their extensive trade in tea was always for the finished product and they knew little about the cultivation of the tea bush and its processing into tea. They knew that tea would grow in the Assam state in the northeastern Himalayas, but they needed to acquire know-how and technology. They had tea varieties from southern China and the native tea bush of Assam, but there was a feeling that both the tea processors they had brought from Calcutta and the quality of the Southern Chinese tea would limit their ability to build a tea industry to compete with China.

Enter John Fortune, a Scottish botanist who was familiar with China and its ways. He was tasked by the tea merchants to go to China and bring back high quality tea plants, experts in tea processing and the necessary equipment to process this tea. Bear in mind that at this point it was believed that green tea and black tea came from different plants. In his account he describes his achievement.

> It was to remedy this and to obtain the best varieties from those districts which furnish the trees of commerce, that the Honourable Court of Directors sent me to China in 1848. Another object was to obtain some good manufacturers and implements from the same districts. As a result of this mission, nearly 20,000 plants the best black and green tea countries have been introduced into the Himalayas. Six first-rate manufacturers, two lead men, and a large supply of implements from the celebrated Hwuy-chow districts were also brought and safely located on the government plantation in the hills.

Given the protectionist nature of China and its obsession with the secrecy of tea leaf processing, this was a dangerous mission and has often been described as a major act of industrial espionage. Fortune was advised to abandon his Western dress and to travel in the local garb. He describes how he had his head shaved not by his assistant Wang but by his coolie, whom he describes as large-boned and clumsy but a native speaker of the district he would visit:

> *Having procured a pair of scissors, he clipped the hair from*
> *the front, back and sides of my head, leaving only a patch at*
> *the crown. He then washed those parts with hot water after*
> *the manner of the Chinese, and having done so, he took up a*
> *small razor and began to shave my head. I suppose I was the*
> *first person upon whom he had ever operated and I am char-*
> *itable enough to wish most sincerely that I may be the last.*

Fortune's team of native Chinese would go ahead from the base camp and enquire from villagers about tea plantations. They would report back to Fortune who would give them money to buy some tea plants. It would be impossible for Fortune to do so in person lest he be caught and punished, most probably expelled. As a result of Fortune's know-how, the importation of tea from India soon completely dominated the English market.

High Tea, Low Tea

Assam tea dominated but the more subtly flavoured Darjeeling tea, being less cultivated, attracted a premium price. Today, teas are not always teas. They are infusions and consumed like tea, but they do not come from *Camelia sinensis*. These include mint, peppermint, chamomile, dandelion and so on. Many of these herbal infusions are very old and provide a fragrant and aromatic hot drink. Some real teas are flavoured, such as Earl Grey which is scented with ber- gamot oil. This oil is from the citrus fruit bergamot and the tea is believed to have been given as a gift to Charles Grey, 2nd Earl Grey, and British Prime Minister in 1830-1834. Jasmine tea is flavoured with the jasmine blossom and was very popular in China as far back as the third century CE.

Photo credit: Toluwalase Omitowoju

Tea, whether herbal, normal or flavoured more so than coffee, is associated with ritual. Anna Russell, the 7th Duchess of Bedford, is credited with the ritual of afternoon tea, also known as 'low tea'. The reason for calling it low tea is that the tea and accompanying foods were served on low tables. With the advent of kerosene lanterns, evening meals began to be served later than tradition, right up to 8.00 pm. The Duchess found that tea with some light snacks took away that afternoon hunger and she started to invite friends to join her. She was also very close to Queen Victoria and when the Queen began to serve afternoon tea, the custom blossomed into a very important social event, almost exclusively for ladies. Taking afternoon or low tea, served with crustless sandwiches, dainty biscuits and cakes, allowed women to meet, chat, debate and indeed gossip at a time when women were not franchised to vote.

The English lace and silver industry did a roaring trade in the many accoutrements that go with the rituals of afternoon tea. High tea is popularly believed to be the most formal of tea occasions involving high society. Not so. Years ago what we call lunch today was dinner, and when we sat down in the evening to dine it was referred to as tea. Because it was served on a high table, this meal was distinguished from afternoon or low tea, and referred to as high tea.

Nowhere is the ritual of tea drinking more formalised than the tea ceremony of Japan. The tea room is small and is built of thatch, bamboo and rough logs, all intended to evoke a sense of the forest. Each tea ceremony should be seen by the guests as unique in the tradition of *ichigo ichie,* one unique meeting at one unique time. Thus even though the host and guest might meet socially, the ritual requires that each person has a sense that the tea ceremony they are attending is utterly unique, never to be repeated. The entrance to the tea house is very low such that all guests have to bow to enter, a sign of humility. Inside the decoration is minimal and it should reflect the season, particularly the flowers that are so sparingly used. The hot water is poured on to the tea leaves in a bowl and each gust sips and, having wiped it, passes the bowl to the next

Photo credit: Oluolu 3

guest. The guests are seated in order of status. When the event is over, all of the utensils used are washed and it is expected that the guests will admire them and ask about their provenance. The tea is absolutely secondary to the ritual.

For this author, a freshly brewed mug of tea at Windy Gap, the halfway point of the old Kenmare road by Mangerton mountain in County Kerry, is my *ichigo ichie*.

Chapter 10

Sugar: Sweet and Slavery

Extract from The Sugar-Plum Tree
By Eugene Field

Have you ever heard of the Sugar-Plum Tree?
'Tis a marvel of great renown!
It blooms on the shore of the Lollypop sea
In the garden of Shut-Eye Town;
The fruit that it bears is so wondrously sweet
(As those who have tasted it say)
That good little children have only to eat
Of that fruit to be happy next day.
. . .

There are marshmallows, gumdrops, and peppermint canes,
With stripings of scarlet or gold,
And you carry away of the treasure that rains,
As much as your apron can hold!
So come, little child, cuddle closer to me
In your dainty white nightcap and gown,
And I'll rock you away to that Sugar-Plum Tree
In the garden of Shut-Eye Town.

The diet of our primate ancestors was particularly high in fruits and berries, and when early hominids came down from the tree tops they maintained that liking for sweet foods. These early hunter-gatherers would also have learned that many of the plants that have a bitter taste are not very pleasant to eat and it has been argued that this bitter taste signalled a potentially harmful food, while the sweet flavoured foods gave an assurance of safety.

This is often used as an explanation for the innate preference of new-born babies for sweetness. When new-born babies are given a drop of a sugar solution on their tongue they smile, but when given a bitter compound like quinine they grimace. The facial reaction to the bitter taste is far stronger than the smiling facial pattern with sugar. Infants may well have a strong preference for sugar to aid in breast feeding with human milk having a very high content of lactose, the sugar of milk. This sweet tooth declines with age. The preferred level of sucrose of young children (5 to 10 years) and adolescents (10 to 20 years) was similar at 12 teaspoons in an 8 ounce glass of water. However, for their adult parents, this preferred level fell to just 7 teaspoons, about the level you'd find in a sugar sweetened soda. Naturally, there is statistical variation about this preference for 7 teaspoons per 8 ounces of water which is reflected in the difference between those with a sweet tooth as opposed to a savoury tooth. This appealing aspect of sugar is reflected in terms of endearment such as sweetheart and honey.

Honey

For early humans the ultimate sweet taste was honey and, like the reverence of tea in Chinese culture, honey was strongly associated with gods and divine healing powers. In the Hindu religion, the sun was seen as God's honey, its rays were its offspring's and bee hives were an intermediate space neither earth nor heaven. Of the five truths of the sacred scripture of Hinduism, one maintained that the rules of our planetary system and our relationship to that system was 'analogous to those existing between honey and bees'. On the Jewish New Year or Yom Teruah, apple slices are dipped in honey to symbolise the advent of a sweet New Year. Buddhists celebrate the feast Madhu Purnima (Honey Full Moon Festival) by giving honey to monks. Christian texts speak of the Promised Land in terms of milk and honey. The Islamic text, the Quran, also mentions honey with Lord Allah saying of bees that '. . . there comes forth from their bellies a drink of varying colour wherein is healing for men'. There are few foods that merit such high prominence in so many religions.

Honey was sweeter than any fruit the ancients might have tasted and of course it was very scarce. Wild hives would have been the first source of honey and apparently their location was held as a great secret. One of the earliest records of honey gathering comes from a prehistoric cave painting in the Cuevas de la Arana in Spain, from about 8,000 to 10,000 years ago. We also know that bee keeping was practiced in ancient Egypt and China. In the days of the Roman empire, honey was highly regarded and both the capturing of bee swarms and the use of smoke to quieten bees are documented by Pliny the Elder who wrote, 'When the honey is taken, it is the best plan to drive away the bees by means of smoke, lest they should become irritated, or else devour the honey themselves'.

Beekeeping evolved over time and was revolutionised by Lorenzo Langstroth, a US clergyman and apiarist with a new version of the traditional hive which to this day is the basis of all beehives. His new hive was designed to allow the beekeeper optimal access to honey with minimum disturbance of the bee colony. It takes eight bees all their life to produce one teaspoon of honey, and in a given day a single bee will visit about 5,000 flowers to

Photo credit: kzenon

yield 70 milligrams of syrupy nectar. Nectar has about 50 per cent sucrose (as in table sugar) and 25 per cent each of glucose and fructose. The bee returns the nectar to the hive where it is swallowed and repeatedly regurgitated to break the sucrose into the simple sugars of glucose and fructose. Each regurgitation is held for a few seconds to allow the nectar solution to lose moisture from about 90 per cent water down to about 50 per cent. Its moisture content is brought down further to just below 20 per cent, an effect achieved by the rapid fanning of the bees' wings.

The honey you see on supermarket shelves is processed honey, meaning that it has been pasteurised to destroy any enzymes and filtered to remove particles of the hive, the bees and of pollen. The pasteurisation makes the colour darker and allows it to be more readily poured into containers. This processing is flexible and can take blends of different honey and process them such that the brand always has a standard colour and texture. Unprocessed honey will eventually crystallise with the sugars building their crystals on small particles of pollen and the like. The flavour of different honeys is due to the scent of the flowers from which the bees obtain the nectar. Some honeys are idolised for their questionable curative properties. New Zealand manuka honey is one such where the bees obtain their nectar from the manuka bush. However, there is roughly six times more manuka honey sold globally than is produced in New Zealand.

Tree Syrup

Maple syrup is as sweet as honey and was treasured by Native American tribes such as the Algonquins, the Iroquois and Ojibways. At the end of the summer and throughout autumn, the growth rate of the maple tree becomes dormant and excess starches are stored in the sapwood which lies just beneath the bark. This starch remains stored so long as the wood temperature falls below about 4° c. But, when the wood temperature rises above this level, enzymes in the sapwood convert the starch to sugars, mainly sucrose. This then passes into the tree's sap at about 2 per cent by volume.

Maple syrup is normally harvested starting on March 1 when night-time temperatures are low and daytime temperatures are milder. The sap rises at night to the outermost branches, which reduces the freezing point of water and protects the integrity of the delicate outlying branches, and flows downwards when the warmer daytime temperature rises. The sap slowly drops from bored holes into buckets and it will take 40 buckets of sap to make one bucket of maple syrup.

Traditionally, the Native Americans would allow the sap to freeze in the very cold nights of what they called 'sugar time'. As the water froze it was gradually discarded leading to a thick, sugary, dark brown maple syrup. In other climates such as in the tropics other tree saps were traditionally harvested. One palm tree could produce 10 to 80 pounds of raw sugar every year. The sap is boiled down and solidified and is known as *gur* in Hindu and jaggery in English.

History of Sugar

Sugar cane is believed to have originated in New Guinea around 4,000 BCE and was then brought to China about 3,500 BCE. It was quite some time before sugar cane arrived in India but when it did, it was the Indians who extracted sugar from the cane and processed it. By the sixth century CE, the Chinese were making exploratory visits to India to better understand its cultivation but, more importantly, its processing. The Greeks who came to India described sugar cane as 'reeds that make honey without the agency of bees'. Sugar cultivation and processing also reached the Arab world but, according to Pliny, it was inferior to that of India.

> *Arabia, too, produces sugar; but that of India is the most esteemed. This substance is a kind of honey, which collects in reeds, white, like gum, and brittle to the teeth. The larger pieces are about the size of a filbert; it is only employed, however, in medicine.*

If we were to seek the global capital of sugar in ancient times it would be India, and especially Kolkata in the province of Bengal. The farming of sugar cane was unique to India and it would take several centuries before it migrated to the Middle East, thence to Turkey and westward with the Ottomans into Europe. Street vendors in Kolkata would repeatedly pass sugar canes into rollers. The resultant sugary liquid is captured in a tray and the vendor fills a cup and sells it to passersby. The Indians' love of sugar created a wide range of sweet dishes, but because of Hindu rules of diet these dishes were dominated by milk from sacred cows and sugar the favoured food of the gods. Writing in his book *Sweet Invention: A History of Dessert,* Michael Krondl describes the sweet milky aroma that pervades the air when approaching temples on holy feasts. Milk and sugar along with ghee and yogurt were the basic elements of all Indian sweet dishes.

The initial Arab conquests of India in the sixth and seventh centuries would have led to the know-how of sugar cane cultivation, and sugar production moved westwards as Arab conquests flowed. It is often said that sugar followed the Quran as the Arabian empire expanded westwards and the earliest sugar industries outside India were established in Palestine, Egypt and Morocco in the eighth and ninth centuries. About a century behind them, sugar industries were established in Spain and in Sicily. In the tenth century, the Arabs established the first commercial sugar refinery on the island of Crete which they referred to as Qandi, the Persian for 'crystallised sugar'. This is the origin of the word candy which is used in the US to describe sugar confectionery.

Northern Europeans first encountered sugar through the Crusades and the Norman conquest, and the demand for sugar began to grow. This led to an expansion of sugar farming into the Christian regions of the eastern Mediterranean, particularly Cyprus. In the Muslim areas, peasant farmers cropped side by side with large ranchers and all labour was fairly treated and remunerated. In contrast, the Christian areas began using corvé and slave labour. The former applied when peasants, unable to pay all or some of their

Photo credit: unknonw

taxes, were forced to work on the sugar plantations to fulfil their fiscal requirements. The fourteenth century Black Death plague decimated the traditional workforce which brought slavery into sugar production for the first time. Slaves were initially taken to the Christian sugar farms from their native Slav homeland, hence the origin of the word 'slave'.

Sugar farms were extended, particularly in Cyprus, mostly with slave labour and financed by the new sugar magnates of Venice. The Marco brothers, Federigo and Fantin, employing 400 sugar workers in Cyprus, were the wealthiest in all of Venice. The Venetians were obsessed with decorative sugar and their banquets featured many elaborate sculptures known as *soteltes* (subtelties) made from sugar, including busts of popes, dukes and generals, and often their plates and cutlery were made of sugar. Elizabeth Abbot in her book *Sugar* describes the installation of Cardinal Thomas Wolsey at Westminster Abbey in 1515:

> *. . . extraordinarily lavish soteltes [subtleties] depicting cas-*
> *tles and churches, beasts and birds, fighting knights and*
> *dancing ladies, even an exquisite chess set, all made of 'spiced*
> *plate' or hardened sugar.*

The Achilles heel of the North African, Cypriot and Cretan sugar industries was the supply of wood for the fuel needed in the process of drying the sugar juice to produce crystallised sugar. This was not a problem in Western and Northern Europe and so sugar processing plants began to emerge in Italy, Belgium and Holland. There was another reason for this. If the sugar cane farmers lacked wood to make sugar and were then forced to export raw sugar cane to western and northern Europe, the commercial shoe, as they say, was now on the other foot, bringing added value to these new sugar barons.

Sugar and the New World

The demand for sugar was beyond the capacity of the Mediterranean and north African countries so, on his return voyage to the New World, Christopher Columbus carried on board his ship sugar cane cuttings. From his first voyage, he had left behind a small garrison to defend the island we now call San Salvador. The garrison was wiped out by the indigenous natives. Columbus carried with him a letter from King Ferdinand outlining to the indigenous peoples how they would be treated. It makes grim reading but it foreshadows what has been described as the American holocaust. It warns the natives that failure to submit to the will of the Spaniards would:

> *. . . enslave your persons, wives and sons, sell you or dispose*
> *of you as the King sees fit; we shall seize your possessions*
> *and harm you as much as we can as disobedient and resist-*
> *ing vassals. And we declare you guilty of resulting deaths and*

injuries, exempting Their Highnesses of such guilt as well as ourselves and the gentlemen who accompany us. We hereby request that legal signatures be affixed to this text and pray those present to bear witness for us.

Columbus started sugar cultivation, which turned out to be a great success. There was a perfect climate, plenty of water and fuel but a dire shortage of labour. The indigenous Taino peoples were enslaved and were wiped out in just five decades through murder, starvation and infection with smallpox, cholera, typhus, yellow fever and all of the other diseases that the Spanish carried but were by then immune to.

The Taino people had to be replaced and so began the horrific era of the slave trade. According to official UK archives, between 1702 and 1808, some 840,000 African slaves were sent to British-controlled Jamaica and, in all, the total trade in slaves from Africa to the Americas was somewhere in the range of 12 to 15 million over the period of the fifteenth to nineteenth century. Interestingly, whilst this archive mentions indentured workers, they refer only to those from the Indian sub-continent. No mention is made of those prisoners of war or the destitute paupers from Ireland that were shipped as indentured servants and agricultural workers to Barbados, which became an English colony in 1625. Hilary Beckles in her paper: 'A riotous and unruly lot: Irish Indentured servants and freemen in the English West Indies, 1644-1713', describes the plight and fight of the Irish indentured workers. It began with Cromwell:

In 1649, after the Battle of Drogheda, Oliver Cromwell informed John Bradshaw, president of the council, that 'the Enemy were about 3,000. . . . They made a stout resistance . . . but those who escaped with their lives . . . are in safe custody for the Barbados.

Cromwellian rule went further than prisoners of war. In 1654, the governors of six Irish counties had orders to arrest and deliver to three English merchants Dudley North, John Johnson and Captain Thomas Morgan:

> ... *all wanderers, men and women, and such other Irish within their precincts as should not prove they had such a settled course of industry as yielded them a means of their own to maintain them, all such children as were in hospitals or workhouses, all prisoners, men and women, to be deported to the West Indie's.*

The majority of the Irish who travelled to the Caribbean as indentured workers went freely, receiving the cost of their passage and subsistence, in return for seven years of labour. At the end, they were free to buy a small parcel of land but in the period 1645-1655, the value of sugar plantation land soared shattering this dream. The English sugar barons abhorred their Irish workers and did all they could to exclude further recruitment.

The Barbadian Governor, Francis Willoughby, wrote a letter to the Privy Council in the English Parliament requesting the arrival of far more Scots and far less Irish. The friction between the English landlords and the indentured Irish workers led to frequent whippings and imprisonment. Ms Beckles describes the punishment issued to two Irish workers, Cornelius Bryan and Daniel Maliglee. Bryan was sentenced to 31 lashes on his bare back by the common hangman, apparently for refusing a tray of meat saying, 'If there was so much English blood in the tray as there was meat, he would eat it all'. Maliglee was punished for similar disrespect to his English landlord by having him roast in the midday sun, naked whilst in the pillory. For decades the Irish workers in the Caribbean sided with the slave revolts or, on the Island of Saint Kitts, sided with the French who shared the island with the British.

The Caribbean sugar industry developed rapidly as did that of the Portuguese colony of Brazil which was also reliant on African slaves. Sugar prices began to fall, and the consumption of sugar grew in tandem with the growth of tea and coffee and was also consumed in great quantities in the rapidly expanding confectionery trade. This dramatic change in diet came with a cost. Frequent ingestion of sugary foods can lead to dental caries and, for example, Queen Elizabeth I was rarely seen with a toothy smile lest she expose a mouth of black teeth. In 1976, work began on the restoration of Christ Church in the parish of Spitalfields in East London, and in the course of this work the remains of 1,000 individuals were removed for burial elsewhere to allow conservation to be completed. Of these, 93 who had been interred between 1729 and 1826 could have their age and sex ascertained by copper plates on the coffins. Some 85 per cent of this group had advanced dental caries.

New Sources of Natural Sweetness

But still the passion for sugar grew. Professor Andreas Marggraf from Berlin showed in 1747 that the sugar in sugar beet was identical to the sugar in sugar cane. Given the riches that could be made from sugar, it is surprising that Marggraf did not pursue it but one of his pupils, Franz Karl Archad, did. He became a very distinguished scientist in the court of Prussia and experimented with different varieties of sugar beet and various cultivation techniques. He also mastered the extraction of sugar from sugar beets thus opening the possibility that a crop that could be grown in Northern Europe might replace sugar cane as the source of this cherished sweetener. Europe was now fully self-sufficient in sugar production and soon

Photo credit: Bill Oxfrod

this agriculture would spread to the US and east to Russia. But sugar production would take another twist.

Sugar prices are highly variable. In 1950, an ounce of sugar cost 8 cents, soaring to 30 cents in 1980 and plummeting to 5 cents in 1999. Such volatility in price posed serious problems for those manufacturing foods and drinks with high sugar content. The huge growth in global demand for sugar-sweetened beverages forced this industry to think outside the box. In the US, there is ample corn grown and corn is made of starch. This starch can be broken down industrially either by heating or enzymes. The net result is pure glucose. But the sweet nature of honey and sugar is due to the presence of two sugars, glucose and fructose, either bound or free. It would take time for science to come up with a way to modify this glucose from all glucose to 50-50 glucose and fructose.

That happened in 1957 when two Californian scientists published the use of a new enzyme obtained from a strain of bacteria that could convert glucose to fructose. High fructose corn syrup (HFCS) was invented, and it came to dominate the sugar-sweetened beverage industry. In fact, the ratio of glucose to fructose in HFCS was identical to honey with about 45 to 55 glucose to fructose, as opposed to cane or beet sugar with a 50-50 ratio. HFCS is a social media bête noir and the internet is awash with all forms of horror stories of addiction and obesity. How something with the same composition of honey can be so misunderstood is difficult to explain, but then again so much of the internet nutrition newsfeed is utter poppycock.

Sugar, Sugars and Morality

Sugar is an integral part of so many desserts and confections but given its bad publicity, recipes are increasingly using sugar in more crude forms than the white crystalline type we find in our sugar bowl, including demerara, muscovado, turbinado and other brown sugars. There is a perception that such sugars are each very distinct, though in fact the differences are subtle. Turbinado is a lightly centrifuged sugar such that some molasses remains and has slightly smaller crystals than demerara. It has only 89 per cent sugar. In contrast, muscovado and demerara have little water while muscovado has a high mineral content.

The reality is that most of these sugars are industrially produced from the pure white sugar crystals which can be soaked in water containing whatever level of molasses or treacle is required to make the product darker or lighter, and where there is some scope to yield granules which differ in size. Golden syrup is like molasses except that it requires the sucrose from either beets or cane to be broken down by acid or enzyme treatment to produce a solution of

Photo credit: Magone

fructose and glucose. This is concentrated and is stable, not prone to crystallisation.

In the sixteenth century, the use of spices in food began to decline. This has been attributed to the snobby attitude of the great and good in France, who now saw spices as vulgar, widely used by the *hoi polloi*. Something similar happened in England where sugar-sweetened tea consumption rose dramatically among the working class and, again, the great and good began to see sugar as somewhat vulgar. The terms 'inappropriate' to define levels of sugar intake began to be replaced by the term 'immoderate', and that term began to stir moral views of sugar consumption. Sugar and morality began to be mixed with sugar and slavery. Somehow, this moral view has never waned.

Chapter 11

Buds, Berries, Beans and Brews: The Story of Coffee

In Praise of Coffee

Translated from the Arabic

O coffee! Doved and fragrant drink, thou drivest care away,
The object thou of that man's wish who studies night and
*   day.*
Thou soothest him, thou giv'st him health, and God doth
*   favor those*
Who walk straight on in wisdom's way, nor seek their own
*   repose.*
Fragrant as musk thy berry is, yet black as ink in sooth!
And he who sips thy fragrant cup can only know the truth.
Insensate they who, tasting not, yet vilify its use;
For when they thirst and seek its help, God will the gift
*   refuse.*
Oh, coffee is our wealth! for see, where'er on earth it grows,
Men live whose aims are noble, true virtues who disclose.

Once upon a time, high in the mountains of Ethiopia, a young goat herder by the name of Kaldi sat playing his flute while his goats grazed the nearby forest. When he called them to return to overnight shelter, he was ignored. Kaldi went to find out why his goats were ignoring him and soon heard them bleating, but not in any normal way. Following the sound of the bleating goats, Kaldi saw that they appeared to have gone mad, leaping, lying, rolling, evidently dancing and engaging in other non-goat like activities. The goats were eating some red berry he had not seen before. Kaldi tasted them and was soon as high as his goats. Being a good boy, he picked some and brought them back to an imam, relating the strange behaviour of the goats. The imam threw them into a smouldering fire and instantly got that 'wake up and smell the coffee' feeing and retrieved them from the fire, ground them, mixed them with hot water et voilà, we had coffee. That is the legend and there are many variations on the theme.

The red berries that Kaldi discovered were the fruit of a plant which would be known as *Coffea Arabica*, a plant native to the highlands in the southwest of Ethiopia by the border of modern Kenya. The plant grows in a narrow strip north and south of the equator, and like the cocoa tree it is intolerant of cold and grows in the shade of the canopies of the great trees of tropical forests. It is strictly speaking a bush, not a tree, and is self-pollinating because of its habitat: high altitude and dense forests. It can grow as high as 10 metres.

Ethiopia lies southwest of the fertile crescent and was greatly influenced by the rulers of the Arabian peninsula, hence the great link between coffee and Arabic cuisine. *Coffea Robusta*, which is native to the Western coast of the African continent along the equator, was cultivated quite some time after *Arabica*. It can grow at a lower altitude and it is not self-pollinating so it relies on wind or insects for propagation.

From Berries to Beans

The fruit of the coffee plant starts off green, then reveals a distinct cherry red colour before turning purple. These three stages represent unripe, ripe and over-ripe fruit. The latter two are harvested and all of this is done by hand and is very labour intensive. Each cherry has two coffee seeds, generally referred to as coffee beans, which lie back to back in the centre of the cherry. Like all fruits and nuts, there is an outer structure overlying several structures underneath. Think of an orange. It has an outer rind which is orange in colour and this overlies an inner white pulp. Each segment of the orange is separated from the next by a wafer thin sheet. Similarly, the fruit of the coffee bush has an outer rind just like an orange and beneath that is a gooey material which in turn overlies the coffee beans. The beans, like the orange segments, are separated by a very thin cover known as a silver skin.

There are two approaches to separating the coffee beans from the rest of the cherry. The most widely used is the dry processing method in which the cherries are laid out on a concrete surface to dry in the sun with regular turning, a process which takes about four weeks and sees the moisture fall five-fold. The wrinkled outer hulls can then be removed mechanically. The next stage involves fermentation in water so that bacteria remove the remaining mush. The beans are then dried, de-skinned and graded at the port just before shipping. One somewhat unusual way to get beans to this stage is to follow palm civet cats in the Indonesian forests and retrieve their faeces. These cats eat coffee cherries, digest the outer covering of the beans and excrete the dehulled beans. Coffee made in this way is known as Kopi Luwak. Coffee aficionados love the exotic and thus the price for this rare coffee soared when it became glamorised. Sadly, that led to the capture and force feeding of these cats and to a loss of credibility in the picky world of coffee drinkers.

The origin of the word 'coffee' has absorbed linguists for centuries. The favourite seems to be the Arabic word *qahwah* and in Arabic the 'hw' is pronounced 'ff'. The Turks, who introduced coffee into Europe, adapted the Arabic word to *kaveh*. The Arab world was very precious about access to their coffee which was highly prized by religious leaders who used coffee to keep themselves awake for their lengthy prayers. According to legend, the earliest migration was to the Indian sub-continent when, around 1,600 CE, a young pilgrim to Mecca, Baba Budan, managed to smuggle out some beans during a stopover in the port of Mocha in Yemen. He set up a coffee plantation in the hills of Chandragiri in Nepal.

The Dutch brought coffee to their colonies in Asia, most notably in Java, in the late seventeenth century. The Portuguese explorer Francisco de Melo Palheta is credited with bringing coffee to the Para region of Brazil in 1727. The French and British brought coffee to the West Indies. In time, coffee would be grown right across the world in the coffee belt, a horizontal band across the globe that lies between the Tropics of Capricorn and Cancer. Coffee is traditionally picked by hand which is very labour intensive and thus coffee has a dark history with slavery. Even today, there are extreme ends of the coffee industry. In a report, 'Poverty in Your Mug', Oxfam point out the difficulties that traditional coffee farmers of Central America face, which makes it impossible for them to compete with the coffee estates of Brazil:

> *To give you an idea of the difference, in some areas of Guatemala, it could take over 1000 people working one day each to fill the equivalent of one container of 275 bags, each bag weighing 69kg. In the Brazilian cerrado, you need five people*

and a mechanical harvester for two or three days to fill a container. One drives, and the others pick.

Decaffeination is fairly straightforward. The beans are soaked in water during which time they swell up. They are then treated with methylene chloride or ethyl acetate, which removes the caffeine and the beans are then washed and steam cleaned. Beans, whether decaffeinated or in their natural state, are drum-roasted to temperatures of 250° C. There are two key sounds that the roaster must listen for. The first, known as the first crack, occurs at about 200° c and has a distinct sound like popcorn popping. The second, which occurs at about 225° c, is much more subtle, sometimes described like the gentle crackle of the breakfast cereal, Rice Krispies.

Photo credit: Jakub Kapusnak

The process of roasting coffee was described to the Royal Society of London in 1699, in what must have been a very dull presentation. As the beans lose their moisture during roasting the green beans turn from yellow to light brown at about the first crack and they get darker up to the second crack. These changes in colour and the sounds of the cracking are due to the loss of moisture and the release of gases. The disruption of the beans causes some oils to cover the outside and thus contribute to the flavour of coffee. After the second crack, the beans are quickly cooled to stop the cooking process. Different coffees with different gastronomic qualities from taste, aroma and mouthfeel are achieved by varying the extent and speed of roasting and through blending different coffees.

The roasted beans are ground, ideally just before preparing the coffee for drinking. Coffee beans can be ground to 45,000 particles for Turkish boiled coffee as opposed to 100 particles for filter coffee and 3,000 for espresso. Turkish coffee is made by putting a scoop of the highly ground beans into a small copper pot with a long handle to which cold water is added. This is placed in a very hot sand pit and the coffee chef can manipulate the temperature by adjusting the depth of the copper coffee pot in the hot sand. The brew is boiled, producing a foam on the top, and in doing so a second roasting is introduced, maximising the flavour. The brew is turned out of the coffee pot into a cup and there should be a balance between the right amount of foam and liquid. Because it is ground so small, the coffee is unfiltered so the coffee grounds remain as a sediment. The coffee needs to settle, allowing the customer to cleanse his or her palate with the glass of water which is always served with such coffee.

From Beans to Brew

The two least technical ways of extracting coffee from ground coffee beans involve either immersion or percolation. In the case of immersion, the French coffee press is used. The ground coffee is put into jug over which boiling water is poured. After a period of time when the coffee is fully extracted, a plunger is used to slowly push the coffee ground to the bottom leaving the coffee on top ready for serving. In 1908, a German housewife by the name of Mellita Bentz tried her hand at designing a coffee filter from paper. Hitherto, linen was used for this purpose. She got a small round copper container and punched holes in it. She then coated the inside of the copper container with blotting paper and poured a pot of boiled coffee into the container allowing it to filter through to a cup. It produced a much nicer flavour then the linen bag which was used often and, although washed, would slowly accumulate flavours. She founded a company named Mellita, which today is the largest coffee filter manufacturer in the world.

In time, electric drip coffee machines were invented, the first in 1972 when Vincent Marotta and Samuel Glazer in the US released their Mr Coffee machine. With the help of the one of baseball's most famous sportsmen, Joe DiMaggio, also known as 'Joltin' Joe', their advertising campaign saw 1 million units sold in just one year.

The stovetop Moka coffee machine with its iconic hour glass shape is believed to have been invented by Luigi De Ponti, an Italian engineer and CEO of a company owned by Alfonso Bialetti. The bottom part has water and above that is a layer of ground coffee covered top and bottom with slim aluminium coverings. A pipe goes through this layer right up almost to the top. The boiled water gives off steam and this creates pressure. Water rises through the

Photo credit: Jakub Kapusnak

pipe creating the familiar gurgling noise to the upper chamber, returning to the lower chamber through the ground coffee. When the gurgling sounds more like a splutter, the coffee is ready.

Pressure is also involved in the espresso machine invented by a Turin engineer Angelo Moriondo in 1884. This machine forces hot water through ground coffee under considerable pressure, 8 to 10 times that of our atmosphere of 14.5 pounds per square inch. That is equivalent to the pressure 100 metres below sea level and drags out every ounce of coffee flavour into a small amount of water. In time, Moriondo's design would be improved and Italian companies have come to dominate the global business of making coffee in cafes: Gaggia, Illy, De'Longhi and Lavazza all spring to mind.

Italy is renowned for coffee drinking and this tradition enjoys many rituals. For example, Italians take their coffee standing up. In 1911, a law was passed which allowed local councils, in consultation with business, to impose a maximum price of goods and services. In the case of cafés, a price was set which was low for coffee 'without service', meaning standing up. This price was deliberately set low to discourage large commercial chains from entering the trade. The practice is now just a tradition. Cappuccino coffee is milk-based and according to Italian beliefs about digestion, it is 'heavy' and suited only for breakfast, which in Italy might just mean a viennoiserie and coffee. It derives its name from another region with a great coffee drinking tradition, Vienna. There, a coffee known as 'kapuziner' is an espresso that is mixed with a small amount of cream and turns brown like the habit worn by Capuchin monks. Grated chocolate or cocoa is sprinkled on top.

The Coffee Shop

The Influx of coffee into Europe began toward the end of the sixteenth century in Venice followed quickly by Amsterdam and Leiden, and across the first six decades of the seventeenth century to Oxford, Marseilles, Vienna, Paris and just about every country in Europe. The arrival of coffee had to compete with two other novel beverages, tea and chocolate. In his book *Coffee: A Drink for the Devil,* Paul Chrystal draws on the writings of the English biologist John Ellis in 1774, and discusses the first coffee houses in Constantinople which opened in 1475 and was patronised by traders from Damascus and Aleppo:

> *When two private persons, whose names were Schems and Hekin, the one coming from Damascus, and the other from Aleppo, each opened a Coffee-house . . . and sold Coffee publicly, in rooms fitted up in an elegant manner; which were presently frequented by men of learning, and particularly poets and other persons, who came to amuse themselves with a game of chess, or draughts; or to make acquaintance, and pass their time.*

Remarkably, when coffee finally arrived in Europe, that formula of a relaxed and comfortable ambiance would be maintained, as would the attraction to such houses of the leading lights in cities across the continent. Floriano Francesconi opened the first coffee house in Europe on St Mark's square in Venice in 1720, originally called Venice the Triumphant. His clientele referred to it as The Florian. In the tradition of the first Turkish coffee house, it attracted all sorts of famous people and among its regulars were Goethe, Casanova, Byron and Dickens. Vienna followed suit with a plethora of comfortable coffee houses each with its own celebrity customers: The Café Sperl was a favourite of Archduke Ferdinand, Café Frauenhuber was the haunt of Mozart while Mahler and Freud were customers at Café Landtman.

In Paris, Suleiman Agha, an ambassador representing Sultan Mehmed IV of the Ottoman Empire, is credited for introducing coffee to the city. The first coffee house in Paris was established by Procopio Cutò, an Italian chef from Sicily. In 1686, he opened a coffee shop, Café Procope, on Rue de l'Ancienne Comédie. He was a limonadier (lemonade vendor) who had a license to sell spices, ices, barley water, lemonade and other such refreshments. Still there today, in its day Café Procope was the favourite of the Parisian intelligentsia from Robespierre to Voltaire, from Balzac to Hugo. Another famous Parisian coffee house of Paris was The Royal Drummer established by Jean Ramponaux. Unlike the high-brow clientele of Café Procope, this coffee house was known for its wicked and naughty ways and was popular with the gentry and the working professional classes of Paris. It merited a little poem which also mentions another famous coffee house, that of Magny:

The pleasures of ease untroubled to taste,
The leisure of home to enjoy without haste,
Perhaps a few hours at Magny's to waste,
Ah, that was the old-fashioned way!
Today all our laborers, everyone knows,
Go running away ere the working hours close,
And why? They must be at Monsieur Ramponaux'!
Behold, the new style of café!

Nathaniel Conopios, a student from Crete, became the first person in recorded history to prepare and serve coffee in England whilst at Balliol College, Oxford. Writing in the Journal *The Plough, the Loom and the Anvil* in 1848, John S. Skinner, a US agriculturalist, wrote thus:

> *It is said to have been first brought to England by Mr. Nathaniel Conopius, a Cretan, who made it his common beverage at Baliol College, at Oxford, in the year 1641 but it must evidently have been a few years prior to this date, as Evelyn says in his Diary 1637, 'There came in my tyme to the Coll: one Nathaniel Conopios out of Greece, sent one from Cyrill the Patriarch of Constantinople who, returning many years after, was made (as I understand) Bishop of Smyrna: he the first I ever saw drink coffee, which custom came not into England till 30 years.'*

Conopios was eventually expelled by 'parliamentary visitors' who were in Oxford to ensure that Cromwellian puritanism was being followed. Perhaps they saw his coffee promotion as a challenge to this puritanism. However, he had started a craving for coffee that would eventually pervade the university. The deans at Oxford sought repeatedly to limit access to coffee houses over many years without success. The first English coffee house, The Angel, was established by be a Jewish entrepreneur by the name of Jacob in Oxford in 1650. Now known as The Grand Café, it still trades today.

Following the new liberalism of King Charles II, who returned as English monarch in 1660, coffee houses in Oxford began to blossom. One such was that of Arthur Tillyard, who at the request of Oxford's leading scientific fellows, established his Oxford Coffee Club in 1655. This was frequented by no less that Sir Robert Boyle, the Irish physicist, and it evolved into a serious centre for discourse in all matters of science. It would eventually lead to the establishment of the Royal Society, London, now a leading global scientific body.

London's first coffee house was established by an Armenian, Pasqua Rosée, in 1652. William Urwin had a coffee house and it is one of the many that Pepys, the diarist, visited. At one such coffee house in Covent Garden, Pepys records meeting the poet Dryden and 'all the wits of the town'.

In Dublin, different coffee houses were favoured by different political parties. Dick's, one of Dublin's most noted coffee house, was favoured by the Tories. It was established by publisher Richard Pue and was a major venue for book auctions. Francis Dickson and his Whig friends favoured Lloyd's coffee house in Oxmantown and the Union coffee house, among others. Both were involved in printing political pamphlets. Máire Kennedy quotes from a history of Dublin in which the clientele of Dick's is described:

> *Ye citizens, gentlemen, lawyers and squires,*
> *Who summer and winter surround our great fires,*
> *Ye quidnuncs! who frequently come into Pue's,*
> *To live upon politicks, coffee, and news;*
> *Ye adepts, ye critics, and orators nice!*
> *Ye grave connoisseurs at the drafts and the dice. . . .*

Photo credit: DA69

Besides the wheeling, dealing, debating and gambling, the clients had access to a wide range of newspapers from around Europe's capitals listed by Máire Kennedy as the:

> *Paris and London Gazettes, Leyden Gazette and Slip, the Paris and Hague Lettres à la main, Daily Courant, Postman, Flying Post, Post-script and Manuscripts.*

Coffee houses everywhere were key venues for the professional classes but they soon faded away in favour of gentlemen's clubs.

Coffee, when first introduced, left sediment in the bottom of the cup, as indeed many modern brews do, which attracted the world of fortune tellers. In the June 1726 issue of the *Dublin Weekly Journal*, a Mrs Cherry offered her services with the following advertisement:

Advice is hereby given that there is lately arrived in this city
the famous Mrs Cherry, the only gentlewoman truly learned in
the occult science of tossing of coffee grounds; who has with
uninterrupted success for some time past practised to the gen-
eral satisfaction of her female visitants. She is to be heard of at
Mrs C-----ks and Mrs. Q---ts, in Angier Street, Dublin.

Commercial Coffee

Nescafé was launched as the first freeze-dried coffee in 1938 with production moved to the USA and at that stage was consumed almost entirely by the US military. After the war, the era of instant coffee boomed. In the 1960s, the US saw the dawn of countercultures and coffee became an important part of this. Jonathan Morris, in his *Global History of Coffee*, outlines the subsequent evolution of US coffee tastes.

Alfred Peet was a Dutch entrepreneur who upon arriving in San Francisco was appalled by the poor quality of American coffee. He opened a coffee shop selling roast and ground beans from a shop he established in nearby Berkeley. The emerging hippy movement frequented small authentic coffee bars run by Italian immigrants around the North Beach area and they bought their coffee for their own brewing from Peet's.

Then, in 1968, Erna Knutsen, an immigrant from Norway, arrived in San Francisco. She had a passion for small roasting and fine coffee and would, in time, set in train a new movement, clearly suited to the Californian counterculture, the concept of a speciality coffee industry. Her efforts led to the establishment of the Speciality Coffee Association of America (SCAA) which facilitated the import of small quantities of high quality green coffee beans to groups of 'cottage' roasters, ideally suited to the bright young US brain boxes seeking an alternative life. They sold high priced speciality coffee to the citizens of San Francisco wherever there was a foot fall, and in 1990 there were over 200 carts operating in the city.

Three college friends, Jerry Baldwin, Gordon Bowker and Zev Siege, started Starbucks in 1971 in Seattle. They bought their beans from Peet's and imported roasting facilities from the Netherlands. By 1980, they had four stores open in Seattle where they sold coffee but not coffee drinks. By 1987, only two of the founders were still with Starbucks and they agreed to sell their share to Howard Schultz who was their chief marketing person. The rest is history. Starbucks served many types of coffee in a relaxed environment but also served top quality coffee to take away. In 2019, there were over 30,000 stores worldwide.

The third wave in coffee fashion, as Jonathan Morris calls it, is the small artisanal coffee shop but with the licence to break free from the traditions of Italian coffee etiquette. Bewley's coffee shop in Dublin's Grafton Street is years old but has been beautifully refurbished with a menu that includes espresso, flat white, mocha, macchiato, cortado, cappuccino and, of course, old fashioned americano.

Chapter 12

Pasta

Remembering of Things Pasta

By Brian Bilston

She blew her fuesili,
My pretty penne,

When she found me watching
Daytime tagliatelle.

Je ne spaghetti rien,
I responded in song'

but she did not linguini
for long,

just walked out
without further retort:

a hard lesson to be tortelloni,
orzo I thought.

And so here I am,
On my macaroni,

And now my days feel
Cannelloni.

If bread in its broadest term is global in its derivation, pasta is the opposite – it is pure Italian in origins. Its history is peppered with various claims as to how it began. A popular, but utterly incorrect, claim is that Marco Polo brought it back to Italy from his travels in China in the fourteenth century. Indeed, the 1938 film *Adventures of Marco Polo* sees Gary Cooper (GC) in the role of Marco Polo, talking to an elderly Chinese servant, Chen Tsu (CT).

> **CT**: *God sees all and he will know that, while our means are poor, our spirit is good. Now. You have never seen food like this before?*
>
> **GC**: *No. What is it? Snakes?*
>
> **CT**: *No, no. It has been eaten by the poor people in China for many generations. We call it 'spaghet'. Now, let me show you how to convey it to your stomach. You grasp the chopstick thus . . .*

It is well documented that the Chinese were eating noodles back in the Han dynasty almost 4,000 years ago, and they came in many forms and shapes. It may well have been that the idea of making a dough, rolling it into flat shapes from which ribbons would be cut, originated in China and then migrated to India where such strings of wheat were called *sevika*, meaning thread. From there it was adopted in Arabian cuisine and it was the Arabian empire that brought it to Sicily, which they ruled from 827 to 902 CE. In 1138 CE, the renowned geographer Muhammad al-Idrisi toured Sicily and described a food called itriyah. This was a noodle made from hard wheat obtained from Africa and would be adopted by the Sicilians and then the Neapolitans. It was, effectively, dried spaghetti and was a major source of food for the many maritime Arabic incursions on Italian cities. Whatever its provenance, pasta is Italian. It is as Italian as Puccini and Verdi or Montepulciano and Gavi.

Like bread, pasta is made from wheat but a different type of wheat than is used for breads, cakes and biscuits. Pasta uses durum wheat from the Latin *durum*, meaning hard. Whereas the kernels of wheat for bread making are white or pearly, those of durum are quite translucent yielding a golden yellow hue due to its high content of plant pigments from the carotene family, the same pigments that give carrots their orange colour. Good quality durum wheat has a higher protein content than bread wheat and these proteins are of the gluten family. It is this higher gluten content that gives durum flour greater capacity to be pulled and twisted into different shapes to make the many pastas we know now. When durum flour is milled to coarse particles, it is known as semolina. This should not be confused with the much detested dessert served in school, semolina pudding, which was a ghastly concoction of crude semolina and milk.

Pasta Dough and Pasta Shapes

Italian flour is graded by colour or the extent to which the bran and the germ are extracted from the flour. It is marked 00 to 04, where 00 is snow white and 04 is brownish grey. In other countries where flour is used to make bread, the flour is graded by both colour (white, brown, whole meal) and by strength (plain, strong, extra strong or words to that effect), the latter reflecting the level of gluten in the flour. Pasta dough is made using 00 flour mixed with water, salt and eggs. The dough is managed much like in bread making, although in bread making the dough is shaped into a circular mound for proving, and the dough for pasta is rolled out into thin sheets. This process is by far the oldest approach to shaping pasta dough into the various forms we know today.

There are many types of pasta and any one type can have strong regional variation. Basically, pasta shapes are sheets, strips, tubes, filled and elaborate. The easiest to imagine is lasagne, where thin sheets of pasta are used to construct the dish. Now if you are careful, you can roll the flat sheet up like a swiss roll and then cut it in sections of about one-quarter of an inch or less. Then unroll the dough and you have tagliatelle. If the sections are wider and cut at say one centimetre, you have pappardelle. Maestro Martino, the fifteenth century Italian culinary expert, described the creation of tubular pasta:

> Take some flour of very fine quality, and mix it with egg white and rosewater, or even with common water. . . and make dough of a firm consistency. Then break off pieces of dough the length of your palm and as thin as a straw. And take a rod of iron the length of your palm, or longer, and as thin as a piece of string. Place this over the said piece of dough, and, using both hands, roll it over on the table. Then remove the iron and the macaroni will have a hollow space down the middle.

The many shapes of pasta evolved for culinary reasons. After the dominance of plain vermicelli with some olive oil and garlic, there arose a demand for other shapes to maximise the pasta with its sauce. Cannelloni derives its name from the Italian word *canna* meaning 'pipe'. The hole should have a diameter of 20 millimetres making it ideal for direct stuffing with whatever the recipe recommends. In the US, cannelloni is often called manicotti and the two differ in that manicotti is larger with ridges, whereas cannelloni is smooth. Cannelloni is one of only a few pastas that is baked rather

Photo credit: Jakub Kapusnak

than boiled. Rigatoni is a tubular pasta for boiling and for use with a strong hearty sauce. It has a diameter of 15 millimetres, well capable of absorbing the sauce into the tubular structure. Penne is now one of the favourite pastas globally and particularly so with young children. How many parents have put pasta tubes on either side of a fork to playfully entice their child to eat the dish? The name penne refers to a quill and pasta has a nib-like endpoint at each end of the tube designed to maximise the uptake of sauce into the pasta. The outer part of penne is generally ridged, again to trap the accompanying sauce. It is narrower than rigatoni, at 10 millimetres.

Bucatini connects the tubular pasta with the stringed pasta in that it might look like a thicker version of spaghetti, but in fact is a tube. It is 3 millimetres in diameter and the diameter of the tubular section is just one millimetre which may seem very small. However, it allows boiling water to enter the inner core of this rather thick string which greatly improves cooking time. Of the non-tubular stringed pastas, spaghetti is the most notable, consumed regularly across the globe. It has a diameter of two millimetres. Of the stringed pasta, cappelli d'angelo (angels' hair) is by far the thinnest with a diameter of just one millimetre. It was recorded in Roman archives back in the seventeenth century. They were the specialty of some convents in the city, and the nuns used to send them to new mothers to promote lactation. Among the ribbon-like pastas, pappardelle is the widest at 16 millimetres, fettucine is next at 13 millimetres and tagliatelle is narrowest at just 10 millimetres.

Turning to the filled pasta, these are as ancient as lasagne and any cook that could roll out a thin pasta dough could cut out squares and circles using small boxes or glasses respectively. One side was filled with whatever was the local speciality and the other laid on top. The air is squeezed out from the centre as the pasta sheets are pushed together and sealed at the edges. According to local legend of the town of Castelfranco Emilia, Venus, the goddess of love, visited the village and stayed at a local inn. The innkeeper was curious to see this goddess and peeked through the keyhole of her room. Stunned by her naked beauty, he ran to the kitchen and made a pasta shape to resemble her navel. Tortellini was born and this scene of a peeping-tom innkeeper is celebrated in the town annually. Tortellini means small tart and reflects the fact that many filled pastas were baked, not boiled.

According to Ortensio Lando in 1548, a Lombard peasant, Libista, invented 'raffioli' wrapped in pasta. Agnolotti is said to be credited to a chef by the name of Angeloto who rustled it up from whatever he could find following the successful defence of a castle in Piedmont. Cappelletti, or little hat, is called after a traditional headdress known as gazola and was first described by no less than the sixteenth century celebrity chef, Bartolomeo Scappi. Recipes for filled pastas travelled and in the ancient English cook book of the fourteenth century, *The Forme of Cury*, a recipe for a ravioli exists but the filling is quite different to that found in Italian ravioli.

> *Take wet cheese and grind it small and mix it with eggs and saffron and a good quantity of butter. Make a thin leaf of dough, and close them up in it like tartlets, and cast them in boiling water, and cook them in it. Take hot melted butter and grated cheese, and lay the raviolis in dishes, and lay hot butter with grated cheese above and below, and put sweet spice mix on it.*

Nuns played a big role in making filled pastas. The Augustinians specialised in making anolini and these were a speciality at Christmas and New Year. Lumachels were made by the Poor Clare and Benedictine orders of nuns in the Marche region southwest of Florence. Both sweet and savoury ravioli were made by the Benedictine nuns of the Church of Santa Maria in Valle di Cividale to celebrate Easter Sunday and the Resurrection. The nuns had several advantages over commercial ventures. Time was less precious in the nunneries and, what's more, they had lower taxes than those in the commercial world.

But the rarest of rare pastas, one that very few readers of this book will ever taste, is called Su Filindeu, 'Veil of God' in the language of Sardinia. It is associated with two feast days in the village of Lula a few kilometres from the city of Nuoro in Sardinia and the capital of the province by that name. Each year in May and October, it hosts a long festival to celebrate the feast of St Francis at the Santuario di San Francesco. Legend has it that the sanctuary was built in the seventeenth century by a notorious thief who was pardoned by Saint Francis in exchange for the promise that he would build him a church in Lula. Pilgrims walk in procession at night from Nuoro to Lula for the start of the nine-day novena. Grazia Deledda, who won the Nobel Prize in literature in 1926, was a regular participant in the pilgrimage and she described the atmosphere in the church:

> *It was night, the lamps swung before the altar, spreading shadows and flickering lights in the empty church: the great saint, dark, seemed asleep among the flowers of every month.*

During this festival, this most rare of pastas, Su Filindeu, is served in a broth of mutton, cheese and herbs. Today, no more than five or six women from Nuoro can make this pasta. Jamie Oliver, never one to dodge a foodie challenge, gave up trying to make it after no less than two hours. First, the pasta is rolled into a metre or so long roll about an inch in diameter. The two ends are held in the left hand and the right hand now pulls the half metre loop to one metre in length. The end is returned and held in the left hand. Now we have two double loops in the left hand measuring half a metre. The loops are stretched again to one meter and returned to the left hand so now we have four loops giving us eight strands. This is repeated in total eight times ending up with 256 strands (2, 4, 8, 16, 32, 64, 128, 256). The 256 strands are laid on a circular board about 1 meter in diameter. Bits hanging over are cut off and the process begins again.

When the next 256 strands are ready, they are laid at right angles to the first layer. The process is repeated a third and final time and the 256-pasta lattice is laid at a 45 degree angle to the first. The board with the pasta lattice is left to dry and the dried pasta lattice is then roughly broken up into quite large pieces, about one foot by one foot. The skill of making this pasta lies, they say, in the hands which are moistened with salty water to help maintain a true feel for the pasta. The few Sardinian women who make Su Filindeu can make this lattice in minutes and, for the bi-annual festive, can make up to 50 kilograms of the pasta for the pilgrims' feast.

The Advent of Mechanisation

Pasta for home consumption was not a very demanding task, but when commercial interests saw a business opportunity producing large amounts of pasta, the kneading of the dough became a chore. To that end, a device was introduced called the brake and is first recorded in the thirteenth century. A big slab of pasta was placed on a flat wooden table and the operator raised and lowered a bar with a punch at the end. The brake would be shifted after each punch to distribute the kneading effect. When sufficiently punched, the operator folded the dough and started all over again. This cumbersome system was the only way that large mounds of pasta could be kneaded.

That was the pasta business until the sixteenth century when its production was revolutionised by the arrival of the torchio, a device which involved a circular wooden plate being screwed through a copper-lined wooden tube, forcing pasta out through a hole in the bottom. Larger presses were devised with horses turning the levers forcing the pasta through the orifice at the base of the press. The first stage in this process, the kneading of the semolina dough, was carried out in a trough called a *madia*, and it wasn't done by hand but rather by the feet of many men who were skilled in the extension, folding and kneading of the dough.

It appears that part of the push to mechanize the making of semolina dough came from a visit by King Ferdinand II to a pasta factory where he was some-what shocked at the sight of men treading dough with scalded feet due to the use of very hot water in the knead-ing process. He set in train a Royal Commission to devel-op a mechanical kneading process and, ultimately, the Neapolitan Salvatore Sava-rese came up with a device to convert 100 pounds of semo-lina into a finished dough in just 30 minutes, one-twelfth the effort of manual work. The advent of the torchio spread into homes and thus the traditional approach to pasta making continued in

Photo credit: Stefano76

line with its industrialisation, which would continue to develop through the nineteenth and twentieth centuries allowing many complex shapes to be made mechanically rather than by hand.

Drying Pasta

Setting out the pasta shape from the dough was one skill but orders of magnitude more complex and technical was the drying of pasta. If it is too slow it can go rancid, if it is too fast it will show cracks. So a balance was sought. Freshly prepared pasta is hygroscopic, meaning that if left alone it will absorb water from the atmosphere. Naples boasted the best pasta and the Neapolitans put this down to their unique climate which they deemed to be ideal for the drying of pasta. The warm, humid Sirocco winds that moved northwards toward Naples across the Mediterranean, coupled with the cool Alpine winds, the Tramontana, that moved southwards, together provided the perfect balance for drying pasta. These winds changed at noon and midnight meaning that the pasta drying racks had to be changed accordingly.

The art of drying pasta was carried out by specialists, the *aizacanne*. There are basically three stages to the drying. In the first phase, *incartamento*, the racks were placed in sunlight to create a crust on the outside of the soft pasta. The second stage, *rinvenimento*, is a recovery phase which is indoors in cooler rooms with a high humidity. This tends to soften the crust. The third and final stage, *essicazzione*, saw the pasta rack moved outdoors, but this time to a shaded area, perhaps a courtyard or alley. At each stage, the pasta racks would be moved to suit the wind and when indoors in the *rinvenimento* stage, windows and doors would be adjusted to maximise the balance of draught and humidity. Drying pasta was truly an art form. Holding pasta by his ear, the *aizacanne* would break a piece of the dried pasta and by the sound know when it was dry and fit for shipping. The process was a closely guarded secret of the Neapolitan vermicelli makers and other parts of Italy struggled to match the quality of the Naples product.

Cooking Pasta

Silvano Serventi and Francoise Sabbah, in their book *Pasta: The History of a Universal Food*, give a detailed account of the many ways that pasta was cooked from earliest time. When pasta first entered the popular cuisine of Sicily and Naples, it was boiled as most of it is today. But unlike the modern preference for pasta *al dente*, for centuries after its introduction to local diets pasta was boiled for up to two hours. The objective was to have it melt in one's mouth. It would not be until the nineteenth century that pasta was cooked more gently, albeit not as we would know al dente today. Boiling of pasta could involve water, a meat broth or almond milk. Pasta was also fried in its early days.

The Romans ate a dish known as laganum which would morph into Italian lasagne. Athenaeus, who lived in the second century CE, outlined a recipe for laganum as fine sheets of a dough flavored with spices, and then deep-fried in oil. Filled pastas such as ravioli were also fried and baked. Lasagne as we know it today is parboiled and when assembled with its meat component then baked.

Many of the filled pastas were baked rather than boiled, and often when boiled were part of a soup. Indeed, pasta has been a component of Italian soups for centuries. It was not until the seventeenth century that the cooking time of boiled pasta was reduced. One chef exploited a shorter cooking time immediately followed by dunking in cold water to stop the cooking process from continuing. Another chef recommended that tagliatelle be boiled for ten minutes, after which it was drained, seasoned and baked for a further ten minutes. By the mid-nineteenth century, the Neapolitan approach to gentle cooking of pasta had become the norm.

Pasta is one of those dishes that can be accompanied by a wide range of sauces, and from its earliest days grated cheese was the accompaniment of choice and parmesan cheese the favourite, often accompanied by cinnamon. The obsessive use of cheese with pasta is parodied in the fourteenth century book, *The Decameron*, in which Giovanni Boccaccio describes a conversation between three artists who were admiring a stone and discussing its origin in a Church in Florence:

> *Maso replied that the most of them were found in Berlinzone,*
> *a city of the Basques, in a country called Bengodi, where the*
> *vines are tied up with sausages and a goose is to be had for*
> *a farthing and a gosling into the bargain, and that there was*
> *a mountain all of grated Parmesan cheese, whereon abode*
> *folk who did nothing but make maccaroni and ravioli and*
> *cook them in capon-broth, after which they threw them down*
> *thence and who so got most thereof had most.*

Grimod de la Reynière, the nineteenth century French food critic observed that:

> *Parmesan cheese, gives an excellent taste to vermicelli, and*
> *it goes very well with all the other types of pasta. One would*
> *almost say that, since they both come from the same country,*
> *they are happy to be together.*

In parts of Italy, sauces were developed without cheese such as one described by Scappi, the Papal cook. It is a mix of crushed walnuts, garlic, peppers and crustless bread which had been soaked in water. Others adapted this to include saffron. Another recipe involved chopped onions fried in lard and soaked in milk, after which it was reduced, added to the macaroni and sprinkled with grated cheese, pepper and cinnamon. Pesto sauces which were based on basil became a speciality of the Genoa region and were rarely used outside the province of Liguria. It was in Naples that the tomato entered the world of pasta. It was first used in a type of salsa based on lightly grilled tomatoes which were then peeled, finely chopped and mixed with a puree of onions, thyme and chilli pepper, and seasoned with oil, vinegar and salt. In time, the tomato would be a dominant element of pasta cuisine.

Pasta Popularity

Pasta comes in a bewildering array of shapes coupled with a bewildering array of sauces. In the early days, the terms vermicelli (little worms) and macaroni appeared and there seems to have been an overlap between the two and, in 1546, the guild of vermicelli makers merged with that of the macaroni makers. In time, those outside Italy used the term macaroni to define all pastas. However, to add to the confusion, foreigners were also using the term pasta. John Ray, a Cambridge naturalist and Fellow of the Royal Society, travelled extensively in Italy in the seventeenth century and noted:

> *Pasta made into strings like pack-thread or thongs of white leather (which if greater call Macaroni, if lesser vermicelli), they cut in pieces and put in their pots as we do oatmeal to make their minestra or broth of, much esteemed by the common people. These boiled and oiled with a little cheese scraped upon them, they eat as we do buttered wheat or rice. The making of these is a trade and mystery; and in every great town you will see several shops of them.*

It is interesting that in the seventeenth century, he uses the generic term pasta and distinguishes the thin vermicelli with the thicker macaroni. In 1787, Goethe commented on pasta in Naples:

> *The macaroni can be bought everywhere and in all shops with very little money. As a rule, it is simply cooked in water and seasoned with grated cheese. . . . This macaroni they served us was exquisite. . . . The pasta seemed unparalleled to me in its whiteness and fineness.*

Vermicelli was sold as a street food in Naples and there are paintings of the time depicting young ruffians holding long strands of vermicelli above their head, feeding it into gaping mouths. In time, pasta was embraced by the well-to-do and it was the port of Genoa in the northwest of Italy that pasta started to spread to the rest of Europe. Genoa had its own very fine pasta, fedelini, a stringed pasta thinner than spaghetti that was very popular with the sailors of that port. But unscrupulous pasta makers began to use chestnut flour or inferior wheat to make fedelini. To control this activity, the city of Genoa introduced a regulation requiring that such traders: '. . . cannot and must not practice said art in the same shop, but in another shop thirty paces away from where they practice said art of fidelaro.'

Photo credit: Gunel Farhardli

Macarone or macoronis were terms used to describe an effeminate type of Englishman that aped the Italian and French cuisine and lifestyle. They were notable for their buffoon hairstyles and ostentatious hats, and were the butt of many jokes in London circles. In *She Stoops to Conquer*, Oliver Goldsmith writes:

> *Let all the old pay homage to your merit;*
> *Give me the young, the gay, the men of spirit.*
> *Ye travell'd tribe, ye macaroni train,*
> *Of French friseurs, and nosegays, justly vain,*
> *Who take a trip to Paris once a year*
> *To dress, and look like awkward Frenchmen here.*

Even in the colonies, the English joked at the colonial settlers who fancied the European way of life and thus the rhyme:

> *Yankee doodle went to town*
> *A-riding on a pony.*
> *He stuck a feather in his cap*
> *And called it macaroni.*

The story of pasta started in Italy and its mechanisation began in the nineteenth century, but it was finished in the United States. Thomas Jefferson spent some time as a US diplomat in Paris before becoming the third US president. He brought back to his Monticello gardens and the White House many plants and cooking techniques of Europe. The Rev. Manasseh Cutler, a member of the House of Representatives, records in his diary details of a dinner with the President where he was served an unusual dish:

> *. . . pie called macaroni, which appeared to be a rich crust filled with strillions of onions, or shallots, which I took it to be, tasted very strong and not agreeable. . . . It was an Italian dish, and what appeared onions was made of flour and butter . . .*

Between 1900 and 1910, over two million Italians had arrived in the US to bolster almost the same number that had started to migrate as early as the 1820s. By the time Italian immigration had reached a decline, over 4 million Italians, mostly from the poorer regions of Naples and Sicily, had come to the United States, accounting for over 10 per cent of the nation's foreign-born population. The food of Italian immigrants was quite different from the prevailing traditions of US food, in turn originating from British colonial times.

The first commercial pasta factory in the US was established by a French immigrant, Antoine Zerega, on the waterfront of Brooklyn. He is said to have used a single horse to turn the pasta press and to dry his pasta on the roof of his premises. Given the New York summer humidity and the freezing winter, one wonders about this. It was in the US that all the significant developments in the mechanisation of pasta were made from kneading to shaping to drying. In 1904, the National Association of Macaroni and Noodle manufacturers recorded 100 pasta factories across the US. As bigger enterprises engulfed lesser enterprises the pasta-making business consolidated as is the norm in commerce.

Nonetheless, for Italians living in the US, there was still a hankering for traditional pasta making and for traditional pasta dishes. In the words of M. Sherman, writing in 1906:

Macaroni is made in every block of the Italian neighbourhoods of New York. In many streets you will find three or four little shops in one block of houses, with the macaroni drying in the doorways and windows. The front room is the shop, the family living in the middle and rear rooms.

Photo credit: Daniel Cuklev

The adherence of US Italians to the traditional Italian cuisine was in stark contrast to the habituated American's perception. To them, pasta was spaghetti and ideally with meat balls in a tomato sauce. This is beautifully illustrated in that great movie *The Big Night*, depicting an Italian restaurant in the 1950s run in the most traditional style of cuisine by two brothers. Below is a conversation between an American customer and Secondo, the maître d':

Customer: *Sir, is this what I ordered?*

Secondo: *Yes, that is the risotto. Is a special recipe that my brother and I bring from Italy. It's delicious, I promise.*

Customer: *It took so long I thought you went all the way back to Italy to get it. Didn't you say that this was going to be rice with seafood?*

Secondo*: It is Italian Arborio rice. The best.*

Customer: *And then with shrimp, and scallop, and . . . I just don't see anything that looks like a shrimp or a scallop. I just . . . Well, I'm . . . I mean, it's just not what I expected. But I get a side order of spaghetti with this, right?*

Secondo: *Why? Well, no . . .*

Customer: *I thought all main courses come with spaghetti.*

Secondo: *Well, some, yes, but, you see, risotto is rice, so it is a starch. And it doesn't go really with pasta.*

Customer's partner: *Honey, honey. Order a side of spaghetti, that's all. And I'll eat your meatballs.*

Customer: *Yeah, she'll have the meatballs.*

Secondo: *Well, the spaghetti comes without meatballs.*

Customer*: There are no meatballs with the spaghetti?*

Secondo: *No. Sometimes spaghetti likes to be alone.*

Customer: *All right, then, I guess we'll also have a side order of meatballs.*

Secondo: *Side of . . .*

Customer: *All right, then no meatballs and we'll just have a side order of spaghetti.*

But just as the US was embracing pasta at the start of the twentieth century, in Italy, moves were afoot to rid that country of pasta. It all began with a manifesto entitled 'The Foundation and Manifesto of Futurism' by an Italian poet by the name of Filippo Tomasso Marinetti, published in *Le Figaro* in February 1909. The futurist movement was besotted with new technologies, from air travel to automobiles, and wanted Italy to move away from its obsession with history and build a new Italy with dynamic art, literature and engineering. Being Italian, it is not surprising that

Marinetti turned to food and developed his own cookery book. He didn't like the old term 'recipe' and replaced it instead with 'a formula', much more technical sounding. Pasta was seen as a food that was decidedly inferior in that it was swallowed quickly and thus digested in the stomach with little salivary breakdown which inhibited the virility of Italian males. The futurists wanted meals to be highly experimental in terms of ingredients and structure. His book describes 'sculpted meat' and presents a formula for one such creation:

> *The Sculpted meat created by the Futurist painter Fillìa, a symbolic interpretation of all the varied landscapes of Italy, is composed of a large cylindrical rissole of minced veal stuffed with eleven different kinds of cooked green vegetables and roasted. This cylinder, standing upright in the centre of the plate, is crowned by a layer of honey and supported at the base by a ring of sausages resting on three golden spheres of chicken.*

Fillia may have painted such a formula but he certainly never actually cooked it. It is an engineering disaster. Thankfully, futurism died with its founder and the world learned to enjoy the wonders of pasta.

Chapter 13

Biscuits, Cakes and Pastries

Extract from **Miss Fogarty's Christmas Cake**
By C. Frank Horn

And there were plums and prunes and cherries
There were citrons and raisins and cinnamon, too
There was nuts, and cloves and berries
And a crust that was nailed on with glue
There were caraway seeds in abundance
Such that work up a fine stomach ache
That could kill a man twice after eating a slice
Of Miss Fogarty's Christmas cake

There was plumbs and grumes and cheriffs and citherers
and raiders and cinemen too
– James Joyce, Finnegans Wake.

(Joyce parodies the lyrics of the song Miss Fogarty's Christmas Cake, which he sang as a child at a concert in 1888 in aid of the local boating club held at Breslin's Hotel on the Esplanade in Bray, County Wicklow.)

Humans have always had a sweet tooth and the opportunity to turn wheat flour into something sweet was grasped with the arrival of honey. Egyptian tomb paintings depict men baking cone-shaped biscuits from tiger nuts, dates, olive oil and honey. *The Deipnosophistae* was an account of dining in third century Greece written by Athenaeus, and in it many references are made to cakes but almost certainly these were, in fact, biscuits. In reply to the question, 'What are biscuits' came the response, 'They are voluptuous loaves'. Quite what is meant by voluptuous is anybody's guess. He also refers to wafer bread which is 'both light and thin, and the so-called epanthrakis'. The latter has been translated as griddle cake or pancake. There is an astronomical number of different cakes and biscuits. Biscuits by and large are crunchy. Some have a very crisp mouthfeel while some are softer and indeed some are chewy. But trying to define a cake is quite difficult. It should be softer and larger than a biscuit, and is generally eaten with a fork whereas biscuits are eaten by hand.

The best way to consider the difference between cakes and biscuits is to consider the recipe. A sponge cake will involve equal quantities of butter, sugar and flour and two or more eggs. A typical biscuit recipe will have twice as much flour as butter and sugar, and no egg or just one. In the cake, the eggs will act as an adjunct to the raising agent to help lift the cake and give it structure. The use of plenty of butter as a shortening provides better control of the gluten network, giving a crumble mouthfeel. It will also be baked in a cake tin to give it an elevated structure.

The biscuits will have no raising agent and will be rolled out flat to end up with a dry structure, 1 to 3 per cent water compared to cakes with 15 to 30 per cent. Biscuits will be cooked at a higher temperature and for shorter periods than cakes. Cakes tend to be soft but the texture can range from a biscuit cake which is hard to a sponge cake which is soft. Nonetheless, there is a wide range of baked sweet goods which straddle the biscuit-cake boundary.

Allied to the development of bread dough is the development of various types of pastry. For the purpose of this chapter, the focus will be on categories of confection.

Sweet Confection: Biscuits and Cakes

Paximadia are biscuits that originated in ancient Greece. The name may have originated from the Greek cookery author Paxamus, but they are also believed to have originated in Crete and thus named after the twin islands known as Paximadia. These biscuits, still popular today in Greece, were originally shaped just like the islands, two halves of a long oval ball. The biscuits were made from barley, chickpeas and honey and were cooked whole, then cut into two halves and cooked a second time, the origin of the word biscuit: *Bis* (twice) *cotus* (cooked).

Biscuits became an essential element of the military. Being dry and portable, they provided high energy foods at times when isolation disconnected troops from the food supply line. The biscuits were baked with a hole in them so that a good number of them could be carried on a string, giving rise to the forerunner of bagels. Biscuits were an essential provision for seafarers with the ship's biscuit known as 'hardtack'. Made with just flour and water, these highly dried biscuits could last for a very long time, assuming they could be kept dry, not always an easy thing on ships.

The Romans also had a similar product called a *bucellatum* and again it was used as a portable food by the Roman military to the extent that the soldiers in the Roman army were referred to as *bucellari*. Throughout Italy, grape must, that is, the stems, seeds and skins of grapes, were blended and incorporated into biscuits known as *mostaccioli*. Biscuits remained a sweet product, made with honey and other sweet produce such as figs, and were twice cooked to yield a simple crunchy, generally flat product to be eaten with one's hand. Bakers were organised into communes or guilds and undertook the beginnings of decorative confectionery. In his book *The Lowly Ancients*, Osborne Ward describes this Roman guild as 'manufacturers of dainty loaves, biscuits, cakes and bon-bons'. By the thirteenth century, biscuits made in Constantinople seemed to have been more sophisticated than these simple twice-cooked biscuits. William of Rubruck, a Dutch geographer who rivals Marco Polo for his account of his eastern travels, mentions getting 'dainty' biscuits in Constantinople around 1250 CE to give as a gift to the Tartars he was to visit.

The Christian sacrament of communion created a demand for the preparation of a special bread which was distributed in this religious event. Those who made these sacramental wafers became

Photo credit: Melanie Dompierre

Photo credit: Melanie Dompierre

known as the oublayeurs and in 1270, Régnaut-Barbon, the Provost of Paris, registered them into a guild. Almost three centuries later this guild, recognising their culinary talent beyond the liturgical host, gave rise to the guild of confectioners. Wafers were made by heating a device with two long handles, each of which had flat round plate-like structure at the bottom. These wafers were crisp and tasty. In time the plates took on a shape leading eventually to the cooking of waffles, known in France as *gaufres*, where eggs, sugar and milk were mixed with the dough. The French King Francois I commissioned the making of a silver waffle iron and the popularity of waffles in Paris was such that King Charles IX ordered that the stalls of oublayeurs be separated by a distance of twenty metres.

In Belgium there were two different forms of waffles, those of the city of Liege and those of Brussels. A Belgian businessman, Maurice Vermersch, brought the waffle to the World Trade Fair in New York in 1964 but decided not to use the term Brussels waffle based on his belief that the average US citizen wouldn't recognise Brussels but would recognise Belgium. Belgian waffles are a street food eaten by hand, whereas in the US they are mainly a breakfast food smothered in maple syrup. The transition from wafers to waffles involved the incorporation of eggs into the recipe, and this use of eggs would transform the preparation of confectionery.

By the seventeenth century, biscuit making in Europe had become more sophisticated. Vincenzo Tamara, in his book *L'Economia del Cittadino in Villa* (The Economy of Citizens in the Countryside), writes of 'pan di Spagna' describing it as 'exotic'. He goes on to say:

> There is another sort of biscotto that is much more delicate and it is this, which is called pan de Spagna (Spanish bread), which is composed of twelve eggs, two pounds raw sugar which you mix together, then add in eight ounces of flour . . . arrange this in the form of a round loaf. . . . They call these small pieces biscottini or in their long form, biscotti alla Savoiarda (Savoy biscuits).

Today we know these as 'ladies fingers'. The transformation in biscuit making and its transition into cake making was the discovery of the properties of eggs to provide a much more sophisticated texture and mouthfeel to both biscuits and cakes. Nicolas de Bonnefons, a French chef of the seventeenth century, lists recipes for biscuit de Roy, de Piedmont, de Savoie and macaroons, and his recipe for biscuit de Roy calls for 'a pound of sugar, three quarters of a pound of butter and eight eggs'. The addition of eggs allows a softer biscuit to be baked and the new guild of confectioners began to develop many sophisticated biscuit recipes spurred on by three factors: the advent of cheap sugar from the West Indies, coffee from Turkey and chocolate from Central America.

Cakes as we know them today did not become available until the seventeenth century, and *The English Huswife*, a cookbook by Gervase Markham in 1615, gives several recipes which tell us a little about baking at that time. Her ingredients include three eggs, a pint of cream and a pint of milk, butter, sugar and barm, from brewers waste. Cloves, mace, cinnamon and nutmegs are mixed in and it should be baked 'according to the thickness'. Typical of cookbooks of the day, many of the measures are absent so we don't know how much flour was used and of course the baking instruction left the cook up to his or her judgement. Cooks were skilled in understanding their wood fired ovens and it would be their judgement as to when to put the mix in the oven. The big advance in cake making was in improved oven technology for cooking which allowed more precise cooking conditions to be maintained. Short, firm twigs were bound together to whisk cream or to blend sugar and butter, but in the mid-nineteenth century the wire whisk was introduced which greatly aided in getting consistency in baked goods.

Structural Confections: Pastry

The history of pastry is complex. In the beginning, pastry was boiled. One recipe from the Forme of Cury describes a Lenten dish and tells us a little about early pastry in 1390. The pastry is made by boiling flour with almond milk until it is thick and is then left to cool. This is a hot water pastry and it is used to make a 'cofyn' which is the word used for a box made of pastry. When the ball of pastry is cold, the pastry is dented with a fist and then worked into a rectangular box. The pastry would be several centimetres in thickness. The filling is made of figs, dates and almond milk and the cofyn would be covered with a thick dry pastry and baked. The pastry would be discarded by the well to do as it was intended simply to act as a container. Two centuries later, in *The English Huswife*, we have a recipe for a prune tart. This time the pastry includes butter, is rolled thin and shapes are cut out to decorate it which clearly shows an intention to eat, not to discard. The edges of the tart are to be delicately pinched with fingers. All in all, this is a much finer pastry.

The evolution of pastry is evident in the seventeenth century book by Edward Kidder, E. *Kidder's Receipts of Pastry and Cookery: For the Use of His Scholars*. First there was hard pastry for a 'high pie' made with hot water:

> *Lay down a peck of flower work it up with 3 pads of butter melted in a sauce pan of boiling water & make it into a stiff paste.*

Then he has a recipe for a pastry for a pasty (pie):

> *Lay down a peck of flower work it up with 6 pads of butter & 4 eggs with cold water.*

Finally, he lists a recipe for puff pastry:

> *Lay down a pound of flower and break into it 2 ounces of but-ter and 2 eggs and make it into paste with cold water and work the other part of the pad of butter to the stiffness of your past and roll out your past into a square piece. Stick it all over with bits of butter. Flower it and roll it up like a collar. Double it up at both ends that they meet in the middle. Roll it out again as aforesaid till all the pad of butter is in.*

The renowned sixteenth century Italian cookbook of Bartolomeo Scappi discusses making elaborate pastry: 'Carefully with a greased hand, put waves into the flaky pastry or else cut it into lacework with a knife'. If you Google 'Who invented puff pastry' you will be told that it was an apprentice pâtissier, Claudius Gele, who gave us puff pastry in 1645 in a tear-jerking tale of how he accidentally discovered this pastry while trying to make a palatable bread for his sick father. However, an anonymous Arabic cookbook from the thirteenth century, translated by the US food historian Charles Perry, shows clearly that puff pastry originated in Arabic cuisine.

One can be a little more confident about the origins of choux pastry. Catherine de Medici's head pâtissier is credited with the discovery of choux pastry in 1540. Marie-Antoine Carême, recognised as the father of modern French cuisine, modified the recipe in the nineteenth century and it is his techniques that are followed today. Choux pastry is very soft and aerated due to the release of steam during baking the dough. In its own right, pastry isn't particularly tasty and its only function is to give a structure to a dish. An apple tart is held in a shallow container of pastry and lacks a covering. On the other hand, an apple pie is similar but with a pastry covering. Puff pastry is used for Danish pastries and other such Viennoiserie and choux pastry provides the structure for éclairs and profiteroles.

Not all pastry structures are vehicles for sweet treats. A quiche Lorraine is a tart and a Cornish pasty is a pie. Dough is not just used for cakes, biscuits and pastries. It is also used for doughnuts and, undoubtedly, they also originated in Arab cuisine. Greek loukamedes, Turkish lokma and Arabic luqma all denote a small ball of liquid dough scooped up and dropped into boiling fat with such skill that as the watery dough hits the hot oil, the cook has skillfully managed to get a hole in the center with adroit use of the thumb.

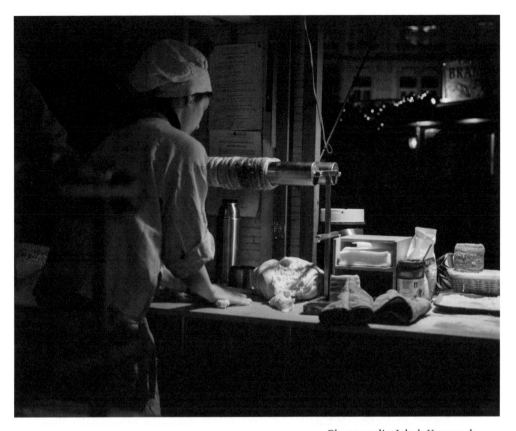

Photo credit: Jakub Kapusnak

Trendy Confections

In the film, *Breakfast at Tiffany's*, Holly Golightly, played by Audrey Hepburn, stares through the window of the famous Fifth Avenue jewellers. She has just finished her nightshift as an escort and is eating her breakfast on the go: coffee and a Danish. Danish pastries and other Viennoiseries such as croissants have their origin in Vienna but they were made popular in Paris. Vienna was besieged by the Ottoman armies in 1683. The bakers of Vienna, who would rise very early in the morning, noted a strange noise near the walls of the city. The Ottomans were intending to tunnel themselves under the wall. Discovering this scheme helped thwart the Ottomans and ultimately King John of Poland led the lifting of the siege. To commemorate this event, the bakers designed a patisserie in the shape of the crescent of the Turkish flag, which today is known as a croissant.

The Viennese went further afield. In 1850, the owners of the large bakeries in Copenhagen locked out their bakers in an industrial dispute and in their place employed Viennese pastry makers. Looking at some traditional baking and pastry commodities of Denmark, the Viennese chefs decided to design a pastry which started as a long, thin string-like dough which was then wound into ever increasing circles then baked and dotted with raisins and sultanas. The Danish pastry was invented and eventually, when the strike was settled, the Danish bakers took up this new recipe. Today, a typical French breakfast involves coffee with a Viennoiserie of which the croissant is the most popular.

Petits fours are perhaps a cross between a cake and a biscuit. The name derives from the French words *petit* for small and *four* for oven. The adjective doesn't refer to size but rather the temperature of the oven. The *grand four* was the raging hot wood fire used for baking bread and confectionery. When this was done, the fire was extinguished and the hot oven began to cool down. This was called the *petit four* and chefs used this to make many forms of pastries, both sweet and savoury

Among the many new biscuits were the macarons, sometimes called macaroons. Almonds are central to the macaron and Venice was the port of call for ships trading almonds. The Venetians apparently devised a type of biscuit containing almonds and called them maccherone, a word denoting paste which would be adopted to macaroni and pasta. Catherine de Medici's chefs brought the macaron tradition to Paris where it quickly became a popular

Photo credit: Jakub Kapusnak

delicacy. Several towns in France developed their own speciality macaron recipe such as macaron de Saint-Jean-de Luz or macaron de Nancy.

Nuns used macarons as a substitute for meat which is understandable in that almonds are an excellent source of protein and many nunneries had their own secret recipes. The daughter of Charles III and the Abbess of Remiremont, Anne Charlotte of Lorraine, founded the monastery of Les Dames du Saint-Sacrement in the town of Nancy and laid down a strict rule that the nuns in the Abbey would not eat meat. They developed their own recipe for a variety of macarons. Following the French revolution, edicts were passed to de-Christianise the country. Two nuns, Sisters Marguerite and Marie-Elisabeth took, refuge in the home of Doctor Gormand on Rue de la Hache, and in return for shelter prepared food for him and his guests. To support themselves, they started to sell their macarons and the rest is history.

Macarons were also popular among Jews who could eat them since they were unleavened. The use of egg white to 'raise' macaron dough meant they were not fermented. The Dutch are accredited with bringing the baking skills of Europe to the new colonies and their little biscuits, *koekje* in Dutch, were popular in New Amsterdam in the eighteenth century. The original Dutch word was adapted in English to 'cookie'.

Confusing Confections

The biscuit industry grew exponentially with the industrial revolution and many of today's brands of biscuit can be directly traced

Photo credit:Nadia Barnard

back to that time: Robert McVitie in Edinburgh, who would go on to make chocolate digestives; William and Robert Jacob in Waterford, famous for their fig rolls; Jonathan Carr in Carlisle, who created water biscuits; Jean-Romain Lefèvre, who created the Lefèvre-Utile (LU) brand in Nantes; Carlo Lazzaroni in Saronno, who created the famous Amaretti di Saronno.

But is it a cake or a biscuit? That is an issue which occupied the British legal system some years ago. Cakes and plain biscuits are zero rated for tax on the grounds that they are dietary necessities, but are deemed luxuries when fully or partly coated in chocolate. McVities made a very popular product, the Jaffa Cake. It is a very soft biscuit flavoured with Jaffa orange and topped with chocolate. The Revenue Commissioners argued that it was luxurious by virtue of the chocolate coating on top, and thus subject to value added tax. The case went to court and the judge ruled thus:

> *Generally, I come to the conclusion that Jaffa Cakes have characteristics of cakes, and also characteristics of biscuits or non-cakes. I conclude that they have sufficient characteristics of cakes to qualify as cakes within the meaning of Sch. 5, Grp. 1, item 1 [schedule 5, group 1, item 1]. If it be relevant, I also determine that the Jaffa Cakes are not biscuits. I therefore allow the appeal. The appellants are at liberty to make an application in respect of costs.*

A year earlier, a similar case was heard in court over the Marks and Spencer product Caramel Shortcake Slices, and the judge ruled thus:

> *We do not attempt to make any definition of 'cake'. We have nonetheless come to the conclusion that there was nothing inconsistent with a cake in either its ingredients or process of manufacture. In appearance the product looked like a cake, it*

was certainly marketed by Marks and Spencer as a cake and would normally if not exclusively be eaten at the times and places where cakes were normally eaten. More decisive in the unanimous view of the tribunal it tasted like a cake and in the unanimous judgment of the members of this tribunal it was a cake. This appeal, therefore, succeeds.

Taxation law is quite complex but whatever the judge might have said, Jaffa cakes and Caramel Shortcake Slices are found in the biscuit aisle, not the cake aisle, in supermarkets.

Chapter 14

The Potato

Extract from Colcannon: The Skillet Pot

By Shaun O'Nolan

Did you ever eat Colcannon, made from lovely
*   pickled cream?*
With the greens and scallions mingled like a
*   picture in a dream.*
Did you ever make a hole on top to hold the
*   melting flake*
Of the creamy, flavoured butter that your mother
*   used to make?*

Chorus

Yes you did, so you did, so did he and so did I.
And the more I think about it sure the nearer
*   I'm to cry.*
Oh, wasn't it the happy days when troubles we
*   had not,*
And our mothers made Colcannon in the little
*   skillet pot.*

The potato was a native crop of the mountainous Andes regions of Bolivia and Peru. Spanish colonists brought the first potatoes to Europe in the late sixteenth century to the Spanish island of Gran Canaria. This Spanish-colonised island was a major junction in world trade, where American-bound expeditions picked up the northeast trade winds. Spain was the first mainland European state to begin to explore the merits of this completely new crop. Records show its use in the market archives of the Hospital de La Sangre in Seville. Some 500 kilometres north of Seville, St Theresa of Avila, the noted Carmelite mystic, is recorded as using potatoes in the care of the sick. From Spain, the potato spread through France, the low countries and Prussia, but its journey to the everyday menu of the masses would take time. But when it did, it had as big an impact on economic growth as did the advent of the industrial revolution.

A Shaky Start

The slow uptake of the potato into everyday cuisine was due to the widespread belief at the time that potatoes were deleterious to health from mild flatulence to the horrors of leprosy and many a malady in between. To begin with, the potato in full bloom looked like it was related to the deadly nightshade family. Extract of deadly nightshade had been used as a cosmetic for ladies, partly to colour their hair and partly because, in tiny amounts, it caused dilation of the eyes which was deemed to be seductive. However, it wasn't long before the Roman gentry realised the lethal nature of even small doses of deadly nightshade, leading to acute toxicity of the nervous system causing confusion, hallucinations, delirium, convulsions and death.

It is also likely that in the early days of potato use, the proper management of harvested potatoes was not appreciated. If potatoes are exposed to light, they go green. That in itself is not a problem since the green pigment on the skin is chlorophyll, the same green pigment of every plant. However, the conditions that make potatoes go green also foster the growth of a group of chemicals known as alkaloids, of which solanine is the most poisonous. Just like the deadly nightshade plant, these potato alkaloids are toxic to our nervous symptoms and there are many known cases of potato toxicity. Thus potato poisoning somewhat resembled that of deadly nightshade, albeit not quite as lethal. Many of these symptoms were mistaken for some of the early symptoms of leprosy, such as tender skin and numbness of the legs and arms.

Aside from the real issue of toxicity and the imagined similarity to early leprosy, there were others reasons why potatoes were shunned. To begin with, potatoes grew underground, unlike oats for porridge or wheat for bread, and that didn't go down well with folks at the time. According to prevailing dietetic principles, potatoes were among the lowliest crops in the Great Chain of Being. Writing in 1548, William Forrest, a noted Catholic priest and poet declared: 'Our English nature cannot live by roots.'

And it wasn't just fear of disease or suspicion of the underground productivity of the potato which hindered its uptake; there were moral issues raised. There is no mention of potatoes in the Bible which was used to argue the case that if God had intended us to eat these underground tubers, He would have given some hint in the Old or New Testament. The Smithsonian Institute in its magazine noted the following:

> In England, 18th-century farmers denounced S. tuberosum as an advance scout for hated Roman Catholicism. 'No Potatoes, No Popery'.

Gentle Persuasion

Potatoes were eaten by the poor and also fed to pigs and this branding of the potato with peasantry and piggery was certain to doom its uptake in the middle and upper classes. All that would change, starting in the military prisons of the King of Prussia, an ardent enthusiast of the potato.

Among his prisoners was a French military pharmacist, Antoine-Augustin Parmentier, who fought with the House of Hanover in the Seven Years War. Captured no less than five times (history does not explain his releases or escapes) he was fed on potatoes and soon realised their nutritional worth. After the war, he returned to France.

In 1769, the grain harvest failed and hunger became widespread at the collapse of the staple food of the French. The Academy at Besancon established a competition to find alternatives to grains. Parmentier won with an essay on the nutritional potential of the

Photo credit: LightFieldStudios

potato. A hungry peasantry can grow angry and create all sorts of bother for the ruling classes so a top-down promotion of the potato was initiated by the royalty. Parmentier had moved to Paris and in 1787 was given the equivalent of 40 acres near Paris by Louis XVI to grow potatoes. The inventive Parmentier had a scheme to slowly encourage the peasants to try potatoes. This cunning plan was described by his collaborator, Julien-Joseph Virey, in a posthumous biography of his friend and colleague:

> *Parmentier arranged for gendarmes to guard them – but only during the day. His intention was for them to be stolen during the night and the populace did not fail to oblige. Every morning these nocturnal thefts were reported to him; he was delighted, and generously rewarded the informants, who were astonished by his inexplicable joy. But public opinion was vanquished and France from that moment was enriched with an enduring resource.*

The royal family are said to have themselves promoted the potato. Promenading around the spacious gardens of Versailles, Marie-Antoinette would wear the purple potato flower in her hair while Louis would wear one in his buttonhole. Very quickly, the potato was adopted in France and then spread across Europe, north to the low countries and the British Isles and East to Russia where its cultivation was championed by Catherine the Great.

The potato is a crop which can grow almost anywhere. The daytime sun promotes the above ground leafy foliage, while the cool nights foster the growth of the starchy underground tubers. At the time that the potato was adopted by European farmers, a three crop rotation system was in use. Crop rotation reduced the scale of pest attacks and allowed soil to better balance its nutrients. Typically, one-third was used for winter and spring cereal, another for beans and other pulses that fix nitrogen from the atmosphere, and the third was left fallow. During that nine month period of fallow, weeds would thrive only to be ploughed back into the soil to restore its nutritional balance. However, that third plot could easily accommodate the cultivation of potatoes with a growing period of just three to four months. The potato was also a crop that could yield more calories and essential nutrients per hectare that any crop prevalent at the time.

Compared to wheat, potatoes had a 50 per cent higher yield, a six-fold output of calories and required less than one-third of the land wheat would need to provide 1,000 calories per day for 365 days.

Driver of Population Growth and Urbanisation

World population began to grow exponentially from 1400 CE. Thus in the next three centuries to 1700 CE, world population grew by 200 million from a baseline vale of 400 million. Then in the next century to 1800 CE it grew by 300 million and in the following century by 700 million. In 1776, the famous economist Adam Smith, in his book *An Enquiry into the Nature and Causes of the Wealth of Nations*, asked whether the potato might foster population growth:

> ... *an acre of potatoes will still produce six thousand weight of solid nourishment, three times the quantity produced by the acre of wheat. ... Should this root ever become in any part of Europe, like rice in some rice countries, the common and favourite vegetable food of the people, so as to occupy the same proportion of the lands in tillage, which wheat and other sorts of grain for human food do at present, the same quantity of cultivated land would maintain a much greater number of people.*

Economic historians recognise that many factors would have influenced population growth, perhaps including mechanisation and new technologies, which in turn required potato production to be expanded. One major study suggested that the potato could explain a quarter of population increase in Europe between 1700 and 1900 CE. Moreover, it is estimated that up to a third of the growth in urbanisation over the same period can be attributed to the potato. This study also demonstrated the direct nutritional effect on the stature of French soldiers from potato growing regions, as opposed to recruits from regions with a low uptake of potatoes in the period 1658 to 1770. Potato consumption increased height up to 0.8 of an inch. Bearing in mind an average height at the time of 65 inches, this represents an increase of 12 per cent. Indeed, the records of the East India Company show that potato-eating Irish recruits were taller than their English counterparts by an inch.

Of all the European countries, Ireland embraced the potato more than any other. In a comparison of potato agriculture across 37 countries, Ireland had the sixth highest production of potatoes, but this was achieved on a very limited acreage with Ireland ranking fourth lowest in per cent of suitable land used for potato production. Most rural labourers had gardens for the growth of potatoes which could feed their family for up to nine months of the year with oats taking over during the late spring and early summer. They would have enough surplus potatoes to feed a pig along with buttermilk following the sale of butter from their one cow. However, English opinion of this reliance on potatoes varied. The Earl of Shrewsbury, Lord High Steward of Ireland, was not at all convinced that the potato would be good for Ireland:

> *The Indians in America live wretchedly enough at times, but they have no knowledge of a better condition, and as they are hunters, they have every now and then a productive chase, and are able to make a number of feast days in the year. Many Irishmen have but one day on which they eat flesh, namely, on Christmas-day. Every other day they feed on potatoes, and nothing but potatoes. Now this is inhuman; for the appetite and stomach of man claim variety in food, and nowhere else do we find human beings gnawing, from year's end to year's end, at the same root, berry, or weed. There are animals who do so, but human beings nowhere except in Ireland.*

In contrast, Arthur Young, the English agriculturist who, unlike the Earl of Shrewsbury, made an extensive visit to Ireland, wrote thus of the reliance of the peasantry on the potato:

> *I heard it stigmatized as being unhealthy, and not sufficiently nourishing for the support of hard labour; but this opinion is amazing in a country, many of whose poor people are as athletic in their form, as robust, and as capable of enduring labour, as any upon earth. . . . When I see the people of a country in spite of political oppression with well-formed vigorous bodies, and their cottages swarming with children; when I see their men athletic, and their women beautiful, I know not how to believe them subsisting on an unwholesome food.*

The population growth of Ireland was spectacular in the eighteenth and early nineteenth centuries: 1.4 million in 1600, 2.9 million in 1718, 6.8 million in 1821 and 8.2 million in 1841. As with Europe as a whole, the question of the pull-push role of the potato in this expansion of Ireland possibly raises complex questions. One study set out to explore the relative importance of many factors on the growth of the Irish population, including potatoes, cottage industry, religion, literacy, urbanisation and income, among others.

As regards net population growth, the role of the potato was by far the most important. Whilst the population had reached 8.2 million in 1841, a decade later it would fall to 6.6 million and a decade after that to 5.8 million.

The potato harvest was devastated by blight. This air-borne fungus played havoc across Europe in the in the mid-1840s. Exactly where the fungus that caused potato blight originated is uncertain, but recent genetic studies using museum specimens suggest that it originated in Mexico and from there travelled via the US to Europe. Potato blight hit seven continental European countries Belgium, Denmark, Sweden, France, Prussia, Netherlands and Spain. For these countries, potatoes occupied about 7 per cent of total arable land, whereas in Ireland that figure was 32 per cent. Again, these seven countries had a mean per capita daily potato intake was 0.5 kilograms. In Ireland it was 2.1 kilograms.

So with a greater concentration of potato cultivation and a higher potato intake, Ireland was poised for a very dramatic effect from the blight. Of course other factors played a role in determining the adverse impact of potato blight on populations such as weather conditions, infectious disease or the escape valve of urban employment. It was in Ireland that the impact of the failure of the potato harvest, and its subsequent gross mismanagement by the English parliament, showed its most horrific consequences. In the mid-1840s the population of Ireland was 8.5 million but between 1845 and 1855, some 1.2 million citizens died and over 2.1 million emigrated. Almost 40 per cent of the population fell victim to this horrific famine. The complexity of the famine, its causes and consequences are beyond the scope of this book.

Fries, Chips and Crisps

Today we see a decline in the intake of potatoes, particularly in favour of pasta. A dish of pasta can be enhanced by pesto or tomato sauce making it more attractive to children than a plate of boiled, mashed, roasted or baked potatoes. But not chips (French fries in the US) or crisps (chips in the US).

The story of chips in Europe is said to originate in Belgium, specifically in the town of Namur. This town in the heart of today's French-speaking regions of Belgium is at the confluence of the Sambre and Meuse rivers. It is said that the locals would fry small fish from these rivers, but when they froze over in winter they would fry small rectangular strips of potato instead. The Belgian frite was born and to this day is the accompaniment to the delicious Belgian treat of French fries and mussels, moules mariniére.

In his description of the dire hunger of pre-revolutionary Paris in *A Tale of Two Cities*, Charles Dickens describes chips or French fries as a food of desperation among the Parisian poor:

> *Hunger was . . . written in every small loaf of his scanty stock of bad bread; at the sausage-shop, in every dead-dog preparation that was offered for sale. Hunger rattled its dry bones among the roasting chestnuts in the turned cylinder; Hunger was shred into atomies in every farthing porringer of husky chips of potato, fried with some reluctant drops of oil.*

In time, the English would embrace deep fried potato chips and sell them with battered fish, the latter believed to have its origins among the Sephardic Jews of London. This Jewish community had lived for centuries in Spain and Portugal but at the very end of the fifteenth century were expelled *en masse* by royal edict. They resettled in North Africa, the New World and across northern Europe.

Prior to their expulsion, these Sephardic Jews were subject to harsh treatment by the authorities such that many hid their Jewish identity. They blended in with Christians by eating fried fish on Fridays and keeping some for cold consumption on their Sabbath. Traditionally, the fish was lightly coated with a mix of flour and ground chickpeas, but in its migration to London it was coated in a batter of flour and eggs. In his book, *Shilling Cookery for the People*, the famed London chef, Alex Soyer, wrote of such fried fish in 1886:

> *This is another excellent way of frying fish, which is constant-ly in use by the children of Israel and I cannot recommend it too highly; so much so, that various kinds of fish which many people despise are excellent cooked by this process; in eating them many persons are deceived, and would suppose them to be the most expensive of fish. . . .*

At the time that fried fish was being sold as a street food in London, chipped fried potatoes were sold by commercial fryers in the new industrial towns in the north of England. However, fried

Photo credit: Dron G

potatoes had permeated throughout England and Soyer describes the cooking of French fries or chips:

> *Peel a pound of potatoes, cut them into very thin slices, almost shavings; put some fat into a frying pan; when very hot but not burning, throw the slices in, not too many at a time as they will stick together; move them about with a skimmer, to prevent it. When a nice brown colour, take them out and sprinkle some salt over them.*

That sounds like a modern day chipper! There is an ongoing argument as to how fish and chips came together. Some argue it was in Lancashire and others that it was in London. It matters little to most people who simply enjoy fish and chips, a very precious food of the British. It was exported to Ireland by Italian immigrants and to this day fish and chip shops in Dublin have a very strong Italian tradition. Dublin's first fish and chip shop was opened by Giuseppe Cervi in the 1880s on Great Brunswick Street. Local lore has it that his wife would point at the fish and then the chips asking, 'Uno di questo, uno de quello?' or 'One of this, one of that?' giving rise to the Dublin slang for fish and chips as a 'one and one'.

Fish and chips dishes, traditionally wrapped in newspaper which is now prohibited for health reasons, were cheap and nutritious, if by that you mean they provided ample amounts of carbohydrates, fat and protein to the otherwise nutritionally challenged poorer classes. A second reason may relate to dentition. In the mid to late nineteenth century when the English chipper boomed, tooth decay and extraction was commonplace and carried out by barbers or blacksmiths until the introduction of The Dentists Act in 1878. Fish and chips are soft and don't require chewing, ideal for those with missing or bad teeth.

The potato chip in the US, or crisp in these parts, is said to have originated in Saratoga Springs, 190 miles upstate from New York city. George Crum was the chef at Moon's Lake House, and on one occasion the steamboat and railroad millionaire, Cornelius Vanderbilt, was among the diners. When his meal arrived, Vanderbilt refused to eat it as the French fries were cut too thick. Crum decided to strike his revenge by preparing the thinnest potato slices he could manage and to deep fry them. Van-

Photo credit: Gunel Farhardli

derbilt, far from being angry at this gesture, raved about the dish. The owner of the restaurant Harriet Moon decided to make these chips a signature dish and served them in paper cones. Of course, this story is disputed but it is still widely cited.

Potatoes remain one of the most widely eaten crops in the world. Unlike grains, pasta and rice, potatoes don't travel and are thus hard to brand to the benefit of the multinational food industry. You will see many advertisements on television for pasta, different rice and cereal products from breads to mueslis, but you won't see an advertisement for potatoes. Sadly, in many European countries the consumption of potatoes by younger consumers is declining with the advent of easily prepared rice or pasta with all sorts of attractive sauces. But when these younger people start to think of food in terms of sustainability and high nutrient density, the local potato will again have its day.

Chapter 15

Chocolate: Sins, Priests and Magic

Chocolate

from My Sister Steals My Toys

By Steve Hanson

*I built my house of chocolate
from the shutters to the walls.
My doors are solid chocolate
at the end of chocolate halls.*

*I dust with chocolate pudding.
I bath in chocolate lakes.
And when I'm feeling tired,
I sleep on chocolate cakes!*

*My chairs are chocolate muffins.
My lamps shine chocolate light.
My grand piano's cocoa. . .
if you're hungry have a bite.*

*I decorate with chocolate
down to the chocolate wreath
I guess that's why my mouth
is filled with chocolate teeth.*

There are every day foods, foods that we should eat sparing-ly and foods we should eat frequently, foods that are festive, foods that are bargains and foods that we might try out. And then there are treats. For some, the treat is very special: champagne, a precious truffle or a hamper of fine delicacies. But there is one treat that is inexpensive, that can be enjoyed by all ages and which can come in many forms and shapes – chocolate. It has a mouthfeel that is simply velvet, an utterly absorbing aroma and a capacity to be treasured, hot as in a chocolate fondant or cold as with sprin-kles on an ice cream. We can make it soft or hard, sweet or bitter, dark or bright. Chocolate is indulgent and comes with a tincture of seduction and magic. 'The Lady loves Milk Tray' is the byline of one famous chocolate advert and yet another iconic brand whis-pers 'Black Magic'. In her book *Chocolat*, Joanne Harris explores the conflict between indulgence and guilt through the eating of chocolate. The chocolate indulgence comes from the small choco-late shop she establishes in a rural French town and the guilt comes from the local Catholic priest. She writes:

> *Before Christ – before Adonis was born in Bethlehem or Osiris sacrificed at Easter – the cocoa bean was revered. Magical properties were attributed to it. Its brew was sipped on the steps of sacrificial temples; its ecstasies were fierce and terri-ble. Is this what he fears? Corruption by pleasure, the subtle transubstantiation of the flesh into a vessel for debauch? Not for him the orgies of the Aztec priesthood. And yet, in the va-pours of the melting chocolate something begins to coalesce – a vision. . . . Scrying [fortune telling] with chocolate is a difficult business. The visions are unclear, troubled by rising perfumes which cloud the mind.*

Chocolate, with its rising perfumes, was the great prize of the Mayans and later the Aztecs. They mastered the cultivation, harvesting and processing of the cocoa bean from whence chocolate is derived. They did so using food technology that we understand today such as aerobic and non-aerobic fermentation and dehydration. But they had to learn these tricks of the trade the hard way and would have invested many centuries perfecting the process. Theirs was one of long, observational-driven and patient understanding of the optimal cocoa pod processing. Their quest for perfection was driven not by profit but for the common good.

Harvesting and Processing the Cocoa Bean

The cacao tree grows in equatorial rainforests 20° north or south of the equator. The formal name of the cacao tree is *Theobroma Cacao, theobroma* coming from the Greek for 'food of the gods'. The pods grow on the bark of the tree, connected by a short bud. When harvesting, care must be taken not to sever the link between the pod and the bud, such that only the pod falls to the ground. The buds will go on to produce another pod. Cacao pods are shaped like a rugby ball, about the length and width of an adult hand. The shell or rind is rough and about 3 centimetres thick. Once harvested, the cocoa pods will begin a lengthy process toward chocolate. The very first thing that must be done is to split the cocoa pod and to scoop out the gooey interior known as baba de cacao, a gelatinous mixture of various sugars, in which 20 to 40 cocoa beans will be found.

The whole of the interior, baba and beans are put in large wooden boxes with some drainage holes in the bottom and covered. Natural yeasts, found on the surface of baba de cocoa, will start the fermentation process, converting the sugars to alcohol. As the oxygen becomes depleted, a second fermentation follows which

Photo credit: Narong Khueankaew

now converts the remaining gooey sugars to lactic acid. The mixture is then moved to a new box which aerates the mass and this now leads to the third stage of fermentation, in which another set of bacteria are fostered converting the ethanol to vinegar. This fermentation process, which is primarily confined to the baba and not the beans, takes about 6 to 10 days. The heat of the fermentative process and the slow appearance of the acidic environment leads to an interaction between the beans, which now have tiny holes etched into their hull by the acids, and the fermented baba. The chemical interactions are complex but are absolutely fundamental to the flavour of chocolate. When fermentation is over, the once purple beans are now a very light shade of lavender. The whole mush is turned out on sheets of wood or large leaves to dry. The quality of the fermentation process determines the quality of the finished product. The beans are now ready for roasting. Up to this point, chocolate production today differs little from that in the ancient Aztec civilisation.

Roasting was carried out by Aztec women in large pans over hot coals for about two hours. The first grinding is coarse and allows the hulls of the beans (also called nibs) to be separated by winnowing. The beans are then finely ground and this process generates sufficient heat to melt the cacao butter in the beans, resulting in a paste rather than a powder. Sugar is added and the mixture is allowed to solidify and is moulded into a square slab. It is important to note that cacao refers to the tree and its fruit, but when the fruit is heated and prepared as a drink it is then referred to as cocoa. Portions of this slab were then mixed with flavourings such as chillies or vanilla and dissolved in hot water. The women would repeatedly pour the liquid from one cup to another to create a foamy broth on top. Instead of mixing the ground paste with water, it could be dried and either stored or transported.

Cacao Beans in the Life of the Aztecs

They say that money doesn't grow on trees but it did for the Mayans. Cacao beans were a currency: 200 beans for a male turkey, 30 beans for a small rabbit or 3 beans for a turkey egg or an avocado.

On August 15, 1502, Christopher Columbus reached what we know today as San Salvador and had his first encounter with Mayan civilisation. His son, Ferdinand, noted in his diary that:

> *They seemed to hold these almonds at a great price; for when they were brought on board ship together with their goods, I observed that when any of these almonds fell, they all stooped to pick it up, as if an eye had fallen.*

These almonds, as he called them, were cacao beans and they were a currency and also strongly associated with their Gods and attendant religious rituals. The Aztecs also had an extraordinary understanding of the therapeutic properties of plants, including cacao, and the Aztec emperor had a botanic garden where this science of apothecary was studied. Bernardo de Sahagun, the Jesuit missionary who studied Mesoamerican food, documented the use of cocoa drinks in the traditional Aztec medicine. Excessive intakes would cause derangement and confusion, while in moderation it was refreshing and invigorating. Other experts of the day attributed many curative properties to cocoa – diseases of the liver and kidney, gout, haemorrhoids, dental diseases to mention a few. Moctezuma II, the Aztec emperor, was very fond of cocoa and the Spanish conquistador, Bernal Diaz del Castillo, wrote:

> *Fruit of all the kinds that the country produced were laid before him; he ate very little, but from time to time a liquor prepared from cocoa, and of an aphrodisiac nature, as we were told, was presented to him in golden cups. . . . I observed a number of jars, above fifty, brought in, filled with foaming chocolate of which he took some.*

Creoles and Chocolate

As ever in wars of conquest, many of the conquered and their conquerors came to form partnerships. Thus Spanish conquistadors inter-married and it was these Creoles who adapted chocolate in ways that would influence Western chocolate habits. In general, the newly arrived Europeans had little time for chocolate. The Italian historian Girolamo Benzoni declared that 'It seemed more a drink for pigs, than a drink for humanity'. In time, however, inter-racial marriage led to the uptake of cocoa drinking, as noted by the Jesuit José Juan de Acosta who described chocolate as 'skumme or froth that is very unpleasant to taste' and then went on to make the point that the Spaniards 'are very greedy of this Chocolate'.

The traditional Aztec chocolate was made as follows: The cocoa beans were ground to a paste and at this point finely ground maize might be added as a thickener as well as flavours such as vanilla, cinnamon, chilli pepper and local flower petals. The paste would be dissolved in water and honey added to sweeten it. It was then poured between two containers from a height to create a foam on top. The creoles made some changes to this process over time but the changes were subtle.

Firstly, the local habit of drinking chocolate cold was abandoned in favour of hot chocolate, and it may be the case that the simultaneous advent of coffee and chocolate to the West, even at a distance from home, co-promoted the popularity of hot drinks with powerful aromas and with a slightly bitter taste.

A second adjustment was to replace honey with sugar and to change some of the spices and flavourings to ones more familiar to Europeans. Thus the chilli pepper lost out to black pepper, while cinnamon and the thickener maize lost out to ingredients such as almonds and egg yolks. Another favourite with the Creoles was the spice blend known as achiote which gave colour and flavour, its ingredients being annatto, cumin, pepper, coriander, oregano, cloves and garlic.

Finally, the habit of creating a foam by repeated pouring the hot drink from vessel to vessel was replaced with a whisk known as a molinillo. The paste that was made from the beans was dried for ocean transport. As chocolate began to pervade Europe, many adaptations to these recipes were introduced. Thus, when Napoleonic embargos on imports limited the availability of chocolate in Italy, the Turin chocolatier Michele Prochet extended cocoa powder with ground hazelnut creating the now famous Piedmont chocolate 'gianduiotto'.

Chocolate and the Catholic Church

The arrival of chocolate into Europe is shrouded in the many disputes as to exactly where and when chocolate appeared. Sophie Coe argues that in 1544, the New World-based Dominican friars took a delegation of Mayan nobles to visit Prince Philip in Spain and presented the King with chocolate. Coe records the first formal customs declaration in 1585 for a shipment of chocolate from Veracruz the Seville, the designated ports through which all trade between Spain and the New World had to travel.

The constant flow of traders, sailors, soldiers, explorers and civil servants between the two worlds meant that there was ample opportunity for the promotion of chocolate as a drink. But one of the big sticking points for Catholic Spain and Italy, where chocolate almost certainly first appeared, was the question of whether taking chocolate broke the fast, be it the Lenten fast or pre-sacramental fast. The Dominicans and the Jesuits were strongly represented among the missionaries of the New World and had opposing views on chocolate. The Jesuits, who had an undeclared interest in the matter, defended chocolate consumption arguing that it was medicinal and would prevent fainting at lengthy high masses.

The Dominicans were much more conservative and regarded chocolate as an aphrodisiac which would undermine moral standing, most particularly of women. This latter view was very strongly held among the Dominicans and harks back to the disputes between the Catholic clergy and the proponents of chocolate as a wholesome beverage. Chocolate had become strongly associated with sex in the early period of the Creole adoption of chocolate.

The English explorer and Dominican friar, Gage, describes how some Creole women insisted on their servants bringing them cocoa drinks to sustain them during lengthy high masses:

> *The women of that City it seems pretend much weaknesses and squeamishness of stomach, which they say is so great, that they are not able to continue in the Church while a Masse is briefly huddled over, much less while a solemn high Masse (as they call it) is sung, and a Sermon preached, unless they drink a cup of hot Chocolatte, and eat a bit of sweet-meats to strengthen their stomachs. For this purpose it was much used by them to make their maids bring to them to Church in the middle of Masse or Sermon a cup of Chocolatte, which could not be done to all, or most of them without a great confusion and interrupting both Masse and Sermon.*

Despite the interventions of Gage and his fellow Dominican friars, the Bishop excommunicated all those who would bring chocolate into his religious services. The women folk responded by abandoning the Bishop and 'took themselves to the Cloister Churches, where by the Nuns and Friers they were not troubled nor resisted'. The Bishop fell ill and all the prestigious physicians were unanimous in their view that he had been poisoned, with the finger of guilt pointed at the women of the city. Dominican Father Page concluded his account of these events thus:

> *The women of this City . . . have learned from the Devill many enticing lessons and baits to draw poor soules to sinne and damnation; and if they cannot have their wills, they will sure-ly work revenge either by Chocolatte or Conserves, or some faire present.*

These conservative prudish attitudes of the Dominicans were in contrast to those of the Jesuits. The two orders detested one another with the Dominican Friar Gage writing: 'But above all, is this envy and hatred found between Dominicans and the Jesuits' and that 'of the two, the Jesuits is more bold and obstinate in malice and hatred'. And so the Vatican was faced with two powerful forces arguing over chocolate and religious fasts. Eventually, a Jesuit leaning Pope, Alexander VII, came down in favour of the Jesuits with the famous law *Liquidum non frangit jejunum* (Liquids do not break the fast). But the argument rumbled on and in time required the opinions of no less than six successive popes before the issue waned. The Jesuits had significant and undeclared commercial interests in the New World as recalled by Joseph McCabe in his history of the Jesuits:

> *Saint Simon tells us that on one occasion a ship from South America discharged at the quays of Cadiz several boxes addressed to 'The Procurator-General of the Society of Jesus (Jesuits).' The contents were said to be chocolate, but the weight was extraordinary and the officials decided to open one of the boxes. It was, apparently, full of bars of chocolate, but the weight of each was so mysterious that they were more closely examined. They were bars of solid gold thickly coated with chocolate.*

The Jesuits were very centrally involved in the harvesting and export of cocoa produce and relied heavily on slave labour, taking native Amazonians and settling them in specially built villages. From these villages, indentured and enslaved natives would move deep into the Amazon region to pick cocoa beans. That same source goes on to point out that between 1743 and 1745, some 80 per cent of the exports from the Amazon region were controlled by the Jesuits with the cocoa produce accounting for four-fifths of their activity. Sophie Coe points out that when these cocoa pickers returned to their Jesuit-controlled villages, the fathers would ring a bell at a given hour to indicate that now was the time for conjugational rights. And to conclude the consideration of chocolate in the annals of the Jesuits, it was rumoured that the death of Pope Sixtus V in 1773, one of their most fierce opponents, was due to poisoning, courtesy of a gift of hot chocolate from the Jesuits.

Chocolate Arrives in Europe

The chocolate drink became a favourite in the Court of King Ferdinand II of Spain and, through the monastic network of the missionaries, cocoa spread rapidly across Europe. In Italy it was made fashionable by the Grand Duke Cosimo III of Tuscany and in France by the court of Louis XIV. Both Marie Antoinette in Versailles

Photo credit: Daniel Cuklev

and King George I in London operated their own chocolate kitchens. The Europeans played around with the ingredients to be added when the cocoa cake was dissolved for drinking. These included ground nuts, milk, sugar and different flavours. As was the case among the Mayans and Aztecs, cocoa became associated with medicinal properties. A flyer for one such chocolate house made audacious claims about the curative properties of chocolate for consumption and claims that it 'maketh Fatt and Corpulent, faire and aimeable'.

Chocolate and coffee arrived in Europe simultaneously and, as with coffee, many chocolate houses sprang up to cater for the social needs of the wealthier classes. In London, White's was the most celebrated chocolate house. William Lecky in his *History of England* in the eighteenth century records the gaming habits of the clientele of London's chocolate houses, most notably Mrs White's in Mayfair, and tells us that Lord Oxford 'never passed it without bestowing on it a curse as 'the bane of English nobility'.

Chocolate: Sex and Drugs

Just as the Spanish suspected that cocoa was used by the Aztecs to improve their sexual drive, so too did the Europeans. Both the Marquis de Sade and Giacomo Casanova used chocolate in their seduction of women. Sophie Coe in *The True History of Chocolate* outlines the writings of Louis Petit de Bachaumont on one of de Sade's parties:

> *M. le Comte de Sade . . . gave a ball. . . . Into the dessert he slipped chocolate pastilles so good that a number of people devoured them. . . . The ball degenerated into one of those licentious orgies for which the Romans were renowned. Even the most respectable of women were unable to resist the*

*uterine rage that stirred within them. And so it was that M.
de Sade enjoyed the favours of his sister-in-law, with whom he
fled to avoid the punishment he deserves.*

And there was a strange belief in the link between chocolate and
magic, perhaps fostered by the Aztec doctors who practised black
magic, which is forever present in the form of the iconic brand of
chocolate: Black Magic. Witchcraft and chocolate feature in accounts of the Spanish inquisition. Nina Haratischvilli, in her novel
The Eighth Life, documenting the history of Georgia, narrates the
story of her great-great grandfather, a chocolatier trained in Buda-
pest and Vienna, who ran a chocolate factory in Tbilisi. It is often
said of this novel that chocolate represented communism, ideal in
small doses but disastrous if overdone. Niza, who narrates the story in the novel, describes her great-great grandfather's chocolate
and its 'magic secret formula that would revolutionise the taste of
hot chocolate':

> *The taste was incomparable: savouring it was like a spiritual
> ecstasy, a supernatural experience. You melted into the sweet
> mass, you became one with this delicious discovery, you for-
> got the world around you, and felt a unique sense of bliss. As
> soon as you tasted this chocolate, everything was exactly as
> it should be. . . . This chocolate can only be enjoyed in small
> amounts.*

It wasn't the chocolate as such that would bring Nina's family
such bliss and calamity, nor was it the chocolate that allegedly poisoned Pope Sixtus and, most likely, it wasn't just simple chocolate
lozenges with which de Sade transfixed his guests or led to such
witchcraft as the Spanish inquisitors would uncover. But chocolate
was the vehicle and whatever myths surrounded its role in such

poisonings and drugging, it is the sinfulness of indulgence in chocolate together with the appropriate comeuppance that fitted the moral model of the time.

The Industrialisation of Chocolate

Cocoa was purchased by the European middle classes as roasted cocoa beans which then had to be ground into the cake that would be dissolved in hot water or milk with whatever flavours and textures the customer preferred. This process was a skill in itself since this is where the heat of the grinding melted the fat in the cocoa beans. This task was often undertaken by workers who would take the necessary equipment from house to house. In France, Sephardic Jews (Jews of Iberian descent) were responsible for this trade. Dried fermented cacao beans contain about 5 per cent water, 55 per cent fat and the rest as protein and starch. To give some idea of the consistency of this, peanut butter is 2 per cent water, 50 per cent fat

Photo credit: Jakub Kapusnak

and the rest is protein and starch. However, the peanut fat is very oily and will stay liquid until about fridge temperature. In contrast cocoa butter is solid at room temperature but melts in the mouth (34° to 38°c).

The industrialisation of chocolate manufacture began in 1761 when Joseph Fry of Bristol established a cocoa mill which was water-powered. The resultant paste was very high in fat with all of the hull material from the bean coverings removed by repeated grinding in the mill. Sixty years later, a Dutch chocolatier, Coenraad van Houten developed a technique for halving the level of cocoa fat in this paste. This meant that whereas half the liquor was fat and roughly half was non-fat solids, now only a quarter was fat and about three-quarters was non-fat solids. Now the product could move from a thick liquor or paste to a powder. Chocolate processing would be transformed.

The new powder could be mixed with water to reconstitute the cocoa liquor and with some cocoa, some vanilla and emulsifiers like egg yolks added back in and, voila, when cooled, you had room temperature solid dark chocolate. In time, another recipe would develop and this would come to totally dominate the popular chocolate market. Once again the lower fat cacao liquor would be reconstituted and this time, along with the sugar, vanilla and emulsifier, milk fat and milk solids were added and you had milk chocolate. And finally we had white chocolate, but is it really chocolate? It was exactly the same as milk chocolate but no cacao liquor, only cacao butter.

The industry grew with names we are all familiar with today: Cadbury, Rowntree, Fry, Hershey, Suchard, Toblerone, Lindt, Leonidas, Nestlé and Cote d'Or to mention a few. Louis XIV of France dabbled in making Easter eggs without any great success.

The breakthrough in the manufacture of chocolate Easter eggs was made by Signora Giambone, a widow in the city of Turin who owned a small shop on Via Roma. She started by filling empty eggshells with melted chocolate, graduating to using hemispherical metal moulds.

In 1873, J.S. Fry & Sons in Bristol were the first to make Easter eggs in Britain, followed two years later by John Cadbury in Birmingham. Today, Brazil is the leader of Chocolate Easter eggs, closely followed South Africa, Germany, the UK, and France. In the UK, 10 per cent of all chocolate consumed occurs at Easter. It is somewhat ironic that the Christian tradition of decorating eggs at Easter, representing the resurrection of Christ, has been taken over by a chocolate Easter egg, the very luxury product that was seen as evil by early Christian missionaries.

Photo credit: Alex Souto Maior

Chapter 16

The Columbian Exchange:
A Miscellany of Foods

I Ate a Chilli Pepper

from Susie Bitner Was Afraid of the Drain

By Barbara Vance

I ate a chilli pepper
On a lunch time dare;
Sandy said I'd burn my mouth,
But I didn't care.

I ate that chilli pepper –
Not a seed to waste –
And won that truly silly bet,
But lost my sense of taste.

The Columbian exchange refers to the development of trade in new foods between the New to the Old World. We have already encountered two, potatoes and chocolate. But the list of foods that we routinely eat today that originated from the conquest of Mesoamerica is vast: tomatoes, maize, cassava, chillies, French beans, Lima beans, avocados, pineapples, artichokes, blueberries, cashews, papayas, pecans, pumpkins, squash, turkey and vanilla, to mention the main ones. Some of these, including potatoes, gave a new source of calories other than wheat and rice. Others enhanced vegetable dishes and desserts, and some enhanced flavour. The list is so long that only a few will be mentioned in this chapter.

Tomatoes

Two related crops were brought back to Spain following the conquest of Central America: the tomato and the tomatillo. Both were small, bitter and green. In time they would evolve to what we know today as tomatoes, but time was needed because on arrival in Europe, the tomato had a tough beginning. Both tomatoes and tomatillos would also feature heavily in Italy, given that Spain controlled Naples, Sicily, Sardinia and Milan. In 1548, Cosimo de Medici, the Grand Duke of Tuscany, was presented with a basket of tomatoes which baffled the Duke and his guests who had never seen them before.

The history of the emergence of the tomato as a culinary delight runs parallel in both the Iberian and Italian peninsulas. The natives of Mexico used what we now call a tomatillo and largely ignored the tomato. The tomatillo is green in colour and it has a soft, paper-like outer husk, not unlike a Chinese lantern, and both belong to the same botanical family. Mexicans used the tomatillo in sauces, salsas and stews. In its raw form it is acidic but when cooked, it imparts a tart taste and a herbal aroma to the dish.

The history of the tomato is befuddled by its confusion with the tomatillo, and the Florentine botanist Giovanvettorio Soderini was one of the few who, in 1590, had a clear distinction between the two. For the rest of this chapter, this confusion is resolved by a focus solely on the tomato. In both Spain and Italy, the tomato would not become a widely cultivated crop, consumed by all, for about

Photo credit: Markus Spiske

another two centuries. David Gentilcore, in his book on the history of the tomato in Italy, lists several reasons why it took so long for the popular uptake of the tomato. The climate and soil conditions in northern Italy were unsuited for its growth, and since wild tomatoes are trailing plants their proximity to the ground meant that they were considered as a 'cold' food, suitable only for the peasants. Tomatoes were highly perishable and lacked any appealing flavour. In addition, tomatoes were not at all filling as was the case with root crops. But it was their perceived toxicity that was the main initial barrier to their uptake. Tomatoes were initially green and were associated with apples, hence the term *pomodoro* meaning golden apples. Historical records show that the green tomato had become 'reddish in colour like flame' by 1583.

The tomato belongs to the *Solanaceae* family of flowering plants, many of which are edible, while others are considered poisonous. The family includes such common foods as eggplant, capsicum (paprika, chilli pepper), potato and tomato. However, many of them are also poisonous such as deadly nightshade (*bella donna*), jimson weed (devil's snare) and mandrake, all of which are rich in neurotoxins. Because of this perceived toxicity, the tomato also attracted the attention of the medical profession who were at that time absorbed in the relative curative properties of foods and herbs. In 1739, the French royal physician, J.B. Chomel, commented on the medicinal properties of the tomato:

> *This plant is about of the same quality as the mandrake, but for internal use, less dangerous; for in some parts of Europe, among others in Italy, its fruit is eaten preserved with vinegar, or salt or pepper; it is bad enough food. I know of persons who steep the fruit in olive oil which they use for contusions, tumours, rheumatism and sciatica. It is a resolutif and anodyne. The juice of the entire plant is used externally in inflammation of the eyes and other parts.*

Hunger, they say, is the best sauce and in both Spain and Italy events would sharpen the appetite of the poor in the seventeenth and eighteenth centuries, a period when the tomato was beginning to attain some acceptability. The seventeenth century saw a major decline in the Spanish empire with the Dutch revolt, the secession of Portugal from the Iberian Union, the problem of maintaining far off colonies and the mass expulsion of Spain's Muslims. The loss of over 300,000 Moriscos (Spanish Muslims and new Christians) led to a collapse in Spanish agriculture with the neglect of the sophisticated irrigation canals and aqueducts that had been brought to Spain by the Arabs. Significant famines followed and in the space of a century, from about 1600 to 1700, the Spanish population fell from under 10 million to 7.5 million.

Food was short and, where they could be found, tomatoes were eaten. Similarly, famines of the eighteenth century in Naples influenced tomato consumption. According to the Italian Gaetano Jerna, 'probably the famous famines of 1745, 1771 and 1774 induced the people of southern Italy to take confidence in the tomato.' In his book, *The Flora of Spain* (1784), the Spanish botanist and physician José Quer described the advance of the tomato from the world of poisons and medicines to a highly regarded food in both Spain and Italy:

> *The majority of the ancient authors are of the opinion that they ought to be included in the ranks of poisonous plants rather than among the medicinal plants. But the experience in our peninsula shows that this is all wrong; and although in Italy, and particularly in Naples, they are eaten with dressing in salads, among us, they are without comparison with other vegetables in their season, for use in sumptuous and delicate dishes, seasonings, the most delightful of foods and forming a delicious sauce which gives an agreeable flavour to cocida and other dishes.*

Slowly but surely, the tomato took off and by the nineteenth century tomatoes were widely consumed all across Italy. Tomatoes are harvested in September and October and although this is entirely a mechanical process today, at the beginning tomatoes were harvested by hand. The enormous volume of perishable tomatoes needed to be preserved and the traditional approach was to make passata. Basically, tomatoes are simmered in hot water to inactivate spoilage enzymes. The water is strained away and the tomatoes are put through a special press which separates the skin and seeds from the juice which is bottled and simmered to pasteurise the liquid, which is then sealed and will last the winter.

In addition to passata, tomatoes could be sundried in the ancient tradition, and for that purpose unripe tomatoes were generally used.

At the heart of many Italian pasta sauces are those based on tomatoes which were introduced into Europe in the sixteenth century. However, it would take several centuries for tomato breeders to produce a tomato with less tartness and more sweetness and for tomatoes to emerge as a component of the Italian diet, eaten for its own properties rather than as a condiment. From the early seventeenth century on, tomatoes were used as a seasoning to replace sour grapes in those recipes which required a tart seasoning. It was not until the eighteenth century that tomatoes appeared in a recipe book, and only in the nineteenth century that pasta and tomatoes began to emerge as a standard dish of the Neapolitan region.

Francesco Cirio was a young entrepreneur who shipped a significant quantity of fresh Italian produce to markets in Paris and London. In 1856, he became one of the first to commercialise the invention of Nicolas Aperture, the canning method of food preservation. Cirio now exported huge volumes of tinned whole tomatoes across the world, most notably to the US where the burgeoning Italian community held the tomato in high regard.

In the US, tomatoes would enter the home in two new ways. The first is with ketchup, originally marketed by the Heinz company. Homogenise a tomato and leave it to stand and it will quickly rot. Thus to supply the mass market with a tomato sauce, it needed to be preserved. The old Italian way was to sun dry or to homogenise and sterilise. Heinz would use salt and vinegar to preserve the ketchup. The tomato is already acidic so the addition of vinegar makes it a very acidic food with a pH of about 3.8, not that much higher than the pH of freshly squeezed lemon juice (pH less than 3). Thus sugar is added as in the traditional cookery approach to balance sweet and sour.

The next great route to the tomato entering the mass US diet was in 1895, when the Campbell company launched its first canned soup using the beefsteak tomato. In 1897, Dr J.T. Dorrance at Campbells developed a condensed soup which effectively meant that water was lowered, increasing its flavour. The colours of the tin were black on top, brown on the bottom with a white circle in the middle with a red tomato. However, in 1898, a Campbell executive by the name of Herberton Williams attended a football game between Cornell University and Penn State and was so taken by the bold red and white colours of the Cornell team that he managed to have a new label designed for Campbell's tomato soup. Andy Warhol made it an icon. Warhol had wanted to create a painting based on comic characters but was beaten to it by his contemporary in the new art movement, Roy Lichtenstein. His friend, Muriel Latow, suggested two new ideas: paint money or a soup can. Apparently, Warhol had consumed Campbell's soup prepared by his mother for 20 years. The rest is history.

Tomatoes have seeds and these seeds are borne with the fruit like apple or orange seeds. The seeds of vegetables on the other hand emerge from flowering parts of the plant, external to the edible part. So tomatoes were fruits for all intents and purposes. However, the common interpretation in the US was that it couldn't be a fruit since no desert was made from it. Rather it was eaten in salads or incorporated into dishes and even made into soups and sauces. All of this is outside the scope of fruits. In 1883, a Commission was appointed in the US to implement the Mongrel Tariff Act and to reconsider tariffs on different goods imported into the US.

A 10 per cent tariff was placed on all vegetables imported into the US. One such importer, Hix from New York, took his case to the Supreme Court to argue that tomatoes were fruits not vegetables but the court ruled against him.

> *Botanically speaking, tomatoes are the fruit of a vine, just as are cucumbers, squashes, beans and peas. But in the common language of the people, whether sellers or consumers of provisions, all these are vegetables, which are grown in kitchen gardens, and which, whether eaten cooked or raw, are, like potatoes, carrots, parsnips, turnips, beets, cauliflower, cabbage, celery and lettuce, usually served at dinner in, with or after the soup, fish or meats which constitute the principal part of the repast, and not, like fruits generally, as dessert.*

As the English humourist and journalist Miles Kington tells us:

> *Knowledge is knowing that a tomato is a fruit. Wisdom is knowing not to put it in a fruit salad.*

Tomatoes remain a very important part of the global diet and because of its vulnerability to post-harvest deterioration, most tomatoes will be consumed in the preserved form as sun dried tomatoes, passata, tomato ketchup or tinned tomatoes. As Elizabeth David wrote in her book *An Omelette and a Glass of Wine*:

> *A world devoid of tomato soup, tomato sauce, tomato ketchup and tomato paste is hard to visualize. Could the tin and processed food industries have got where they have without the benefit of the tomato compounds which colour, flavour, thicken and conceal so many deficiencies? How did the Italians eat spaghetti before the advent of the tomato? Was there such a thing as tomato-less Neapolitan pizza?*

And tomatoes have always been a good source of humour. Uma Thurman in the movie *Pulp Fiction* tells the joke:

> *Three tomatoes are walking down the street – a papa tomato,*
> *a mama tomato and a little baby tomato. Baby tomato starts*
> *lagging behind. Papa tomato gets angry, goes over to Baby*
> *tomato and squishes him . . . and says 'Ketchup!'*

Maize

Maize was unknown in Europe prior to the Columbian exchange. The Spanish colonists called it Indian corn but its native name was *mahiz*. Maize wasn't a staple food just for the Aztecs and Incas. Many native tribes in North America cultivated maize from the Iroquois in the northeast to the Navaho in the southwest. The colonising English would not have survived their early entry to the US without maize. However, it would be the Spanish who would take it to Europe.

Maize was abundant when the Spanish armies entered the Aztec empire and they noted the great reverence the natives paid to this crop and its dominant role in their diet. Maize kernels were softened by cooking in boiling water. In the case of the Aztecs and other natives of Central and South America, lime was added to the water, while in North America, the native tribes cooked these kernels with added ash from burned wood. The two most popular foods made from maize were tortillas and tamales. Maize does not contain gluten and so cannot be made into a dough to rise and form a bread. Instead, small balls of maize dough are flattened and cooked to produce a tortilla, which were then filled with turkey and vegetables and undoubtedly chillies.

Tamales involve wrapping a dough around some filling and binding it together with leaves such as banana leaves for steaming.

Photo credit: bhofack2

There is a detailed account of the Aztec food chain in the 12 volume *Historia General de las Cosas de Nueva España* (General history of the Things of New Spain)' compiled by a Spanish Franciscan missionary, Fray Bernardino de Sahagún (1499–1590). Generally referred to as the Florentine Codex, it is regarded as one of the finest manuscripts of its day. It is presented in two columns per page, one in Spanish and the other in Nahuatl, the native language of the Aztecs. It describes the many foods of the Aztecs: maize, potatoes, chillies, squash, chocolate, turkey, avocados, beans and spices such as vanilla and oregano. Avocados were often eaten in the form of guacamole, disparagingly referred to by the Spaniards as 'poor man's butter'. Indeed, de Sahagún described the use of maize to make popcorn which was a central part of Aztec ceremonies and writes:

And also a number of young women danced, having so vowed,
a popcorn dance. As thick as tassels of maize were their pop-
corn garlands. And these they placed upon their heads.

However, when the Spaniards took maize back to Europe it wasn't very well received. Its origins were somewhat misunderstood. In many parts of Europe it was referred to as Turkish corn, possibly because the merchants were from Turkey and all things Turkish were regarded as somewhat exotic. In the year 1597, the English naturalist John Gerarde declared that maize lacked nutrients and was 'a more convenient food for swine than men'.

However, in certain regions of Europe, in the northwestern region of the Iberian Peninsula and in the Lombardy region of Italy, poor soil conditions made maize an attractive new crop, easy to farm and with a hefty yield of nutritious starch. The easiest dish to prepare from maize was a simple gruel or porridge. In Italy, the cooks took it further and made polenta. This consists of a hot gruel which is poured on to a cold wooden board and eaten when cool. The exterior would be crusty and the interior soft and can be adorned with cheese and various sauces. However, for the peasants of Italy, in the northwest Iberian Peninsula and in southern France, maize was often eaten just as polenta or as a gruel. In North America, maize became a major crop and was eaten as grits in the southern states.

Maize in the human diet was about to generate a major medical problem that would haunt public health experts for centuries. Pellagra is a disease of the four 'Ds': dermatitis, diarrhoea, dementia and death, and today we know that it is due to a deficiency of the B-vitamin, niacin. In Italy, in the last decade of the nineteenth century, around 2,000 to 3,000 deaths occurred annually from pellagra. The disease was associated with poverty and poor sanitary conditions. The Italian authorities believed that some noxious or infectious agent, found in poor quality maize, was responsible for the disease for it was almost exclusively associated with reliance on polenta. However, the best data on this condition would come from the US where, as in Italy, the poor of the southern states relied heavily on maize with their diet described as the three 'Ms', maize, molasses and meat, where the meat was low quality fatty pork. As in Italy, it was believed to be a transmissible disease and fostered by the poor conditions of the peasantry.

Alfred Bollet MD, writing in the *Yale Journal of Biology and Medicine*, charts the history of pellagra in the US. From 1906 to 1940, when the cause of pellagra was discovered, Bollet estimates that about 3 million cases occurred with about 100,000 deaths. In 1914, the Surgeon General appointed the epidemiologist Dr Joseph Goldberg to explore the cause of the epidemic, and from the outset he suspected that it was caused by a poor diet. He noted that staff members at the Georgia State Sanatorium, caring for the pellagrins, those suffering from pellagra, did not themselves get the disease. He also noticed that they drank milk twice a day while the pellagra patients rarely got milk and were fed the monotonous three Ms diet. He started two studies among pellagrins, where their diet was enhanced by ample milk and the pellagra disappeared. The medics in the Association for the Study of Pellagra were not impressed and the idea that the diets of southerners were inadequate was ridiculed: 'Famine does not exist anywhere in the South and we fail to find a general increase in pellagra', wrote the United Daughters of the Confederacy to President Warren Harding.

But some were inclined to believe Goldberg and one was the Governor of Mississippi. He offered a pardon to prisoners at Rankin Prison Farm if they would take part in a study. Twelve prisoners, isolated in their own apartment to minimise any entry of infectious agents, were fed a diet of cornbread, grits, rice, collards and yams. Six volunteers developed pellagra and begged for an end to their suffering, one saying, 'I have been through a thousand hells'. And still his work was vilified with the governor accused of staging the whole exercise to get a pardon for one of his friends. Goldberg went on to hold 'filth parties' where he and his colleagues were daubed in faeces, skin scales and the urine of pellagrins with no case of pellagra ever arising from these parties. Finally, agricultural chemists working at the University of Wisconsin identified a new B-vitamin, niacin, which if absent from the diet would cause pellagra.

But why didn't the Aztecs and the Native Americans develop this condition? There are two likely reasons. The first is that the Incas used lime water to boil maize while the Native Americans added wood ash to the water. Both had the effect of making the water alkaline, the opposite of acidic, and under these conditions, niacin (vitamin B_3) in maize becomes less bound and more available to the consumer. This process is known as nixtamalization and, when the culinary traditions of the Aztecs were exported east to Europe and North to the US, the accompanying cooking technology was left behind! In the southern states of the US, grits, from coarsely ground maize is a very popular dish, indeed a signature dish of the Carolinas. Today, grits are referred to as hominy grits which are soaked in alkali-treated water. Perhaps an equally important reason was that these Mesoamerican peoples ate a varied diet, including turkey, squash and beans, all providing adequate intakes of niacin.

Besides the potato and maize, another starch crop that left South America for Europe was cassava, also known as manioc. Portuguese explorers took it to Africa where it was quickly adopted by local farmers, given that cassava can grow readily under poor soil conditions. When ground and processed, the product is called tapioca. But like maize, cassava needs to be carefully processed. Like many plants, it contains a neurotoxin to protect itself from herbivorous predators. The toxin in this case is a cyanide releasing compound and raw cassava is very toxic. The proper processing of cassava – drying, soaking in water, rinsing or baking eliminates this toxicity.

Beans, Nuts and Spices

Beans were part of the European food chain diet prior to the arrival of some new varieties as part of the Columbian exchange. Chick-peas, fava beans and lentils had their origins in the fertile crescent and were the only beans used in Greek, Roman and Persian empires and by the countries of Europe up until the late medieval period. The Columbian exchange would change that. Beans were part of the so-called trinity of foods that underlay the Aztec diet: maize, squash and beans. The two dominant families of beans (*Phaseolus*) were that of vulgaris and lunatus. The former included French beans, kidney beans, runner beans, string beans, haricot bean, navy bean, flageolet bean and many other lesser known varieties. The lunatus family was the Lima bean also known as butter beans.

Prior to the Columbian exchange, the range of nuts in the Medieval diet included walnuts, hazelnuts, pistachios, chestnuts, pine-nuts and almond. The New world would give us Brazil nuts, cashew nuts and peanuts which are not really nuts but belong to the pea family. That being said, peanuts are the dominant nuts of the modern western food chain. It was in Peru where peanuts were most extensively cultivated. The peanut would travel rapidly around the world. The Portuguese took them to West Africa and Spain to Asia. In Africa, ground peanuts were incorporated into soups to

Photo credit: Jenn Kosar

thicken them, and in Asia, ground peanuts were used to make the now famous satay sauce of Indonesia and Thailand. Peanuts, also known as groundnuts since they grow underground, yield peanut oil which can be heated to quite high temperatures, useful for rapid pan frying in Asian cuisine.

When west African slaves were transported to the US, they took with them peanuts and cultivated them in their little patches of land. The locals had little regard for peanuts and generally thought they would be best fed to livestock. The slaves brought with them the local Bantu word for peanut, *nguba*. During the American civil war, when food was limited, troops on both sides of the conflict took to eating peanuts with the Bantu name *nguba* now called goober by the confederate soldiers. When the civil war ended, peanuts became popular as a snack food all across the US and were sold roasted, as street food. From there they became the snack of choice at football and baseball games, and in vaudeville theatres where the cheap seats became known as the 'peanut galleries'.

In 1884, a Canadian, Marcellus Gilmore Edson, transformed roasted peanuts into a paste which would become peanut butter. Eleven years later, John Harvey Kellogg, the man who invented breakfast cereals, patented a peanut butter made from ground peanuts which had been boiled. Kellogg ran a sanitorium with a strict vegetarian ethos. The peanut butter offered an excellent way to deliver protein and calories to elderly patients who had lost teeth and could not eat hard food. In 1903, a businessman, Ambrose Straub of St. Louis, patented a peanut butter-making machine. The rest is history. The average daily intake of peanut butter in the US is 10 grams per day, or five teaspoons per week. In contrast, the average US daily intake of dairy butter is just six grams.

The voyages of Christopher Columbus were financed on the basis that he would 'not only propagate the Christian religion, but also certainly bring back pearls, spices and gold beyond anything ever imagined'. As regards spices, his search was in fact a dismal failure. It would be the conquistador Hernando Cortés who would find vanilla deep in the jungles of Central America and allspice in Jamaica. Vanilla is unique in that it is the only edible part of any of its family, the orchid. When picked, fresh vanilla has no aroma. That is produced during a lengthy curing process.

The second great spice that came from the west was the chilli. The history of the chilli goes back 8,000 years. The chilli belongs to the Capsicum family of which three dominated different regions of South America: the *C.Annuum* variety in Mexico, the *C.Pubescens* variety in the Andean regions of Bolivia and the *C.chinense* variety in the Amazonian region. Columbus and his team first encountered chillis on the island he called Hispaniola (today's Dominican and Haitian republics). The indigenous islanders, the Taíno, introduced the Europeans to the spice they called *ají* and Columbus chose to name them pimientos, after the term pimiento or black pepper. Herein starts the confusion over the terms chillies and peppers. Today we would describe the pimiento as a sweet bell pepper. We do know that Columbus brought back hot chillies to the Spanish monarchs because the conquistador Cortés recorded that the *ají* (chilli peppers) 'burned their tongue'.

The worldwide spread of the chilli was due to the Portuguese who colonised the eastern part of South America where the *capsicum chinense* was the dominant chilli. They first brought it to their African colonies and, following the rounding of the Cape of Good Hope by their explorer Vasco da Gama, the chilli made its way into the cuisine of India and South East Asia, most notably Thailand. As

Photo credit:Tang Yubing

with the peanut, its arrival in the southern US states was through the slaves from Portuguese and African colonies.

Chillies contain significant quantities of capsaicin compounds which are responsible for their very fiery mouthfeel. They are primarily located in the white membrane inside the chilli. Contrary to popular belief, the seeds do not contain capsaicin but can be contaminated by the proximity to the membrane or placenta.

The heat of chilli peppers is measured on the Scoville scale. A fixed amount of dried chilli is dissolved in alcohol to extract the capsaicin and naturally this alcohol extract is fiery hot. It is diluted gradually with sugary water until such time as the spiciness disappears. Thus a sweet pepper scores zero on the Scoville scale because it simply does not produce capsaicins. The jalapeño might score up to 10,000 on this scale while a habanero chilli could reach nearly 400,000. There is a global competition to find the hottest chilli and annually, the *Guinness Book of Records* is re-written with chillies now scoring over 2 million Scoville units. The ability to eat hot chillies is also competitive. The Carolina Reaper averages about 1.5 million Scoville units, and a New Yorker managed to eat 22 of these in just sixty seconds!

Chapter 17

Building the Larder

The Cupboard

By Walter de la Mare

I know a little cupboard,
With a teeny tiny key,
And there's a jar of Lollipops
For me, me, me.

It has a little shelf, my dear,
As dark as dark can be,
And there's a dish of Banbury Cakes
For me, me, me.

I have a small fat grandmamma,
With a very slippery knee,
And she's Keeper of the Cupboard,
With the key, key, key.

And when I'm very good, my dear,
As good as good can be,
There's Banbury Cakes, and Lollipops
For me, me, me.

For plants to survive, they need to develop ways to discourage the animal kingdom from eating them into extinction. To do that many plants have developed chemicals which are toxic to predators. Virtually all great poisons that bedevilled the rulers of old were plant extracts, such as hemlock, and almost all mind-altering substances were also plant-derived such as opium. Traditional Chinese medicine is based on the natural chemicals in plants and their impact on our various bodily functions. But not all of the plants chemical defences are repellents. Some use colour and aroma to encourage consumption of their seeds to have the outer half-digested by the predator, leaving the active seed to drop to the ground in their faeces. Almost all of our herbs and spices are part of the plants defensive and propagative mechanisms.

Herbs and Spices

Herbs are grouped around a small number of plant families. Herbs of the mint family include basil, bergamot, lavender, lemon balm, marjoram, mint itself, oregano, rosemary, sage and thyme and that list is not exhaustive. The cabbage family of plants include mustards, horseradish and wasabi. Herbs were never as precious as spices because they were native to Europe and abundant. The dry and rocky land of the Mediterranean was ideal for the growth of herbs, and thus it is not surprising that a lot of Mediterranean dishes rely much more on herbs than spices (basil, fennel, mint, oregano, tarragon, sage, garlic, thyme etc). We also have well known mixtures of herbs. From France come bouquet garni, comprising bay leaves, thyme and parsley; fines herbes, involving tarragon, chervil and chives; and herbes de Provence, comprising thyme, marjoram, fennel, basil, rosemary and lavender.

Spices were an entirely different matter as most would require considerable maritime trade. The ancient Greeks had access to the port of Aden and from there they would sail south in great sailing ships hugging the east coast of Africa as far as Mozambique and out to the nearby island of Madagascar. The Greek mariner and geographer Hippalus is credited with the discovery that the monsoon winds would facilitate sailing to the Malabar region of South India. Ships would sail from Aden around May, June and July, catching the early season monsoon winds that blew in a southeasterly direction, allowing them to reach India in just 40 days. There they would pick up precious stones, textiles and pepper, the spice that would dominate as a flavouring agent for millennia to come. Then in the period from November to March, the monsoon winds would reverse and they followed the northwesterlies back to Aden. The Romans eventually took over this route, sailing homeward up the Red Sea, then across land to the port of Alexandria and onwards across the Mediterranean to Rome.

These routes would eventually connect with the maritime trade of the far east, right to Macau on the eastern coast of China, creating what we now call the Spice Route. Goods were traded starting from China, then east to the Philippines, south to the Spice Islands (today's Maluku), then west through Borneo and Indonesia and then, hugging the coastlines of Malaysia, Thailand and Bangladesh, on to India and Sri Lanka then onwards to ancient Persia and to Egypt and along the coast of the Gulf of Arabia, south to Zanzibar and on to Madagascar. The reason for this complex trade route was that each highly valued spice was limited to growth and harvesting in just one location. Thus the Spice Islands specialised in the harvesting of nutmeg, mace and cloves, while cinnamon was what put Sri Lanka on the Spice Route. India and surrounding regions were a source of curry leaves, turmeric, cardamom, pepper, lemon grass, vanilla, ginger and the like. Cloves were an abundant crop in Zanzibar. Spices attracted great tales of how they were harvested, all involving great risk and the taller the tale the better, since the greater the risk of their procurement, the greater the price.

Cinnamon was held to be taken from the bark of trees by mythical birds from a distant unknown land. These birds then built nests so high in the forests or on the sheer faces of the mountainous cliffs of Sri Lanka that remarkable feats were needed to get the cinnamon from their nests. The poet Thomas Moore, who never set foot in South Asia, wrote a poem about the fabled royal beauty, 'Lalla Rookh' (tulip cheeks), in which he referred to the cinnamon bird:

> *Those golden birds that in the spice time drop*
> *About the gardens, drunk with that sweet food*
> *Whose scent hath lured them o'er the summer flood;*
> *And those that under Araby's soft sun*
> *Build their high nests of budding cinnamon.*

Just as herbs are commonly combined to orchestrate their individual flavours, so too are spices. From India we have garam masala which combines cumin, coriander, cardamom, black pepper, cloves, mace and cinnamon, and from China we have 5-spice: star anise, Sichuan pepper, cassia, cloves and fennel. Spices were much sought after in ancient times, not just for food but for natural Ayurvedic medicinal purposes, as aphrodisiacs, as embellishments to alcoholic drinks and as scents to escort the dead to Nirvana.

The Flavours of Herbs and Spices

Daniel Patterson and Mandy Aftel have proposed a compass to explain how herbs and spices contribute to the flavour of foods.

Photo credit: Melanie Dompierre

Spices lie at the north and are divided into four groups and I'll cite two examples of each: (1) earthy, such as saffron and cumin, (2) fresh, such as ginger and lemongrass, (3) sharp, such as the peppers and (4) sweet, such as anise and cinnamon; citrus is at the east comprising lemon and limes; herbs are at the south and are divided into two groups, the sweet such as dill, tarragon and basil and savoury such as sage, rosemary and thyme; flowers such as lavender or rose lie at the west. These categories help guide us in the use of herbs and spices in food preparation according to their four rules of flavour.

- Rule One is that similar ingredients need a contrasting flavour. Thus, a sweet herb with a sweet spice is not a good idea. Thus parsley and coriander have sweet flavours while parsley can be combined with three savoury flavours, rosemary, sage and thyme in the ancient recipe for stuffing.

- Rule Two states that contrasting flavours need a unifying flavour. They give an example of roasted cauliflower which is sweet, paired with roast cumin which is earthy with these two contrasting flavours unified with some lime juice.

- Rule Three states that heavy flavours need a lifting note. The example here is of braised greens which are described as bass or earthy, which are lifted with a citrus flavour, a typical example being boiled spinach with lemon juice.

- Rule Four states that light flavours need to be grounded. An example would be real balsamic vinegar which starts light and perky but with a loss of moisture gets an earthy and somewhat sweet flavour.

Sauces, Fats and Oils

Spices are generally incorporated into a dish during its preparation and cooking. Sauces on the other hand are part of the dish but are a complement to its main element. It is almost impossible to define sauces. Some are very liquid such as a vinaigrette. Others are pourable but much thicker such as gravy. Some are simply pastes such as horseradish sauce. But sauces have been an integral part of all cuisines worldwide and from very ancient times. Soy sauce was used by the Chinese many millennia ago. Fish sauce was widely used in Asia and was known by its Chinese name, *kê-tsiap*. Eventually, *kê-tsiap* would enter the English language as ketchup. French cuisine is renowned for its sauces and, in fine dining restaurants, the saucier or sauce maker plays a key role in the kitchen. The French cook Marie-Antoine Carême in the nineteenth century created a classification of sauces with four mother sauces: sauce tomat, béchamel, velouté, and espagnole. In the twentieth century, the distinguished chef August Escoffier added a fifth, hollandaise sauce. Each is a base sauce from which many others are created. For example, béchamel gives rise to mornay sauce, cheddar cheese sauce and mustard sauce along with many others. Hollandaise is the base for several sauces including béarnaise and dijon sauces.

While classic sauces were fundamental to French cuisine, the British stuck with gravy and it is said that it was anti-Catholic sentiment which protected Britain from French classic sauces. Gravies are widely used in all the former colonies of Britain but rarely elsewhere. Italian and French cuisine considered English food as bland and boring. The French politician Talleyrand stated:

> In France, we have three hundred sauces and three religions.
> In England they have three sauces and sixty religions.

Alberto Denti di Pirajno wrote that English cuisine was so poor in flavour that they 'call on sauces to furnish their dishes with that which they do not have'. Voltaire is believed to have said, 'the English have only one sauce, melted butter'. The French poet Paul Claudel wrote:

> There is only one word to say when faced with English cuisine: Pass!'

Of course, there was much derision in the opposite direction as well, with Norman Douglas, the English novelist claiming:

> Bouillabaisse is only good because cooked by the French, who, if they cared to try, could produce an excellent and nutritious substitute out of cigar stumps and empty matchboxes.

The English groaned at the thought of eating snails, frogs' legs and of course horses. Today, things are quite different and English restaurants win many Michelin stars.

Many of the most widely used sauces are commercially produced. Lea & Perrins Worcester sauce first appeared in the early 1800s. Its exact recipe remains a secret but includes vinegar, anchovies, molasses, tamarind extract and spices. Apparently, Lord Sandy returned from Bengal and asked two chemists, Mr Lea and Mr Perrins, to concoct a sauce for him according to a recipe he had discovered in Bengal. They were not impressed with the concoction and put the bottle into storage. Two years later they opened the bottle and noted a very interesting aroma. They dared to taste it and were thrilled with the sauce. Fermentation over that two-year period had transformed the sauce. The rest is history.

Tabasco sauce is attributed to Edward McIlhenny who allegedly invented it in 1868. Tabasco sauce is made up of mashed peppers which are salted and put in oak barrels for three years. The mash is strained, mixed with vinegar and stirred for several weeks. As noted earlier, the spiciness of food is measured in Scoville units and tabasco sauce rates at about 40,000 units, which makes it mildly hot. It is used to add zest and spiciness to meats and only a few drops are used at a time. People who eat spicy food on a regular basis will use up a small bottle of tabasco sauce fairly quickly. However, it has been said that among non-Hispanic, non-Cajun Americans, a standard bottle of tabasco sauce lasts longer that the average US marriage (12 years!).

Henry J. Heinz was born in Pittsburgh in 1844, one of eight children whose parents had emigrated to the US from Karlstad in Germany. By the age of nine, Heinz was selling his own horseradish sauce. He formed his own company and sold horseradish sauce and pickles in clear glass bottles, believing that would enhance consumer confidence in the product's quality. In 1876, he introduced his famous ketchup in iconic octagonal glass bottles and today almost 2 million are sold daily across the world. Another great Heinz product is mayonnaise, which is typically made with egg yolks, dijon mustard, oil and white wine vinegar or lemon juice. After the Duke de Richelieu had defeated the British at Port Mahon on the island of Menorca, his chef panicked at the absence of cream with which to make a sauce. He was obliged to create something using olive oil and came up with what we know today as mayonnaise. However, because this sauce was developed in Port Mahon, it was originally called mahonaise.

The list of sauces used in modern cooking is a long one: Pesto from Italy, salsa from Mexico, ponzu from Japan, pebre from Chile, curry from India and tahini from the middle east, just to mention a few. In contrast, the fats and oils used in cooking are much less numerous. Butter is the most widely used fat in cooking and has been covered in Chapter 4. It was traditionally the fat of northern Europe along with lard, tallow and duck fat. But in southern Europe it is olive oil that was dominant and this oil is now regarded as a key and essential component of every larder.

Olive Oil

Olive tree cultivation is ancient and olive oil is strongly associated with faith and legend. Odysseus was found lost and covered in brine and mire and was given clothes and olive oil by Nausicaa, who was enjoying the beach with her handmaids. He bathed in the sea and coated himself with olive oil and this haggard looking wanderer was transformed into a tall handsome athletic man by Athena, the goddess of olive oil. In Christian scripture, olive oil is extensively mentioned as in Exodus 30:23-25:

> *Take the finest spices: of liquid myrrh 500 shekels, and of sweet-smelling cinnamon half as much, that is, 250, and 250 of aromatic cane, 24 and 500 of cassia, according to the shekel*

of the sanctuary, and a hin of olive oil. And you shall make of these a sacred anointing oil blended as by the perfumer; it shall be a holy anointing oil.

Olive oil, wine and bread are the holy trinity of foods in early religions. Prophet Muhammad said, 'Eat olive oil and massage it over your bodies since it is a holy tree'. He also stated that olive oil cures 70 diseases. Seed oils require solvents to extract the oil from the seed and subsequent evaporation of the solvent leaving a core oil such as maize oil, sunflower oil or rapeseed oil. The olive is, however, a fruit and its pulp contains both oil and water and the oil is extracted mechanically rather than chemically.

For centuries, olive presses were used to extract the oil. First the olives are crushed using a stone grinder. The crushed olives form a slushy paste which is divided into hemp bags, each containing about 6 kilograms of the paste. The sides of the hemp bags are brought together to cover the top and these are then placed one on top of the other within a vertical press and slowly the screw is turned. The press begins to apply pressure and the oil and water seep out into a tank. The oil-water mixture is left to settle so that the oil floats to the top. It is then decanted into a centrifuge and spun to remove the last traces of water. This is cold pressed virgin olive oil.

To merit the term extra virgin olive oil, it must undergo taste evaluation to ensure that it is free from defects in taste and odour which is completed by a registered trained taste panel. They smell the

Photo credit: Alex Souto Maior

oil to detect odours through the nose, just like a wine buff, and then take a small amount into their mouth, hold it there and, opening the gums at the side, rapidly suck in air, a process known as strippaggio. This creates an emulsion of the oil and saliva and allows odours to reach the back of the nasal passage at the roof of the mouth.

The European Union regulates the classification of olive oil with three different categories of virgin olive oils:

- Extra virgin olive oil is the category with the highest quality. From an organoleptic point of view, it has no defects and is fruity. Its acidity level must not exceed 0.8 per cent.

- Virgin olive oil may have some sensory defects but at very low level. Its acidity must not exceed 2 per cent.

- Lampante olive oil is a lower quality virgin olive oil with an acidity of more than 2 per cent, with no fruity characteristics and substantial sensory defects. Lampante olive oil is used for industrial purposes and is not intended for the retail market.

An additional four categories are regulated: Refined olive oil; oil composed of refined olive oil and virgin olive oils; crude olive-pomace oil; and refined olive-pomace oil. So basically, there is extra virgin olive oil at the top with the lowest acidity (>0.8 per cent), then virgin olive oil with a higher acidity (<2 per cent) and then olive oil which is a blend of oils probably with refined olive oil (chemically extracted) and virgin olive oil. Extra virgin olive oil is best used in dressings and for marinades, while other oils are used for cooking.

Vinegar

All larders have one or more vinegars and basically vinegar is created when plant material is first fermented into alcohol and then into vinegar, the name coming from the French *vin aigre*, sour wine. The vinegars are ancient and arose because the harvest of perishable fruits and grapes would inevitably yield a surplus which, if left to its own devices, would rot. If the excess fruit was used to make vinegar it would yield a relish to many dishes and also act as a preservative for other foods through pickling. Grapes, apples, pears and the like are pressed to release a juice which can be fermented respectively into wine, cider and poire. What is left behind, mostly skin and seeds, is referred to as must. It is this must when twice fermented which yields vinegar. Cider vinegar is made from apple must, grape must is used to make red and white wine vinegar, and that of rice forms rice wine vinegar. But if there is a champagne of vinegars it is balsamic vinegar. A balm is a creamy substance used in ancient medicine and when derived from the sap of plants and trees is known as balsam, a balm with a very fruity, floral aroma. Balsamic vinegar concentrates and modifies the aroma of wine must, giving it a very distinctive flavour. Wine vinegars have an acidic taste while balsamic vinegar has a milder element of acidity. Balsamic vinegar hails specifically from the city of Modena in the northern region of the Italian province of Emilia-Romagna.

The traditional balsamic vinegars produced in these provinces are either the Aceto Balsamico Tradizionale di Modena or Aceto Balsamico Tradizionale di Reggio Emilia. Traditional balsamic vinegar takes up to a decade to produce and was, for centuries, a simple family venture. The must is first boiled to reduce it down and in so doing it intensifies the flavour and the colour and releases sugars for fermentation. The reduced must is then double fermented and aged in wooden barrels. As the material is stored in the barrels, water is lost, further intensifying flavour, aroma and colour. To reduce exposure to air, the contents of the barrel are transferred to a smaller barrel, and this is repeated several times with ever smaller types of wooden barrels, such as chestnut, cherry wood, ash, mulberry, and juniper. After 12 years or so, it is at last bottled and used in cooking.

The two traditional balsamic vinegars demand a premium price when sold, but they are mostly used by the family that lovingly created the product. However, the recent modern demand for balsamic vinegar required its commercial production and such vinegars are what most people buy when they buy a bottle of balsamic vinegar. On a commercial basis they try to follow the traditional method, but they use colouring and thickening agents and some flavours.

Between these two lies a superior balsamic vinegar but which does not include the word 'tradizionale', known just as Balsamic Vinegar of Modena. It has to contain a minimum of 20 per cent grape must with the additional use of red wine vinegar. It is fermented for a minimum of two months, not necessarily in wooden barrels, and uses ingredients such as caramel to darken the colour and a thickening agent to simulate the traditional product. The product has to be made in the city of Modena and enjoys European PGI (Protected Geographical Indication) status. The traditional balsamic vinegar of Modena enjoys POD (Protected Designation of Origin) status, a higher rank than PGI. An online Italian food store, Pepegusto, sells the traditional balsamic vinegar of Modena at €120 for 100 millimetres, whereas the non-traditional sells at €14 for 250 millimetres, a staggering 300-fold difference! The traditional balsamic vinegar of Modena is priced at about the same level as Chanel's Eau de Parfum No 5. There is also a white balsamic vinegar which is fermented and aged in stainless steel containers, but it is not a regulated balsamic vinegar.

Salt, Pepper and Mustard

Salt and pepper are standard features of most dining tables today. Salt is either drawn from beneath the earth's surface as brine wells or as salt mines, or from the sea and from salt lakes. The extraction of salt is ancient and, by and large, methods haven't changed much over time. Heat is used to dry salt and this can be with wind and sun or it can be by the use of fire. In the modern world dehydration is also achieved by vacuum treatment.

Salt was highly sought after for millennia both for its culinary purposes and for its preservative properties. Many foods are traditionally preserved in salt and salted fish was a very important part of the diet of ordinary Europeans for centuries.

There are many different types of salt. Normal table salt is very finely crystalline, and to keep it from clumping, anti-caking agents are added which allow the salt to flow freely. Sea salt is a flaky salt obtained from the seas and it has a crunchiness which adds to its appeal. Salt isn't always pure white. Hawaiian salt is mixed with red clay from the Waimea mountains, giving the salt a reddish tinge. Himalayan salt is derived from very ancient sea deposits and its mineral content gives it a slightly pink colour. Finally, kala namak is a black Indian salt which is heated with charcoal and mixed with local spices. However, the champagne of salts is fleur de sel. It is harvested from sea side marshes where, through natural climatic conditions, the salt begins to crystallise on the surface of the water. The salt is harvested by hand and it is believed that this was first perfected by Benedictines in the tenth century. What makes this salt so expensive is the harvesting by hand and the vagaries of weather since sunshine and wind are needed to dry up the shallow waters of the marshes and of course, rain is most unwelcome.

Standard table salt will cost €0.22 per 125 gram while Le Guerandais Fleur De Sel will be €8.99, a 40-fold price difference.

Salt is one of the five tastes we have and one that we enjoy. Sodium is after all an essential nutrient. We like salt to taste. For me there are three foods that would be unthinkable without salt: fresh tomatoes, eggs and mushrooms. But salt threshold is a personal taste and so it is always advisable to taste before adding salt. Ideally, salt is served on the table in a salt cellar and because salt was so precious, expensive and scarce, it was contained in very elaborate salt cellars. At a dining table of a noble person, the salt cellar would be placed perhaps a third the way down the table. Those below this mark would never dream of taking the salt for they were 'below the salt', simply as a consequence of the civil rank. The Bishop of Norwich, Joseph Hall, a well-known satirist, wrote thus in 1602:

> *A Gentle Squire would gladly entertain*
> *Into his house, some trencher-Chaplain:*
> *Some willing man that might instruct his sons,*
> *And that would stand to good conditions.*
> *First that He lie upon the Truckle-bed,*
> *Whiles his young master lieth ore his head*
> *Second, that he do, on no default,*
> *Ever presume to sit above the salt.*

Pepper is the world's most commonly used spice. *Piper nigrum* starts life as berries on a flowering shrub, native to south India but now grown across the world. It is an ancient spice going back to 2000 BCE. After the fall of the Roman empire, it was the Arabian empires that cornered this sought-after spice and they embellished the stories of the origin of the pepper claiming it was grown high in the Caucus mountains, protected by snakes, requiring the trees to be burned to frighten off the snakes and turning the white berry black.

Photo credit: Karolina Grabowska

The merchants of Genoa and Venice entered the pepper trade as did the Dutch and Portuguese, but it would eventually be the British East India Company that would dominate this trade. The pepper plant, *Piper nigrum*, gives us both black and white pepper. White pepper comes from berries that are picked at full ripeness following which they are soaked in water to ferment after which the outer hull is removed. This process yields a less pungent pepper.

Another essential component of any larder is mustard, probably of several varieties. The ground mustard seeds used are fiery hot and this flour is mixed with water to yield English mustard. The Romans were the first to mix mustard seeds with grape must vinegar to produce the hot condiment of mustard which they named 'burning must' or 'mustum ardens'. The Monks of St Germain des Pres in Paris are credited with maintaining the Roman mustard recipe. In 1752, a French mustard producer, Jean Naigeon, replaced the vinegar with verjuice, which is simply a pressed juice of unripe green grapes. The latter, whilst acidic, has a more gentle flavour than vinegar. Thus was Dijon mustard born. All in all, it is far milder than English mustard. American mustard is the least fiery of all and it gets its strong yellow colour from the addition of turmeric.

Epilogue

I am tomorrow, or some future day, what I establish today. I am today what I established yesterday or some previous day.
– James Joyce

The foods that have been covered in this book dominate the modern food chain, and it is somewhat humbling to think that hundreds of centuries ago these same foods were also eaten then. The manner in which they are cooked also remains largely the same: boiling, baking, roasting, steaming, cooling, grilling, toasting and frying. Their processing will also remain the same: peeling, shredding, dicing, slicing, mincing, blending and kneading. The mixing of food in dishes between proteins such as meats, fish and beans with carbohydrates, vegetables and sauces hasn't dramatically changed. So what of the future of these foods and their use in the kitchen or factory?

New recipes have come and gone but few new foods rarely appear. Margarine was invented in the nineteenth century and became, in time, a credible substitute but was always second fiddle to butter. Indeed, the butter-margarine dispute illustrates in a nutshell the problem of introducing an entirely new food into any traditional food chain. Margarine served the same function as butter, a spreadable fat. It cost a fraction of the price and was adopted by those for whom price was critical. But those who could afford butter had a decidedly snobbish attitude to it, scorning the inferior taste of margarine. The famed American chef Julia Child wrote:

> *I cooked artichokes with hollandaise sauce which is melted butter that's been whipped into a frenzy with egg yolks until it's died and gone to heaven. And let me say this. Is there anything better than butter? Think it over. Every time you taste something that's delicious beyond imagining, and you say, 'What is in this?' The answer is always going to be 'butter'. It's incredible. It's been whisked into submission, that's why. The day there's a meteorite heading toward the earth and we have 30 days to live, I am going to spend it eating butter. Here's my final word on the subject. You can never have too much butter.*

In the movie *Julie & Julia*, a story partly about Julia Child's life, her husband, a US diplomat in Paris, raises a toast to his wife at a Valentine's day dinner part they hosted:

> *Julia, you are the butter to my bread and the breath to my life. I love you, darling girl. Happy Valentine's Day.*

They were comfortably middle class and committed to the higher priced and then nutritionally risqué butter. So butter represents the 'natural' and margarine 'the technological'.

We are now facing a challenge to our choice of what to eat in order to reduce our animal-based foods, meat and dairy, to reduce greenhouse gas emissions from agriculture. We can choose either of two routes to achieve this aspiration. One route takes the 'natural' approach to achieve this goal using traditional foods: pulses, fruits, vegetables, mushrooms. Others will take the 'technological' solution and continue to eat 'animal products' but as analogue meat, lab-grown meat, clever plant-based burgers and sausages, plant-based fish and sushi and plant-based milk. Both solutions will prevail. The 'natural' route will be predominantly adopted by those who have the time, money, knowledge and wherewithal to serve up imaginative dishes based on plant foods. The 'technology' route will be mainly adopted by those who have significant time constraints and who prefer convenience. The tension between the two routes will be very much along the old butter-margarine lines.

This tension will spread into the local globalisation debate. Those opting for the natural approach will eschew globalisation solutions and favour locally sourced foods. But therein lies a problem. Farmers' markets will provide traditional foods, locally grown and suitable to the local agricultural systems, but there will be foods which will not be locally available. Where I live, citrus fruits, plus many nuts and pulses, have to be imported since they are not suited to the climate of this region.

The technological solutions will be championed by large multinational companies with an eye on the global market, and will hit the growing consumer concern about processed food, the erosion of traditional food chains with such foods and the perceived growing power of such companies. In reality, all these issues will prevail, one way or another.

People will continue to enjoy food, to enjoy the conviviality of shared meals, many of which will embrace the foods covered in this book. We will move toward more plant-based foods, embracing the natural versus processed and local versus global tensions, just as we do at present. As water finds its own level, so do different socio-economic groupings. *Bon Appétit*.

> *One cannot think well, love well, sleep well, if one has not dined well.* – Virginia Woolf

References

This is a book in the popular rather than academic genre and for that reason I have chosen not to pepper the text with references. In the interests of transparency, the following are the main books and scientific papers consulted. I have visited so many websites, read so many media reports and downloaded so many e-books, many of very old texts, that to include them all would serve little purpose.

Books

Abbott, E. (2009) *Sugar: A Bittersweet History*. London: Duckworth publishers.

Albala, K. (2014) *Nuts: A Global History*. London: Reaktion Books.

Anderson, H.A. (2018) *Berries: A Global* History. London: Reaktion Books.

Anderson, H.A. (2013). *Breakfast: A History*. Maryland: Alta Mira Press.

Beeton, I. (1861) *Mrs Beeton's Book of Household Management*. London: S.O. Beeton Publishing.

Bertelsen, C. (2013) *Mushroom: A Global* History. London: Reaktion Books.

Blanc, R. (2019) *The Lost Orchard: A French chef rediscovers a great British food heritage*. London: Headline.

Boesch, M.J. (1967) *The World of Rice*. New York: E.P. Dutton.

Book of Deuteronomy. xxiv. 6

Bosanquet, C. (1806) *A letter to W. Manning on the proposition submitted to the government, for taking the duties on Muscovado sugar ad valorem*. Florida: Hardcore.

Capatti, A. and Montanari, M. (2003) *Italian Cuisine (Arts and Traditions of the Table: Perspectives on Culinary History*. New York: Columbia University Press.

Chrystal, P. (2016) *Coffee: A Drink for the Devil*. Stroud: Amberly.

Clarkson, J. (2010) *Soup: A Global History*. London: Reaktion Books.

Clutton, A. (2019) *The Vinegar Cupboard*. London: Bloomsbury Publishing.

Coe, S.D. and Coe, M.D. (2013). *The True History of Chocolate*. New York: Thames and Hudson Ltd.

Columella, L. (2017) *Of Husbandry: In Twelve Books: and His Book Concerning Trees Chapter VIII, Of the method of making cheese*. Florida: Hardpress.

Czarra, F. (2009) *Spices: A Global History*. London: Reaktion Books.

Danchev, A. (ed.) (2016), *100 Artists' Manifestos*. London: Penguin Modern Classics.

Daniel, H. (2019) *The History of Vegetarianism and Veganism: Short, concise and easy to digest*. Translated by Masser, D. Babelcube Inc.

Darwin, C. (1989) *Voyage of the Beagle*. New York: Penguin Classics.

David, E. (2009) *An Omelette and a Glass of Wine*. London: Grub Street Publishing.

Davidson, A. (1999) *The Penguin Companion to Food*. New York: Penguin.

Davidson, S.R., Passmore, J.F.B. and Truswell, A.S. (1979) *Human Nutrition and Dietetics*. New York: Churchill Livingstone.

De Vita, O.Z. (2009) *Encyclopaedia of Pasta* (California Studies in Food and Culture Book) Los Angeles: University of California Press.

Della Croce, J. (1987) *Pasta Classica: The Art of Italian Cooking*. San Francisco: Chronicle Books.

Dickens, Charles (1859) *A Tale of Two Cities* The Planet. Kindle Edition

Edwards, A. (2019) *Biscuits and Cookies: A global history*. London: Reaktion books.

Elizabeth, A. (2010) *Sugar*. London: Duckworth Publishers.

Fagan, B. (2017) Fishing: *How the Sea Fed Civilization*. London: Yale University Press.

Farr, E. (1848) *History of England, from the earliest period to the Eleventh Year of the Reign of Queen Victoria*. Longman, Brown, Green and Longman.

References

Fernandez-Armesto, F. (2001) *Food: A History.* London: Pan Books.

Fischler, C. (1987) *Attitudes Towards Sugar and Sweetness* in *Historical and Social Perspective. In Sweetness.* J. Dobbing, ed. Berlin: Springer-Verlag, 83.

Fitzgibbon, T. (1983) *Irish Traditional Food.* Dublin: Gill & Macmillan.

Foley, C. (2014) *Of Cabbages and Kings: The history of allotments.* London: Francis Lincoln, 53.

Forbes, S. (2018) *Print and Party Politics in Ireland, 1689-1714.* London: Palgrave Macmillan.

Fortune, R. (1852) *A Journey to the Tea Countries of China.* London: John Murray.

Franklin, B. (1791) *Benjamin Franklin: An Autobiography.* Salt Lake City: Project Gutenburg.

Gentilcore, D. (2010) *Pomodoro! (Arts and Traditions of the Table: Perspectives on Culinary History.* New York: Columbia University Press.

Gies, F. and Gies, J. (1990)J. *Life in a Medieval Village.* London: Harper Row.

Gladwell, M. (2011) *Outliers: The Story of Success.* Boston: Little, Brown and Company.

Grieco, A.J. (2019) *Food, Social Politics and the Order of Nature in Renaissance Italy.* Boston: Harvard University Press.

Grivetti, L.E. and Shapiro, H-Y (2009) *Chocolate: History, Culture, and Heritage.* New Jersey: John Wiley.

Harari, Y.N. (2014) *Sapiens: A Brief History of Humankind.* New York: Harpers.

Haratischvili, N. (2019) *The Eighth Life.* London: Scribe Publications.

Harbison, P. (1994) *Pre-Christian Ireland App: From the First Settlers to the Early Celts (Ancient Peoples & Places).* London: Greener Books.

Harris, J. (2010) *Chocolat.* London: Transworld.

House of Lords (1849) *The sessional papers printed by order of the House of Lords, or presented by Royal command, in the Session 1849, (12° & 13° VICTORIÆ).*

Johnson, S. (1997) *Tomatoes, Potatoes, Corn and Beans: How Foods of the Americas Changed Eating around the world.* New York: Atheneum books.

Krondl, M. (2011) *Sweet Invention: A history of dessert.* Chicago: Chicago Review Press.

Kurlansky, M. (2003) *Salt: A world history*. London: Vintage.

Kurlansky, M. *Salmon* (2020). London: Oneworld Publications.

Langstroth, L.L. (2004) *Langstroth's Hive and the Honey-Bee: The Classic Beekeeper's Manual*. New York: Dover Publications.

Laws, B. (2017) *Fifty Tales from the Kitchen Garden: A Social History of Vegetables*. London: Albert Bridge Books.

Lecky, W. (1904) *A History of England in the Eighteenth Century*. Volume ii. London: Longmans, Greene and company.

Linford, J. (2018) *The Seven Culinary Wonders of the World: A History of Pork, Honey, Salt, Chilli, Rice, Cacao and Tomato*. London: White Lion Publishing.

Mahon, B. (1991) *Land of Milk and Honey. The story of traditional food and drink*. Colorado: American Book Company.

Marinetti, F.T. (2014) *The Futurist Cookbook*. London: Penguin.

Marti, L.C. (2018) *A History of Tea*. Vermont: Tuttle Publishing.

Marton, R. (2014) Rice: *A Global History*. London: Reaktion Books.

McCabe, J. (1913) *A Candid History of the Jesuits*. London: Eveleigh.

McGee, H. (1984) *On Food And Cooking: The Science and Lore of the Kitchen*, New York: Charles Scribner.

McWilliams, M. (2012) *The Story behind the Dish: Classic American Foods, Classic American Foods*. Santa Barbara CA; Greenwood.

Mitscher, L.A. (2008) *The Green Tea Book*. New York: Avery.

Montgomery, D. (2003) *King of Fish: The Thousand-Year Run of Salmon*. Boulder, CO: Westview Press.

Morris, J. (2019) *Coffee: A Global History*. London: Reaktion Books.

Moss, S. (2009) *Chocolate: A Global History*. London: Reaktion Books.

Mueller, T. (2012) *Extra Virginity: The Sublime and Scandalous World of Olive Oil*. London: Atlantic Books.

Murray, D.S. (2016). *Herring Tales*. London: Bloomsbury Publishing.

Orwell, G. (1937) *The Road to Wigan Pier*. New Delhi: Delphi Open Books.

Patterson, D. and Aftel, M. (2017) *The Art of Flavour: Practices and principles for creating delicious food*, London: Riverhead Books.

Paul, C. (2016) *Coffee: A Drink for the Devil*. Stroud: Amberley Publishing.

Pell, R.C. (1857) *Milledulcia: A thousand pleasant things. Selected from Notes and a thousand pleasant thing.* New York: Appleton.

Pendergrast, M. (2019) *Uncommon Grounds: The History of Coffee and How It Transformed Our World.* New York: Basic Books.

Pepys, S. (1659-1669) *The Diary of Samuel Pepys.* London: Frederick Warne & Co.

Pliny the Elder (2015) *The Complete Works of Pliny the Elder, Book 53.* London: Delphi Publishing Ltd.

Rolph, G.M. (1917) *Something about Sugar: Its history, growth, manufacture and distribution.* Florida: Hardpress.

Rose, S. (2010) *For All the Tea in China.* London: Penguin.

Roux, M. (2018) *Eggs.* London: Quadrille Publishing Ltd.

Rubel, W. (2015) *Bread: A Global History.* London: Reaktion books.

Saffron, I. (2002). *Caviar.* New York: Broadway Books.

Salaman, R. (1985) *The History and Social Influence of the Potato.* Cambridge: Cambridge University Press.

Sattar, M., Sharma, S.D. and Pokharia, A.K. (2010) *History of Rice in South Asia (Up to 1947).* In Sharma SD. *Rice: Origin, Antiquity and History.* Florida: CRC Press.

Schapira, J., Schapira, D, and Schapira, K. (1996) *The Book of Coffee and Tea.* New York: St Martin's Press.

Serventi, S. and Sabban, F. (2000) *Pasta (Arts and Traditions of the Table: Perspectives on Culinary History).* New York: Columbia University Press.

Sharma S.D. (2010) *Rice: Origin, antiquity and history.* Florida: CRC Press.

Shelke, K. (2006) *Pasta and Noodles. A Global History.* London: Reaktion books.

Shephard, S. (2006) *Pickled, Potted, and Canned: How the Art and Science of Food Preserving Changed the World.* London: Simon & Schuster.

Silverman, K. (2003) *Lightning Man.* New York: Knopf Doubleday Publishing Group.

Smith, A. (1775) *An Inquiry into the Nature and Causes of the Wealth of Nations.* Chicago: University Of Chicago Press.

Smith, A.F. (2008) *Hamburger: A Global History.* London: Reaktion Books.

Snapes, R., Harrington, G. and Hemingway, E. (2018) *Bread & Butter* London: Quadrille Publishing Ltd.

Soyers, A. (1855) *Shilling Cookery Book for the People.* London: Routledge.

Sponsel, L.E. (1989). 'Farming and foraging: A necessary complementarity in Amazonia'. *In Farmers as Hunters: The implications of sedentism* (ed. S. Kent), Cambridge: Cambridge University Press.

Stannard, D.E. (1992) *American Holocaust: Columbus and the Conquest of the New World.* Oxford: Oxford University Press.

Talbot, A., Earl of Shrewsbury (1844). *Hints towards the pacification of Ireland: Addressed more particularly, to the ruling powers of the day.* 2nd edition. London: Charles Dolmen.

Tannahill, R. (1973) *Food in History*. New York: Three rivers Press.

Tebben, M. (2014) *Sauces: A Global History*. London: Reaktion Books.

The Domesday book. Available from https://www.nationalarchives.gov.uk.

The Duchess of Northumberland (2013) *The Duchess of Northumberland's Little Book of Jams, Jellies and Preserves.* London: The History Press.

Thirsk J. (2006). *Food in Early Modern England: Phases, fads and fashions 1500-1760.* New York: Hambledon continuum.

Toussaint-Samat, M. (1926) *History of Food.* Oxford: Blackwell Press.

Tully, J. (1999) *The Crimes of Charlotte Bronte, The Secret History of the Mysterious Events at Haworth.* London: Constable and Robinson.

Turner, J. (2004) *Spice: The History of a Temptation.* London: Harper Collins Publishers.

Ukers, W.H. (1922) *All About Coffee.* Gillingham: Zellerz Publishing Company, 122.

Valenze, D. (2011) *Milk: A Local and Global History.* New Haven: Yale University Press.

Walton, J.K. (1992) *Fish & Chips and the British Working Class 1870-1940.* Leicester: Leicester University Press.

Ward, C.O. (1888). *A History of the Ancient Working Peoples.* Washington: W.H. Lowdermilk & Co.

Watkins, S-B. (2016) *Catherine of Braganza. Charles II restoration Queen.* Winchester: Cronos.

Weiss, L.B. (2011) *Ice Cream: A Global History*. London: Reaktion Books.

Wilson, H. (1913) *A Naturalist in Western China: With Vasculum, Camera, and Gun; Being Some Account of Eleven Years' Travel, Exploration, and Observation in the More Remote Parts of the Flowery Kingdom*. London: Methuen & co.

Wrangham, R. (2012) *Capturing Fire*. London: Profile Books.

Young, A. (1897) *A Tour in Ireland 1776-1779*. London: Cassell and Company.

Zola, M. (1873)*The Belly of Paris (also known as The Fat and The Thin)*. Stanford: e-artnow.

Academic and related articles

Angelakis, A.N, and Zheng, X.Y. (2015) 'Evolution of water supply, sanitation, wastewater and stormwater technologies globally'. *Water*, 7:455-463.

Behan, B. (1962) 'The confirmation suit'. *The Spectator*, April 27.

Bharucha, Z. and Pretty, J. (2010) 'The roles and values of wild foods in agricultural systems'. *Philosophical Transactions of the Royal Society*, B365: 2913-2926.

Bollett, A.J. (1992) 'Politics and Pellagra: The Epidemic of Pellagra in the U.S. in the Early Twentieth Century'. *The Yale journal of biology and medicine*. 65:211-221.

Brandes, S. (1992) 'Maize as a Culinary Mystery', *Ethnology*, 31:331-336.

Burkett M.E. (1977) 'An Early Date for the Origin of Felt'. *Anatolian Studies*, 27: 111-115.Chicken soup inhibits neutrophil chemotaxis in vitro. *Chest*, 118:1150-1157.

Colledge, S. and Conolly, J. (2014) 'Wild plant use in European Neolithic subsistence economies: a formal assessment of preservation bias in archaeobotanical assemblages and the implications for understanding changes in plant diet breadth'. *Quaternary Science Reviews*, 101:193–206.

Currie, C.K. (1991) The Early History of the carp and Its economic significance in England, *The Agricultural History Review*. 39, 97-107.

Davis, J. (2004) 'Baking for the Common Good: A Reassessment of the Assize of Bread in Medieval England'. *The Economic History Review*, 57: 465-503.

Eaton S.B., Eaton S.B III. and Konner M.J. (1997) 'Palaeolithic nutrition revisited: A twelve-year retrospective on its nature and implications'. *European Journal of Clinical Nutrition*, 51:207-216.

Elliot, R.C. (1963) 'The shape of utopia' *English Literary History*, 30:317-334.

Engs, R.C. (1991) 'The 19th century clean living movement. *J School Health*, 61: 155.

Finlay, M.R. (1992) 'Quackery and cookery: Justus von Liebig's extract of meat and the theory of nutrition in the Victorian age'. *Bulletin of the History of Medicine*, 66: 404-418.

Fisberg, M. and Machado, R. (2015) 'History of yogurt and current patterns of consumption'. *Nutrition Reviews*, 73 (Supplement 1):4-7.

Gopal, L.(1964) 'Sugar making in Ancient Indi'. *Journal of the Economic and Social History of the Orient*, 7: 57-72.

Gowlett J. A.J. (2016) The discovery of fire by humans: a long and convoluted process. *Philosophical Transactions of the Royal Society*, B 371: 20150164.

Gubb, A.S. (1908) 'Raw Meat Juice in the Treatment of Haemophilia and Allied States'. *The British Medical Journal*, 2486:502.

Hajar, R. (2012) 'The Air of History (Part II) Medicine in the Middle Ages'. *Journal of the Gulf Heart Association*, 13: 158-62.

Hawkes, J.G. and Francisco-Ortega, F. (1992) 'The Potato in Spain during the Late 16th Century'. *Economic Botany*, 46: 86-97.

Houghton, J. (1699) 'A discourse of coffee'. *Philosophical Transactions of the Royal Society of London*,1:311-317.

https://hartley-botanic.co.uk/magazine/a-history-of-the-english-glasshouse (Accessed December 2020).

Jørgensen, D. (2013) 'Running Amuck? Urban Swine Management in Late Medieval England'. *Agricultural History*, 87: 429-451.

Kaufman, D.B. (1932) 'Poisons and Poisoning among the Romans.' *Classical Philology*, 27: 156-167.

Kindstedt, P.S. (2013) 'The basics of cheesemaking'. *Microbiology Spectrum* 1(1):CM-0002-2012.

Marzano, A. (2018) 'Fish and fishing in the Roman world'. *Journal of Maritime Archaeology*. 13:437–447

McComb, A.M.G. and Simpson, D. (1999) 'The Wild Bunch: Exploitation of the Hazel in Prehistoric Ireland'. *Ulster Journal of Archaeology*, 58: 1-16.

McCue, G.A. (1952) 'The History of the Use of the Tomato: An Annotated Bibliography'. *Annals of the Missouri Botanical Garden*, 39: 289-348.

McD Beckles, H. (1990) 'A riotous and unruly lot: Irish Indentured servants and freemen in the English West Indies, 1644-1713'. *The William and Mary Quarterly,* 47:503-522

McKenzzie, A.T. (1971) 'The Lamentation of Glumdalclitch for the Loss of Grildrig. A Pastoral: What We Have Been Missing'. *Texas Studies in Literature and Language,* 12: pp. 583-59.

Mennella, J.A., Lukasiewicz, L.D., Griffith, J.W. and Beauchamp, G.K. (2011) 'Evaluation of the Monell Forced-Choice, Paired-Comparison Tracking Procedure for Determining Sweet Taste Preferences across the Lifespan'. *Chem Senses,* 36: 345–355.

Mercader, J. (2009) 'Mozambican Grass Seed Consumption during the Middle Stone Age'. *Science,* 326: 1680-1683.

Mokyr, J. and O'Grada, C. (1981) 'The height of Irish and English in the 1770's: Some evidence from the East India Company records'. *Eighteenth-century Ireland,* 4:83-92.

Mokyr, J. (1981) 'Irish History with the Potato'. *Irish Economic and Social History,* 8: 8-29.

Morris, J. (2013) 'Why Espresso? Explaining changes in European coffee preferences from a production of culture perspective'. *European Review of History,* 20: 881-901.

Nayik, G.A., Shah, T.R., Muzafffar, K., Wani, S.A., Gull, A., Majid, I. and Bhat, F.M. (2014) 'Honey: Its history and religious significance: A review'. *Universal Journal of pharmacy,*3: 5-8.

Nunn, N. and Qian, N. (2011) 'The potato's contribution to population and urbanization: Evidence for a historical experiment' *Quarterly Journal of Economics,* 126: 503-650.

O'Grada, C. (1979) 'The Population of Ireland 1700-1900: A survey' *Annales de Démographie Historique Année,* 1:281-299.

O'Kelly, M.J. (1954) 'Excavations and experiments in Ancient Irish Cooking Places'. *The Journal of the Royal Society of Antiquaries of Ireland,* 84: 105-155.

Ramón-Laca L. (2003) 'The Introduction of Cultivated Citrus to Europe via Northern Africa and the Iberian Peninsula'. *Economic Botany,* 57: 502-514.

Rebecca, E. (2017) 'Promoting Potatoes in Eighteenth-Century Europe'. *Eighteenth-Century Studies,* 51: 147-162.

Rowley-Conwy P. (2011) 'Westward Ho! The spread of agriculture from central Europe to the Atlantic'. *Current Anthropology*, 52: S431-S451.

Saleh, A.S.M., Wang, P., Wang, N., Yang, L. and Xiao, Z. (2019) 'Brown Rice Versus White Rice: Nutritional Quality, Potential Health Benefits'. *Reviews in Food Science and Food Safety*, 18: 1070-1096.

Sayers, K. and Lovejoy, C.O. (2014) 'Blood, Bulbs, and Bunodonts: On Evolutionary Ecology and the Diets of Ardipithecus, Australopithecus, and Early Homo'. *The Quarterly Review of Biology*, 89:319-357.

Squarcina, E. and Maletesta, S. (2012) 'The geography of Carlo Collodi's "Journey through Italy of Geannettino" as a tool for the construction of the Italian national. *Revista electronica de geografia y ciencias sociale*, 16: 418.

Steiner, J.E., Glaser, D. and Hawilo, M.E. (2001) 'Comparative expression of hedonic impact: affective reactions to taste by human infants and other primates' *Neuroscience Biobehaviour Review*, 25:53-74.

Testart, A., Forbes, R.G., Hayden, B., Ingold, T., Perlman, S.M., Pokotylo, D.L., Rowley-Conwy, P. and Stuart, D. E. (1982) 'The significance of food storage among hunter gatherers: Residence patterns, population densities and social inequalities'. *Current Anthropology*, 25: 23-537.

Walford C. (1878) 'The Famines of the World: Past and Present'. *Journal of the Statistical Society of London*, 41: 433-535.

Whittaker, D.K. and Molleson, T. (1996) 'Caries prevalence in the dentition of a late eighteenth century population'. *Archives of Oral Biology*, 41: 55-61.

Wollenberg, R.A.C. (1909) 'Pellagra in Italy'. *Health Reports (1896-1970)*, 24: 1051-1054.

Wood, J.D., Enser, M., Fisher, A.V., Nute, G.R,, Richardson, R.I. Sheard PR. (1999) Manipulating meat quality and composition. *Proceedings of the Nutrition Society*, 58:363-370.

Y.Li,J.-F.Liang,M.-Y.Yang,J.-Y.Chen, B.-Z.Han (2015) 'Traditional Chinese Rice Noodles: History, Classification, and Processing Methods'. *Cereal Foods*, 60:123-127.

Zakari, A. and Abizar, A-Z. (2008) 'Ramadan fasting alters food patterns, dietary diversity and body weight among Ghanaian adolescents', *Nutrition Journal*, 17:75.

Zhanga, N. and Mab, G. (2016) 'Noodles, traditionally and today', *Journal of Ethnic Foods*, 3:209-212.

Index